TALK YOUR WAY AROUND EUROPE

FRENCH

SPANISH

ITALIAN

GERMAN

W9-BWJ-528

TALK YOUR WAY AROUND EUROPE

FRENCH

SPANISH

ITALIAN

GERMAN

SHAUN DOWLING

PASSPORT BOOKS
a division of *NTC Publishing Group*
Lincolnwood, Illinois USA

CONTENTS

PREFACE

This book provides a new, but simpler, method of learning a language. Not just one language, but any one of four that you are likely to need when you travel abroad —French, Spanish, Italian, and German—all set out in an easy-to-read format.

The method described here aims to take the drudgery out of learning and teach you language in the most natural way. It allows you to absorb the language through single words, just as a child learns to build up vocabulary quite naturally and develop speaking skills. It will show you how to grasp any one of the four languages in 15 sessions, and with a little practice you should get by anywhere in Europe.

You start off with a simple list of 500 basic words, very carefully chosen, which enable you to build up phrases and sentences, express ideas, and communicate messages. These are the basic language tools, many of which you will remember if you read them through, whenever you have a spare half-hour or so. In addition, there is a list of about 100 key words on food that you may need when you are shopping or eating out, and a further 150 words that you may need if you are traveling on business.

The next stage is to build up these words into phrases or short sentences, for which I have provided a list of just 80 frequently used "*message builders*." You can practice these by yourself, until you feel comfortable using them in conversation.

You then move on to the grammar itself, which has been pruned down to the main essentials. One complete grammar can be read right through in an hour but, for the purpose of learning, it has been split up into 15 sessions, each covering two or three aspects of the language. Each language is presented in exactly the same format, so if you have grasped one language, it is a simple matter to move on to the next. The grammar has also been carefully tabulated, so that you can quickly turn to the section you need.

You should pick up the book at least a week before you travel, then keep it with you in your pocket, briefcase, or handbag, until your journey is finished. Dip into the book at all times of the day or night until you are thoroughly familiar with the vocabulary and the layout of the grammar. Browse through the book at the airport, on the train, in the restaurant, or at the hotel. Pull

Preface

it out when you are shopping, or you have forgotten a word, or you want to translate something that you have seen or has been said to you. Treat the book as your companion to stay with you throughout your journey. You will soon find you are speaking a foreign language with confidence.

If you want to learn a language from scratch, or refresh your memory, rusted from disuse since you last went abroad or finished studying at school, turn to the next section, which will show you how to learn a language in the quickest and most efficient way.

HOW TO LEARN MORE QUICKLY

You can use this book in a variety of ways: for browsing, for reference or for learning a new language. If you need to brush up old skills, or you are starting from scratch, you will get on much quicker if you follow the instructions set out below, working through the vocabulary and language structure in a systematic way. To help you through this process, each language has been broken down into 15 sessions. Sessions 1–4 deal with sounds, words and sentence building. Sessions 5–15 deal with the language structure, each split up into two or three sections covering a particular aspect of the grammar.

A brief description of each session is shown in the notes which follow. Read through these carefully before turning to each session.

Session 1 – Your Word List

Turn to p. 20 (French), p. 76 (Spanish), p. 134 (Italian) or p. 197 (German).

There are only 500 or so words in each vocabulary, of which almost half are nouns. Every noun, whether subject or object, provides a key to a message.

Consider, for a minute, a child learning to speak. He does not say 'Excuse me, mother, can I please have a drink?' He uses one word – 'drink' – sometimes not even that, but the message is understood. So too, if you stopped your car and said the word 'airport' to a passerby, you would very likely be directed to the airport. Or, if you were in a taxi, you would get taken there. One word is often sufficient to get the message across.

The first objective, therefore, is to learn as many words as you can. So, go through the main vocabulary in Section 1A and see how many words you recognize which are similar to English, or you can remember from the past.

Now write down on a piece of paper all the words that *you* think are important. You will need this list in Session 2. If you want to run through words for food or business by all means do so, but don't overload the memory.

Session 2 – Pronunciation

Turn to p. 32 (French), p. 88 (Spanish), p. 146 (Italian) or p. 210 (German).

Read aloud each sound and the example shown alongside. Don't forget to look at the notes on 'accents and stress' shown in Section 2B at the end.

How to Learn More Quickly

Go through the pronunciation two or three times.

Now pick up the word list which you wrote in Session 1, and read through this list as well. Check the guide to pronunciation if you get stuck.

Don't be put off by the rules for pronouncing certain letters differently according to their position in the word, or the letters they are next to. This is because there are far more sounds than there are letters in the Roman alphabet. Similar rules of pronunciation apply to all European languages. In this respect, at least, you are fortunate, as English is the most difficult language of the lot!

Remember to speak slowly and clearly at all times. It will greatly increase the chance of your being properly understood when you are speaking to a stranger. All foreigners appear to speak quickly at first. Tell them to slow down, so you can understand what they are saying. It will take time for your ear to become attuned to the sounds and the rhythm of a foreign language.

Session 3 – Absorbing the Language

Turn back to p. 20 (French), p. 76 (Spanish), p. 134 (Italian) or p. 197 (German).

Go through the main vocabulary in Section 1A and read all the words aloud.

Go through a second time, covering up the English and see how many words you can translate. If this takes too much time, have a break and pick the rest up later.

Now go through a third time, this time covering up the foreign language you are studying and see how many words you can translate. Don't worry if there are only a few. Your vocabulary will develop with regular practice. Tomorrow or the next day, you will find that you know a whole lot more, and each word will build up your communication skills.

Session 4 – Message Builders

You can now use a number of foreign words. Indeed, you are already speaking the language.

The next step is to build these words into short messages, or what are known in modern jargon as *'communication bytes'*. You can do this by using a handful of key *'message carriers'* or *'message builders'* which have been mostly lifted from the text. These are shown on p. 36 (French), p. 91 (Spanish), p. 149 (Italian) or p. 213 (German).

All you have to do is to add the words you have learned, or you have written down on your word list, to these *'message builders'* and your message is complete.

For example, add the words 'one tea' to the *'message builder'* 'Could I have . . . ?' and you have now completed a sentence in a foreign language.

Don't try to learn phrases out of a phrase book: they will only overload your memory and they will not improve your language skills. Make up your own phrases and sentences, using these *'message builders'*.

Finally, spend a few minutes learning how to address friends and strangers. This is shown on p. 39 (French), p. 94 (Spanish), p. 152 (Italian) or p. 216 (German).

Once you have read this section, you can 'top and tail' your message by adding, for example, 'Excuse me, madam (miss), could I have one tea please?' – or anything else you want to order.

Session 5 – Language Structure

This session is designed to prepare you for language structure. Note that we have used the word 'structure' and not 'grammar' as all languages, including English, have the same structure. The use of nouns and pronouns, verbs and adverbs, main sentences and subordinate clauses, is just the same in French, Spanish or Italian as it is in English. Only the words and word endings differ.

The other reason for not using the word 'grammar' is that it reminds you of school and the classroom. In this book there are no questions and answers, no examinations. You go at your own speed, making up your own messages, just as you do in English.

For the three 'romance' languages (French, Spanish and Italian), the word order is pretty similar to English, although there are a few rules which you should look at on p. 40 (French), p. 95 (Spanish) or p. 153 (Italian).

If you are learning German, turn to p. 217. Here the rules do look a little complex, but if you try to grasp the main principles, you will find that you quickly get into the habit of using German, rather than English word order. To start off, just move the verb around the sentence and fit in the other parts of speech as they naturally fall into place. Don't worry too much about the order at first. If you speak clearly, you will still be perfectly understood even if you get the word order wrong.

Session 6 – Nouns, Adjectives and The Two Articles

Turn to p. 40 (French), p. 96 (Spanish), p.154 (Italian) or p. 219 (German).

Here we go straight to the heart of the language. By now, you will have noticed that all nouns in the vocabulary are marked m (masculine), f (feminine), or n (neuter).

Every noun has a gender which should be memorized along with the word itself.

Any word relating to a noun, including the definite article ('the'), the indefinite article ('a'), or an adjective, has to agree with it. This often means that the word ending has to be changed. This differs from English where articles and adjectives don't change at all; for example,

a good boy – a good girl

In the plural all languages change their endings, including English; for example,

house – houses   mouse – mice

Both French and Spanish are fairly straightforward, but Italian plurals take a little longer to get used to.

German students need to give this session more time, preferably breaking it up into two parts, the first on p. 219 dealing with the principles of nouns, gender and 'cases'. Make certain you understand why the word endings change before moving on to the following sections dealing with The Two Articles, Noun Case Endings and Adjectives starting on p. 222.

Although German word endings are more difficult than in the other languages, comfort yourself that the remaining sessions become easier, particularly the next session on German verbs, which are easier than French, Spanish or Italian ones. Meanwhile, here are three tips to help you through the session:

i)   The umlaut (¨) over a vowel in the middle of a word changes the pronunciation. If in doubt, refer back to p. 210.

ii) The majority of words, where the endings do change, add -e or -er, both of which sound similar in speech.

iii) Feminine nouns and adjectives usually add -en in the plural.

Finally, don't worry too much over the endings. If you make a mistake, the message will get through just the same.

Session 7 – Personal Pronouns and Verbs

Turn to p. 42 (French), p. 98 (Spanish), p. 157 (Italian) or p. 226 (German).

In this session, the sections on pronouns and regular verbs are largely self-explanatory. As you will see in the text, the tenses of regular verbs have been stripped down to the 'present', the 'imperfect' and the 'future', whilst the 'perfect' tense (for all except German), is shown in Session 8. Here the word endings *do* matter as they indicate both the time of the action and the person speaking or writing. Many of the little words used in English like 'am', 'do', 'was', 'will', 'have', 'would' and 'should', are incorporated in the verb itself.

Session 8 – To Be and To Have

Turn to p. 45 (French), p. 101 (Spanish), p. 161 (Italian) or p. 230 (German).

There are two essential verbs which you need to learn. These are 'to be' and 'to have' which can either be used on their own, or serve as auxiliary verbs to build up the past tense. For example,

I *have* spoken   It *is* finished

If you are studying German, you will have covered 'haben' (to have) in Session 7 and you should concentrate here on the use of 'sein' (to be).

Session 9 – Object Pronouns

Turn to p. 47 (French), p. 104 (Spanish), p. 164 (Italian) or p. 231 (German).

The distinction between personal pronouns (I, she, we, they, etc) and object pronouns (me, her, us, them, etc) provides a regular trap for those learning a foreign language. The main difference in English is that we make more use of the word 'to' (to her, to us, to them, etc) in the indirect case, where the other languages generally only use a single pronoun. In French, Spanish and Italian, object pronouns are generally positioned before, not after the verb.

Session 10 – Imperatives, Reflexives and Irregular Verbs

Turn to p. 48 (French), p. 106 (Spanish), p. 166 (Italian) or p. 232 (German).

This session is designed to extend your knowledge of verbs. We start off with the imperatives (words of command) and how to recognize reflexive verbs (e.g. I dress *myself*). We then move on to irregular verbs.

Many students have a fear of irregular verbs which derives from 'over-kill' in the classroom, so it is worthwhile pausing for a minute before studying the text. All languages have some irregular verbs, including English. They derive from centuries of corrupted or abbreviated speech, differences in regional speech, or a desire to improve the sound of the word, particularly among the 'romance' languages (French, Spanish and Italian).

In reality, there are only about 50 irregular verbs in common use, many of them changing only a single letter in the stem, or the verb ending. These verbs are all set out in the text. Unless you have a very good memory, don't try to learn them, just read them through a few times. Recognize the deviations and see how these run in patterns. If you keep up your reading, you will assimilate all the irregularities in time and they will not create the obstacle you remember from school.

There is one final section for German students on 'modal' and 'separable' verbs. 'Modal' verbs (may, can, should, must or want to) are more like English than any of the 'romance' languages and they too are irregular. Many of the 'separable' verbs which hive off the prefix (ab-, an-, auf-, etc) to another part of the sentence, are otherwise regular.

Session 11 – Questions and Negatives

Turn to p. 55 (French), p. 113 (Spanish), p. 174 (Italian) or p. 240 (German).

In this session you will find out how to ask questions and turn a question or a statement into a negative. You will find that you really do need interrogatives (who? what? why? when? how?) to find your way round. So practise them to yourself, using the *'message builders'* and your own word list.

Session 12 – More Adjectives

Turn to p. 59 (French), p. 116 (Spanish), p. 177 (Italian) or p. 242 (German).

You briefly covered adjectives in Session 6 as they related to, and agreed with nouns. But they deserve a whole session to themselves, as there are about 80 in the word list. In this session you will also be introduced to possessives (my, mine) and comparatives (easy, easier, easiest).

Session 13 – Adverbs, Prepositions and Conjunctions

Turn to p. 61 (French), p. 119 (Spanish), p. 181 (Italian) or p. 244 (German).

Most of us don't remember the difference between an adverb, a preposition and a conjunction, or realize that some words such as 'before' and 'after' can be any one of these in a different context. So, before you start on the text, just refresh your memory on their usage in English, shown below. (As you will find out later on, the use of an adverb, preposition or conjunction may well qualify, or change the ending of a verb, noun or pronoun which follows it.)

Adverbs usually describe an action or state (e.g. quickly, always, here) but sometimes qualify a statement (so, therefore, thus).

Prepositions indicate position (of, with), purpose (for, in order to) or a spatial or time relationship (at, in, on, before, opposite).

Conjunctions (and, or, but, since) do just what they say: conjoin, or join up phrases and sentences.

Session 14 – Prepositions and Link Words

Turn to p. 63 (French), p. 121 (Spanish), p. 183 (Italian) or p. 247 (German).

This session covers the use of some of the commonest prepositions (to, at, in, from, of, for) which differ from one language to another; also some of the relative pronouns (words which link sentences) and *'message builders'* such as 'here is'.

Session 15 – Numbers and Time

Turn to p. 67 (French), p. 124 (Spanish), p. 187 (Italian) or p. 249 (German).

This is the last of the programmed sessions, in which you will find out how to deal with numbers, measures, dates, time and the weather.

There are two further Appendices for reference only, the first on the formation of subjunctives, the second on the use of second person pronouns (Italian and German only).

Conclusion

If you have worked your way systematically through the book, you should have grasped the language structure and memorized a reasonable amount of vocabulary. From now on, it is all about listening, reading and talking in the language you are learning.

To get your listening ear in tune, try listening to the local radio, or better still, watching local television or films. If you have a video, borrow a foreign film.

To improve your vocabulary and translation skills, pick up a local paper every day. Its topicality will help you with the translation and you may, at this stage, use a dictionary to learn new words.

Finally, keep on talking. Mix with local people and get in as much conversation as you can. Remember to speak slowly and confidently yourself, and don't hesitate to tell the other speakers to slow down. If you have forgotten how to do that, turn back to *'message builders'* (Session 4).

Meanwhile, happy travelling!

FRENCH

CONTENTS

French

SESSION ONE
Your Word List

1A   500 Word Vocabulary

a/an **un** (m), **une** (f)
able, to be **pouvoir**
accept, to **accepter**
accident **accident** (m)
according to **selon**
account **compte** (m)
address **adresse** (f)
advise, to **conseiller**
aeroplane **avion** (m)
after **après**
afternoon **après-midi** (m)
again **de nouveau**
against **contre**
age **âge** (m)
ago **il y a**
agree, to (be of same
  opinion) **être d'accord**
air **air** (m)
airmail, by **par avion**
airport **aéroport** (m)
all **tout**
allow (let), to **permettre à**
  (de + verb)
almost **presque**
alone **seul**
already **déjà**
also (too) **aussi**
always **toujours**
amuse, to **amuser**
animal **animal** (m)
and **et**
angry **fâché**
another **un autre**
answer, to **répondre à**
anyone **quelqu'un**
arrive, to **arriver** *E
art **art** (m)
as . . . as **aussi . . . que**

ask, to **demander (à/de)**
at **à**
attention **attention** (f)
avenue **avenue** (f)

bad/worse **mauvais/pire**
bag **sac** (m)
baggage (luggage)
  bagage (m)
bank **banque** (f)
bath **bain** (m)
be, to **être**
beach **plage** (f)
beautiful **beau/belle**
because **parce que**
become, to **devenir** *E
bed **lit** (m)
before **avant** (de)
begin, to (start/commence
  commencer (à + verb)
behind **derrière**
believe, to **croire**
between **entre**
bicycle **bicyclette** (f)
big **grand** or **gros**(se)
bill (account) **addition** (f)

black **noir**
blue **bleu**
boat **bateau** (m)
book **livre** (m)
born, to be **naître** *E
bottle **bouteille** (f)
box **boîte** (f)
boy **garçon** (m)
break, to **rompre**
bridge **pont** (m)
bring, to **apporter**

*E indicates verbs which use 'être': see p. 46

brother **frère** (m)
brown **brun**
building **bâtiment** (m)
bus **autobus** (m)
business **affaire** (f)
but **mais**
buy, to **acheter**

cafe/bar **café** (m)
call **appeler**
camera
 appareil-photo (m)
can (verb: be able)
 pouvoir
car **voiture** (f)
car park **parking** (m)
caravan **roulotte** (f)
careful, be! **attention!**
carry, to **porter**
castle **château** (m)
cat **chat** (m)
certain **certain**
chair **chaise** (f)
change, to **changer**
cheap **à bon marché**
cheque **chèque** (m)
chemist's (pharmacy)
 pharmacie (f)
child **enfant** (m, f)
choose, to **choisir**
church **église** (f)
cigarette **cigarette** (f)
class **classe** (f)
clean, to **nettoyer**
clear **clair**
clock **horloge** (f)
close, to **fermer**
clothes **vêtements** (m. pl)
coat **manteau** (m)
cold **froid**
colour **couleur** (f)
come, to **venir** *E
comfortable **confortable**
complete **complet/**
 complète
concert **concert** (m)
continue, to **continuer (à)**

conversation
 conversation (f)
cook, to **cuire**
corner **coin** (m)
correct **correct**
cost, to **coûter**
cotton **coton** (m)
count, to **compter**
country **pays** (m)
cover, to **couvrir**
cry, to **pleurer**
customs **douane** (f)
cut, to **couper**

damage **dommage** (m)
dance, to **danser**
dangerous **dangereux**
dark **sombre**
date **date** (f)
daughter **fille** (f)
day **jour** (m)
dear (expensive) **cher/**
 chère
decide, to **décider (de)**
defend, to **défendre**
dentist **dentiste** (m)
depart, to (leave)
 partir *E
descend, to (go down)
 descendre *E
desire, to (want) **désirer**
die, to **mourir** *E
different **différent**
difficult **difficile**
direction (way)
 direction (f)
dirty **sale**
distance **distance** (f)
do, to **faire**
doctor **médecin** (m)
door **porte** (f)
dress **robe** (f)
drink, to **boire**
drive, to (a car) **conduire**
dry **sec/sèche**
during **pendant**
duty **devoir** (m)

French

each (every) **chaque**
early **de bonne heure**
eat, to **manger**
empty **vide**
end **fin** (f)
engine **machine** (f)
English **anglais**
enough **assez (de)**
enter, to **entrer** *E
equal **égal**
evening **soir** (m)
every **chaque**
everything **tout**
excellent **excellent**
exchange, to **échanger**
excuse, to **excuser**
exit **sortie** (f)
expensive (dear) **cher/ chère**
eye **oeil** (m) **yeux** (pl)

face **figure** (f)
fall, to **tomber** *E
family **famille** (f)
far **loin (de)**
fast (quick) **vite**
fat **gras(se)**
father **père** (m)
feel, to **sentir**
field **champ** (m)
film **film** (m)
fight, to **combattre**
fill, to **remplir**
find, to **trouver**
finish, to **finir**
fire **feu** (m)
fix, to **fixer**
floor **étage** (m)
flight (by air) **vol** (m)
fly, to **voler**
follow, to **suivre**
food **nourriture** (f)
foot **pied** (m)
football **football** (m)
for (in order to) **pour**
for (because of) **pour**

forget, to **oublier (de + verb)**
free **libre**
French **français**
fresh **frais/fraîche**
friend **ami/e** (m/f)
from **de**
fruit **fruit** (m)
full **plein**

garage **garage** (m)
garden **jardin** (m)
German **allemand**
gift **cadeau** (m)
girl **fille** (f)
give, to **donner**
glasses **lunettes** (f. pl)
glove **gant** (m)
go, to **aller** *E
go down, to **descendre** *E
go out, to **sortir** *E
go up/climb, to **monter** *E
gold **or** (m)
good **bon(ne)**
great **grand**
ground **terre** (f)
group **groupe** (m)

hairdresser **coiffeur** (m)
hand **main** (f)
handbag **sac à main** (f)
handkerchief **mouchoir** (m)
happen, to **passer**
happy **heureux/heureuse**
hard **dur**
hat **chapeau** (m)
have (possession of), to **avoir**
have, to (auxiliary) **avoir**
hear, to **entendre**
heavy **lourd**
healthy **sain**
help, to **aider (à + verb)**
here **ici**
high **haut**
hill **colline** (f)

hold, to **tenir**
holiday (vacation) **vacances** (f. pl)
hope, to **espérer**
hospital **hôpital** (m)
hot **chaud**
hotel **hôtel** (m)
hour **heure** (f)
house **maison** (f)
how **comment**
how much/how many? **combien de?**
husband **mari** (m)

ice **glace** (f)
if **si**
ill **malade**
immediately **immédiatement**
important **important**
in **dans**
include, to **inclure**
industry **industrie** (f)
information **renseignements** (m. pl)
inside **dedans**
intelligent **intelligent**
interesting **intéressant**
is (verb: to be) **est**
Italian **italien**

join, to (be part of) **s'associer (à)**
journey **voyage** (m)

keep, to **tenir**
key **clef** (f)
kind **gentil(le)**
king **roi** (m)
kiss, to **embrasser**
know, to (something) **savoir**
know, to (somebody) **connaître**

lady **dame** (f)
language **langue** (f)

last **dernier/dernièr**
late **tard**
lawyer **avocat** (m)
learn, to **apprendre (à + verb)**
leave, to (go out) **sortir** *E
leave, to (depart) **partir** *E
left **gauche**
lend, to **prêter**
less **moins**
let, to (permit) **permettre à (de + verb)**
letter **lettre** (f)
lift **ascenseur** (m)
light **lumière** (f)
like, to/wish, to **vouloir**
liquid **liquide** (m)
list **liste** (f)
little (small) **petit**
little (a) **peu** (m)
live, to **vivre**
live in, to **habiter**
long **long/longue**
look at, to **regarder**
lorry **camion** (m)
lose, to **perdre**
loud **fort**
love, to **aimer**
luggage (baggage) **bagages** (m. pl)

mad **fou/folle**
make, to **faire**
man **homme** (m)
manner **manière** (f)
many **beaucoup de**
map **carte** (f)
market **marché** (m)
match **allumette** (f)
medicine **médicine** (f)
meet, to **rencontrer**
meeting **réunion** (f)
middle **milieu** (m)
million **million** (m)
minute **minute** (f)
mirror **miroir** (m)
mistake **erreur** (f)

23

money **argent** (m)
more **plus**
morning **matin** (m)
motorway **autoroute** (f)
mother **mère** (f)
mountain **montagne** (f)
mouth **bouche** (f)
move, to **mouvoir**
much **beaucoup**
museum **musée** (m)
music **musique** (f)
must (verb: to be obliged) **devoir**

name **nom** (m)
near **proche à**
necessary **nécessaire**
need, to **avoir besoin de**
never **jamais**
new **nouveau/nouvelle**
newspaper **journal** (m)
next **prochain**
night **nuit** (f)
no **non**
noise **bruit** (m)
nothing **rien**
now **maintenant**
number (figure) **numéro** (m)

obtain, to **obtenir**
of **de**
offer, to **offrir (de + verb)**
office **bureau** (m)
often **souvent**
oil **huile** (f)
old **vieux/vieille**
on **sur**
once **une fois**
only (adv.) **seulement**
open, to **ouvrir**
opposite **en face de**
or **ou**
ordinary **ordinaire**
other **autre**
over **au-dessus de**

owe, to (be obliged) **devoir**

package **paquet** (m)
pain **douleur** (f)
paper **papier** (m)
park **parc** (m)
part **partie** (f)
pass, to **passer**
passenger **passager/ passagère** (m/f)
passport **passeport** (m)
path **sentier** (m)
pay, to **payer**
pen **plume** (f)
pencil **crayon** (m)
perhaps **peut-être**
permit (let) **permettre à (de + verb)**
persuade, to **persuader**
person/people **personne/s** (f)
petrol **essence** (f)
pharmacy **pharmacie** (f)
photograph **photographie** (f)
piece **morceau** (m)
place **endroit** (m)
play, to (games) **jouer (à)**
please **s'il vous plaît**
police **police** (f)
point out, to **indiquer**
poor **pauvre**
port (harbour) **port** (m)
porter **porteur** (m)
possible **possible**
postcard **carte postale** (f)
post office **bureau de poste** (m)
prefer, to **préférer**
prepare, to **préparer**
price **prix** (m)
private (not public) **privé**
probable **probable**
profession **profession** (f)
programme **programme** (m)

promise, to **promettre à (de + verb)**
put, to (place) **mettre**

quality **qualité** (f)
quantity **quantité** (f)
question **question** (f)
quick (fast) **vite**
quiet **tranquille**

rain, to **pleuvoir**
read, to **lire**
ready **prêt**
receive, to **recevoir**
reception (hotel) **réception** (f)
red **rouge**
regret, to (be sorry) **regretter**
remember, to **se souvenir de**
repeat, to **répéter**
reply, to **répondre**
report, to **rapporter**
responsible **responsable**
restaurant **restaurant** (m)
return, to **revenir** *E
rich **riche**
right (direction) **droite** (f)
right, to be **avoir raison**
river **fleuve** (m)
road **route** (f)
room **chambre** (f)
run, to **courir**

sad **triste**
same **même**
save, to **sauver**
say, to **dire**
school **école** (f)
sea **mer** (f)
see, to **voir**
seem, to **sembler**
sell, to **vendre**
send, to **envoyer**
serve, to **servir**
service **service** (m)

shoe **chaussure** (f)
shop **magasin** (m)
short **court**
show, to **montrer**
shower **douche** (f)
shut, to **fermer**
sign **signe** (m)
silver **d'argent**
since **depuis (que)**
sing, to **chanter**
sister **soeur** (f)
sit down, to **s'asseoir** *E
skiing (noun) **ski** (m)
sky **ciel** (m)
sleep, to **dormir**
slowly **lentement**
small **petit**
snow **neige** (f)
so, thus **ainsi**
soap **savon** (m)
soft **doux/douce**
some **quelque**
someone **quelqu'un**
sometimes **quelquefois**
son **fils** (m)
soon **bientôt**
speak, to **parler**
square (town) **place** (f)
stairs **escalier** (m)
stamp **timbre** (f)
start, to (begin) **commencer (à)**
station (railway) **gare** (f)
stay, remain, to **rester** *E
step (pace) **pas** (m)
stop, to **arrêter**
street **rue** (f)
strong **fort**
student **étudiant** (m)
study, to **étudier**
suddenly **soudain**
suitcase **valise** (f)
summer **été** (m)
sun **soleil** (m)
suntan **hâle** (m)
sweet **doux/douce**
swim, to **nager**

French

swimming pool **piscine** (f)

table **table** (f)
take, to **prendre**
tariff (customs) **tarif** (m)
taste, to **goûter**
taxi **taxi** (m)
tea **thé** (m)
teach (to), to **enseigner** (à)
teacher **professeur** (m)
telegram **télégramme** (m)
telephone, to **téléphoner** (à)
television **télévision** (f)
tell, to **dire à (de + verb)**
tennis **tennis** (m)
thank you **merci**
theatre **théâtre** (m)
then **donc**
there **là**
there is/are **il y a**
therefore **donc**
thing **chose** (f)
think, to **penser**
this, that **ce**
through **par**
ticket **billet** (m)
time **temps** (m)
time (what time?) **quelle heure?**
time (one or more) **fois** (f)
tip **pourboire** (m)
tired **fatigué**
to (towards) **à**
to (in order to) **pour**
too (also) **aussi**
too much/many **trop**
today **aujourd'hui**
toilet **toilette** (f)
tomorrow **demain**
tourist **touriste** (m, f)
towards **vers**
towel **serviette** (f)
town **ville** (f)
traffic **circulation** (f)

train (express) **train** (m)
translate, to **traduire**
travel, to **voyager**
travel agent **agent de voyages** (m)
tree **arbre** (m)
true **vrai**
try, to **essayer (de + verb)**
typical **typique**
tyre **pneu** (m)

umbrella **parapluie** (m)
under **sous**
underground (railway) **métro** (m)
understand, to **comprendre**
unfortunately **malheureusement**
university **université** (f)
use, to **employer (à + verb)**
useful **utile**

vacation (holiday) **vacances** (f. pl)
very **très**
village **village** (m)
visit, to (a place) **visiter**
voice **voix** (f)

wait for, to **attendre**
waiter **garçon** (m)
walk, to **marcher**
wall **mur** (m)
want/wish for, to **vouloir**
wash, to (oneself) **(se) laver**
watch **montre** (f)
water **eau** (f)
way (direction) **côté** (m)
wedding **mariage** (m)
week **semaine** (f)
weekend **week-end** (m)
well **bien**
what! **quoi!**

26

when? **quand?**
where? **où?**
which? **quel/quelle?**
which/whom **que**
white **blanc/blanche**
who **qui**
why? **pourquoi?**
wide **large**
wife **femme** (f)
wind **vent** (m)
window **fenêtre** (f)
wine **vin** (m)
winter **hiver** (m)
wish/want, to **vouloir**

with **avec**
without **sans**
wood **bois** (m)
word **mot** (m)
work, to **travailler**
world **monde** (m)
write, to **écrire**

year **an** (m)
yellow **jaune**
yes **oui**
yesterday **hier**
young **jeune**

1B 100 Words for Buying Food and Eating Out

Shops

bakery **boulangerie** (f)
butcher's **boucherie** (f)
fishmonger's
  poissonnerie (f)
grocer's **épicerie** (f)
market **marché** (m)
self service **libre-service**
shop **magasin** (m)
supermarket
  supermarché (m)
tobacconist's **bureau de
  tabac** (m)

Meals

breakfast **petit
  déjeuner** (m)
dining room **salle à
  manger** (f)
dinner **dîner** (m)
drink **boisson** (f)
food **nourriture** (f)
lunch **déjeuner** (m)
meal **repas** (m)

Table setting

bottle **bouteille** (f)
chair **chaise** (f)
cup **tasse** (f)
fork **fourchette** (f)
glass **verre** (m)
jug **pot** (m)
knife **couteau** (m)
menu **menu** (m)
oil **huile** (f)
pepper **poivre** (m)
plate **assiette** (f)
salt **sel** (m)
spoon **cuillère** (f)
sugar **sucre** (m)
table **table** (f)
tip **pourboire** (m)

vinegar **vinaigre** (m)
waiter **garçon** (m)

Drinks

I'm thirsty **j'ai soif**
beer **bière** (f)
brandy **cognac** (m)
cider **cidre** (m)
coffee **café** (m)
cream **crème** (f)
lemonade **limonade** (f)
milk **lait** (m)
orangeade **orangina** (m)
tea **thé** (m)
tomato juice **jus de
  tomates** (m)
water/sparkling water **eau
  minérale/gazeuse** (f)
whisky **whisky** (m)
wine **vin** (m)

Food

I'm hungry **j'ai faim**
apple **pomme** (f)
asparagus **asperges** (f. pl)
aubergine **aubergine** (f)
bacon **bacon** (m)
banana **banane** (f)
bean (French) **haricot
  vert** (m)
bean (haricot) **haricot** (m)
beef **boeuf** (m)
bread **pain** (m)
broccoli **brocoli** (m)
butter **beurre** (m)
cabbage **chou** (m)
cake **gâteau** (m)
cauliflower **chou-
  fleur** (m)
celery **céleri** (m)
cheese **fromage** (m)
chicken **poulet** (m)
chocolate **chocolat** (m)

coffee **café** (m)
cucumber **concombre** (m)
curry **curry** (m)
egg **oeuf** (m)
fish **poisson** (m)
flour **farine** (f)
fruit **fruit** (m)
ham **jambon** (m)
hors d'oeuvre **hors
 d'oeuvre** (m)
ice cream **glace** (f)
jam **confiture** (f)
lemon **citron** (m)
meat **viande** (f)
melon **melon** (m)
milk **lait** (m)
mushroom
 champignon (m)
nectarine **brugnon** (m)
oil **huile** (f)
omelette **omelette** (f)
onion **oignon** (m)
orange **orange** (f)
pancake **crêpe** (f)
pâté **pâté** (m)
peach **pêche** (f)
pear **poire** (f)
peas **petits-pois** (m)
pepper **poivre** (m)
pork **porc** (m)
potato **pomme de terre** (f)
 chipped potatoes
 frites (f. pl)
prawns **crevettes** (f. pl)
ravioli **ravioli** (m)
rice **riz** (m)
salad **salade** (f)

sauce **sauce** (f)
sausage **saucisse** (f)
soup **soupe** (f)
spaghetti
 spaghetti (m. pl)
spinach **épinards** (m. pl)
tart **tarte** (f)
tea **thé** (m)
toast **pain grillé** (m)
tomato **tomate** (f)
vegetables
 légumes (m. pl)
vinegar **vinaigre** (m)

Cooking

boiled **cuit**
fresh **frais/fraîche**
fried **frit**
grilled **grillé**
rare **saignant**
raw **cru**
sour **aigre**
sweet **sucré**
well cooked **bien cuit**

Containers

bag **sac** (m)
bottle **bouteille** (f)
bottle opener **ouvre-
 bouteille** (m)
can **boîte** (f)
can opener **ouvre-
 boîtes** (m)
corkscrew **tire-
 bouchon** (m)

29

1C   150 Words for Business Use

interpreter **interprète** (m)
translate, to **traduire**

Organization **Organisation** (f)

accountant
 comptable (m, f)
authority **autorisation** (f)
chairman **président** (m)
company **compagnie** (f)
company secretary
 secrétaire général
director **directeur** (m)
director (board)
 administrateur (m)
employee
 employé(e) (m/f)
executive **cadre** (m)
management
 cadres (m. pl)
manager **directeur** (m)
managing director **P.D.G.**
 **(président directeur-
 général)**
responsible **responsable**
secretary **secrétaire** (m, f)

Office **Bureau** (m)

agreement **accord** (m)
airmail **par avion**
authorize, to **autoriser**
bank **banque** (f)
business **commerce** (m)
computer **ordinateur** (m)
contract **contrat** (m)
copy **copie** (f)
data processing
 informatique (f)
documentation
 documentation (f)
fax **télécopie** (f)
invoice **facture** (f)
lease **bail** (m)
legal **légal**

official **officiel**
post **poste** (m)
private, confidential **privé**
receipt **reçu** (m)
regulations **normes** (f. pl)
rent **loyer** (m)
report **rapport** (m)
requisition **réquisition** (f)
shares (in a company)
 actions (m. pl)
sign, to **signer**
signatory **signataire** (m, f)
tariff (customs) **tarif** (m)

Works/factory **Usine** (f)

chemical **produit chimique**
 (m)
development
 développement (m)
electrician **électricien** (m)
electricity **électricité** (f)
engineer **ingénieur** (m)
foreman **contremaître** (m)
fuel **combustible** (m)
gas **gaz** (m)
laboratory **laboratoire** (m)
machinery
 machines (f. pl)
maintenance
 maintien (m)
manual worker **ouvrier/
 ouvrière** (m/f)
metal **métal** (m)
oil (lubricating) **huile** (f)
raw materials **matières
 premières** (f. pl)
research **recherche** (f)
services (works)
 révisions (f. pl)
site **emplacement** (m)
stores (warehouse)
 magasin (m)
tool room **salle à outils**
warehouse **entrepôt** (m)

Production **Production** (f)

automation
 automatisation (f)
batch **lot** (m)
budget **budget** (m)
construction
 construction (f)
consumption
 consommation (f)
control, to **contrôler**
effluent **effluent** (m)
increase, to **augmenter**
invest, to **investir**
job (to be done)
 travail (m)
new product **nouveau
 produit** (m)
output **production** (f)
performance
 performance (f)
plan **plan** (m)
productivity
 productivité (f)
quantity **quantité** (f)
reduce, to **réduire**
schedule **programme** (m)
timetable **horaire** (m)
ton **tonne** (f)
utilization **utilisation** (f)
volume **volume** (m)
waste **déchets** (m. pl)
works order
 commande (f)

Marketing **Marketing** (m)

achieve, to **accomplir**
advertise, to **faire de la
 publicité**
agent (sales) **agent** (m)
agree/accept, to **convenir**
assess, to **estimer**
brand **marque** (f)
commission (payment)
 commission (f)
competition
 concurrence (f)

customer **client** (m)
delivery **livraison** (f)
demand **demande** (f)
distribution
 distribution (f)
economic **économique**
forecast, to **prévoir**
market objective **objectif
 de marché** (m)
market research **étude de
 marché** (f)
opportunity **occasion** (f)
packaging **emballage** (m)
presentation
 présentation (f)
price **prix** (m)
product test **essai** (m)
promote, to **promouvoir**
quality **qualité** (f)
representative
 représentant (m, f)
sales **ventes** (f. pl)
sales force **ensemble des
 représentants** (m. pl)
service (customer)
 service (m)
share (of market)
 participation (f)
target **objectif** (m)

Employment **Emploi** (m)

assessment **estimation** (f)
benefit **avantage** (m)
bonus **gratification** (f)
canteen **cantine** (f)
job (for person)
 emploi (m)
pension **pension** (f)
personnel **personnel** (m)
salary **traitement** (m)
skill **habileté** (f)
social security **services
 sociaux** (m. pl)
training **formation** (f)
unemployed **en chômage**
vacancy **poste vacant** (m)
wage **salaire** (m)

31

French

Accounts *Comptes* (m. pl)

actual **réel**
asset, net **net actif** (m)
bad debt **créance irrécouvrable** (f)
balance sheet **bilan** (m)
borrow, to (from) **emprunter (à)**
capital **capital** (m)
capital expenditure **dépenses en capital** (f. pl)
cash **argent liquide** (m)
cash flow **cash-flow** (m)
cost of sales **prix coûtant** (m) .
credit control **contrôle des crédits** (m)
creditor **créancier/ creancière** (m/f)
debtor **débiteur/ débitrice** (m/f)
depreciation **dépréciation** (f)

dividend **dividende** (m)
expenditure **dépenses** (f. pl)
grant **subvention** (f)
interest (bank) **intérêt** (m)
labour cost **main d'oeuvre** (f)
liability (balance sheet) **passif** (m)
liability (damages) **engagement** (m)
loan **prêt** (m)
margin, gross **marge brut** (f)
profit, net **bénéfice nette** (f)
share capital **capital en actions** (m)
stocks **réserve** (f)
taxation **taxation** (f)
variance **variation** (f)
working capital **capital de travail** (m)

SESSION TWO
Pronunciation

2A Letters and Sounds

French	Sounds like	Example
a	a in hat	avenue
â	a in father	âge
au	o in no	auberge
b	b in bat	bon
c	c in cat	café
	but c in nice before e, i and y *or* when shown with a cedilla (ç) underneath	Nice français

ch	**sh** in **sh**ip	Champagne
d	**d** in **d**og *but* silent at word end	**d**eux gran**d**
e	**er** as in fath**er**	j**e**
é	**ay** as in m**ay**	sant**é**
ê	**e** as in b**e**t	f**ê**te
è	**ai** as in **ai**r	m**è**re
eau	**o** in n**o**	**eau**
eu	between **ur** and **er** as in m**ur**d**er**	d**eu**x
f	**f** in **f**ix	**f**ine
g	**g** in **g**ot *but* **g** in bei**g**e before e, i and y *and* almost silent at word end, (modifies the previous n)	**g**arage san**g**
gn	**ni** in on**i**on (softens the n)	a**gn**eau
h	lightly sounded or silent	**h**omme
i or **î**	**ee** in f**ee**t Note that **ie** written together are sounded separately	s**i**x p**i**ed
j	**g** in bei**g**e	**J**ean
k	**k** in **k**it	**k**ilo
l or **ll**	**l** in **l**it or a**ll**ow *but* **y** in **y**es after i (except ville, mille and village)	**l**it, A**ll**ô! fi**ll**e
m	**m** in **m**an *but* almost silent after vowels (see nasal sounds below)	**m**ère e**m**ballage
n	**n** in **n**ot *but* almost silent after vowels (see nasal sounds below)	**n**e u**n**
o	**o** in h**o**t	d**o**cument
ô	**o** in h**o**le	comp**ô**te

French

œu	**ur** in f**ur**	**œu**f
oi	**wa** in b**wa**na	tr**oi**s
p	**p** in **P**aris *but* silent at word end	**P**aris cham**p**
ph	**ph** in **ph**ase	**ph**ysique
qu	**c** in **c**art	**qu**atre
r	**r** in **r**at *but* trilled slightly (try vibrating the tongue at the back of the mouth and growling!) *but* silent in verb ending -er	**r**ien tromp**er**
s	**s** in **s**ave	**s**auf
	z in bla**z**e between two vowels *but* silent at word end	phra**s**e gra**s**
t	**t** in **t**in *but* silent at word end	**t**rente es**t**
u	between **oo** in p**oo**l and **ew** in ph**ew**!	**u**tile
ui	**we** in **we**	cond**ui**re
v	**v** in sa**v**e	**v**ase
w	not used (w) except in words of foreign origin	–
x	**x** in e**x**it *but* not in 'six' or 'dix' which have a variable pronunciation	e**x**trême
y	**ee** in f**ee**t *but* **y** in **y**es, followed by another vowel	t**y**pe **y**eux
z	**z** in bla**z**e *but* silent at word end	dou**z**e ne**z**

Nasal Sounds

A vowel followed by m or n, should be pronounced through the mouth and nose together. The m and n letters themselves are almost silent.

Letter combinations	Sounds like
on, om	**or** in **horn**
un, um	**er** in **fern**
im, in, ein, aim, ain	**ar** in **barn**
am, an, en, ean	**o** in **on**

Liaison

Consonants at the end of a word are often carried forward to the next word if it starts with a vowel, just as in English. Thus 'un petit enfant' is pronounced 'un peti t'enfant'.

Letter combinations like ts, ds, rs and rt are not usually sounded at the end of a word, but they are sounded and rolled on to the next word if it starts with a vowel.

2B   Accents and Stress

Let's deal with stress first, as it is easy to describe. Although some letters are not sounded, there is *no* real stress given to different syllables in French. The French articulate all their syllables evenly, clearly and precisely, perhaps with a slightly greater emphasis on the last syllable; they raise the pitch of the voice at the end of each phrase and lower it at the end of a sentence, unless expressing doubt or surprise.

Accents are a little more difficult, the two most common being the acute (´) and the grave (`) accents which are used over the a and e vowels. The acute accent shortens the sound as in 'café', the grave accent generally lengthens the sound as in 'père' (father).

Sometimes you see a circumflex (^) like a hat over the a, e, i or o vowels. The circumflex generally lengthens the sound of a, as in 'father', and modifies the sound of e and o. Ê sounds as it does in 'fête', ô as in 'hole'. The i sound does not change.

Occasionally we see a cedilla (ç) shown under a c consonant. This softens the c like an s, otherwise c is hard, as in 'cat'.

French

SESSION THREE
Absorbing the Language

This is a practice session, for you to try in your own time.

Go through the main vocabulary in Section 1A and read all the words aloud.

Go through a second time, covering up the English and see how many words you can translate.

Now go through a third time, this time covering up the French and see how many words you can translate from the English. Don't worry if there are only a few. Your vocabulary will develop with regular practice.

SESSION FOUR
Message Builders

4A   Message Builders

The 80 or so *'message builders'* shown below comprise part-phrases, interrogatives or verbs in everyday use, which you can use to build up questions and messages. You can use these *'message builders'* with your own list of key words to find your way round and to give yourself practice in speaking the language. There are no nouns shown in the list below; you get these from your own word list, or the main vocabulary. (Note that the nouns in the vocabulary are shown only in the singular, and the adjectives are shown in their masculine form, but you will find out in Session Six how to deal with the word endings.)

In Section 4B (p. 39) you will find the commonest forms of address and greetings which will 'top and tail' your messages. Liberal use of 'please' and 'thank you' will add considerably to your communication skills!

English	French
Today is	**Aujourd'hui c'est** . . . . .
I speak	**Je parle** . . . . .
Do you speak	**Parlez-vous** . . . . .
Yes . . . . . no	**Oui** . . . . . **non**

My name is	**Je m'appelle** . . . . .
My number is	**Mon numéro est le** . . . . .
I live in	**J'habite à** . . . . .
This is my	**C'est mon*** . . . . .
Who is/who are	**Qui est/qui sont** . . . . .
I am/we are	**Je suis/nous sommes** . . . . .
Why are we	**Pourquoi est-ce que nous sommes** . . . . .
Are you	**Est-ce que vous êtes** . . . . .
Where is/Where are	**Où est/où sont** . . . . .
a	**un** (m), **une** (f)
the	**le** (m), **la** (f), **les** (pl)
my	**mon** (m), **ma** (f), **mes** (pl)
Where can I find	**Où se trouve** . . . . .
I have lost	**J'ai perdu** . . . . .
I have broken	**J'ai cassé** . . . . .
I have forgotten	**J'ai oublié** . . . . .
When does . . . . . open	**À quelle heure ouvre** . . . . .
When does . . . . . start	**À quelle heure commence** . . . . .
When does . . . . . close	**À quelle heure ferme** . . . . .
Excuse me	**Pardonnez-moi** . . . . .
What is the way to	**Pour aller à** . . . . .
I want to go to	**Je veux aller à** . . . . .
Is it far to	**C'est loin** . . . . .
Is it	**Est-ce que c'est** . . . . .
It is	**C'est** . . . . .
It is not	**Ce n'est pas** . . . . .
Here is/here are	**Voici** . . . . .
Is there	**Y a-t-il** . . . . .
There is/there are	**Il y a** . . . . .
Is there . . . . . near here	**Y a-t-il** . . . . . **près d'ici**
Do you have/have you got	**Avez-vous** . . . . .
I have reserved	**J'ai réservé** . . . . .
It's for	**C'est pour** . . . . .
Does it have	**A-t-il*** . . . . .
I have/we have	**J'ai/nous avons** . . . . .
Can I have	**Puis-je avoir** . . . . .
Can you	**Pouvez-vous (+ infinitive)** . . . . .
Would you like	**Voulez-vous** . . . . .

French

I would like/we would like	Je voudrais/nous voudrions . . . . .
Another	Un/une autre . . . . .
I am sorry that	Je regrette que . . . . .
There is no	Il n'y a pas de . . . . .
What . . . . . do you have	Quel* . . . . . avez vous
How many . . . . . do you have	Combien de . . . . . avez vous
Anything else?	Encore quelque chose?
I would prefer	Je préférerais . . . . .
It is too	C'est trop . . . . .
I need/we need	J'ai besoin de/nous avons besoin de . . . . .
I will take/we will take	Je prends/nous prendrons . . . . .
I like . . . . . very much	J'aime bien . . . . .
Give me	Donnez-moi . . . . .
How much is	C'est combien . . . . .
More/less	Plus/moins . . . . .
One/two/three/four/five	Un/deux/trois/quatre/cinq . . . . .
Ten/twenty/fifty	Dix/vingt/cinquante . . . . .
One hundred/one thousand	Cent/mille . . . . .
Tell me	Dîtes-moi . . . . .
What time is it?	Quelle heure est-il?
When does . . . . . leave	À quelle heure part . . . . .
When does . . . . . arrive	À quelle heure arrive . . . . .
When do we	Quand est-ce que nous . . . . .
How do we	Comment (verb) -nous . . . . .
I am going to	Je vais (+ infinitive) . . . . .
I have just	Je viens de (+ infinitive) . . . . .
Don't go!	Ne vous en allez pas!
Let's go to	Allons à . . . . .
Meet me at	Rencontrez-moi à . . . . .
Telephone me at	Téléphonez-moi à . . . . .
I ought to/we must	Je dois/nous devons (+ infinitive) . . . . .
I can/we can	Je peux/nous pouvons (+ infinitive) . . . . .
Take care!	Prenez garde!
I will come back on	Je reviendrai le . . . . .

* masculine only

I can't understand	**Je ne comprends pas**
Speak more slowly	**Parlez plus lentement, s'il vous plaît**
Could you repeat that!	**Répétez, s'il vous plaît!**

4B   Addressing Friends and Strangers

French is more formal and polite than English. So:
● Shake hands when you meet and part company every day.
● Address adult strangers as **'monsieur'** (sir) or **'madame'** (madam), and girls as **'mademoiselle'** (miss), thus:

Excusez-moi, monsieur, puis-je trouver . . . (Excuse me, sir, can I find . . .)

● **'S'il vous plaît'** (please) literally means 'if it pleases you'. 'Thank you' is **'merci'**.
● The time of day to the French is rather like the subject of weather to the English, so:

Good morning, good day	**Bonjour**
Good evening	**Bonsoir**
Goodnight	**Bonne nuit**
Delighted to meet you	**Enchanté**
Goodbye	**Au revoir**
Until we meet again	**A bientôt/A la prochaine**

● Useful words of greeting include **'Bonjour!'** or **'Salut!'** (Hello!) and **'Comment ça va'** (literally, 'How goes it' or 'How are you') to which you could reply **'Ça va bien'** (It goes well).
● To toast your friends, use **'Santé!'** (Good health!) for drinks, and **'Bon appétit'** (Enjoy your meal) before a meal.

SESSION FIVE
Language Structure

5 Word Order

Similar to English, but with these main differences:

1 Longer adjectives usually follow nouns; shorter adjectives usually precede them. Thus **'Un livre intéressant'** literally means 'a book interesting', but **'un grand animal'** is 'a big animal'.

2 Object pronouns, reflexive pronouns and the negative **'ne'** are positioned *before* the verb, except after an imperative. When there are two pronouns, the following order should be observed:

me nous vous	} *before*	le la les	} *before*	lui leur

Je *le lui* donne (I give it to him) means literally 'I *it to him* give'

Je *ne le lui* ai *pas* donné (I have not given it to him) means 'I it to him have not given'

3 In asking a question, the verb and subject (noun or pronoun) are usually reversed, but not when you start the sentence **'est-ce que'**.

Parlez-vous français? (literally, Speak you French?), but **Est-ce que vous êtes anglais?** (Is it that you are English?)

SESSION SIX
Nouns, Adjectives and The Two Articles

6A Nouns and Gender

Every noun in French is either masculine (m) or feminine (f), and so are the definite and indefinite articles:

the = **le** (m) or **la** (f)
a = **un** (m) or **une** (f)

Examples are:

the boy – **le garçon**
the girl – **la jeune fille**
a boy – **un garçon**
a girl – **une jeune fille**

But, if the noun starts with a vowel (or a silent h) and it would sound awkward after **'le'** or **'la'**, you knock off the e or a and run the two together, e.g.

l'accident (m), **l'auberge** (f) (inn), or **l'homme** (m) (man)

There are no easy rules for masculine or feminine, except that masculine objects are usually masculine, and many nouns ending in -e are feminine. So try to learn the gender at the same time as you learn the word. Once you have heard the word in French or used it a few times, the gender can be memorized automatically with the word itself.

6B   Adjectives Must Agree

In Section 5, you will have read that longer adjectives generally follow the nouns, shorter ones precede them. But adjectives also have to agree. If the noun is feminine, so is the adjective. Thus **'bon'** (good) changes from

Un bon garçon (A good boy) to
Une bonne fille (A good girl)

Most adjectives just add a single e when they become feminine, unless there is an e there already. (Words ending in -é add another e.)
But words ending in -l, -n, -s and -t generally double up the final consonant and add an e, thus:

naturel becomes **naturelle**
bon becomes **bonne**
gros becomes **grosse**
net becomes **nette**

while those ending in -f and -x change to -ve and -se:

neuf (new) becomes **neuve**
faux (false) becomes **fausse**

There are some common exceptions shown in Section 12A (p. 59). In the word list we also show the feminine of any adjective which does not follow these rules.

6C Plurals

Most nouns in French add s in the plural, just as in English (unless there is one there already). Adjectives have a plural form too, which must agree with the noun. Very logical, but easy to forget.

The definite article also changes from **'l' '**, **'le'** or **'la'**, to **'les'**:

le frère (brother) becomes **les frères**
la bonne fille (the good girl) becomes **les bonnes filles**
l'enfant terrible (the terrible child) becomes **les enfants terribles**

There are one or two exceptions. Words ending in -eau add -x:

château (castle) becomes **châteaux**

If we assume that the plural of 'a' is 'some', this changes in French from **'un'** or **'une'** to **'des'** or **'de'** when followed by an adjective (see Section 14B, p. 64).

SESSION SEVEN
Personal Pronouns and Verbs

7A Subject Pronouns

Before moving on to verbs, we should run through the personal pronouns – I, he, we, you and they – which are the *subject* of the verb. We usually describe the subject pronouns as being in the 1st, 2nd or 3rd person singular, or plural, and modify the verb endings accordingly. The subject pronouns are as follows:

1st person singular	I	**je**
3rd person singular	he/it (m)	**il**
	she/it (f)	**elle**
	one	**on**
1st person plural	we	**nous**
2nd person plural	you	**vous**
3rd person plural	they (m)	**ils**
	they (f)	**elles**

42

'Je' drops its e before a verb starting with a vowel, thus **'j'aime'** (I love or I like).

Note that we have left out the singular form for 'you' ('tu' in French) and only use the plural. Until you get to know French people well, it is impolite to use the singular, so we have omitted it entirely. However, we have included the pronoun **'on'** (one) which is 3rd person singular.

7B   Regular Verbs

Present, Imperfect and Future Tenses

In this section we start with the regular verbs, then move on to some of the irregular verbs. To make it easier, we have restricted the tenses to the present (I am doing), the imperfect (I was doing), the future (I will do) and the past (I have done). We shall therefore leave out the tenses which mean 'I did' (historic), 'I would or could do' (conditional), 'I may or might do' (subjunctive) and a few other tenses which are less frequently used, even though their use in many sentences would be grammatically correct. However, a note does appear on the use of the subjunctive in the Appendix, which we have left right to the end (p. 71).

In French, as in English, the verb endings change, both with the pronoun used and the tense. However, the French do not use different words to indicate tense such as 'am', 'was', 'will', 'shall', 'had', 'have', 'should', 'could', 'may' or 'might'. These are all incorporated in the verb itself, and indicated by the verb ending.

We saw the subject pronouns in Section 7A (facing page). These require five verb endings, one each for I, he/she/it, we, you and they. Remember, we are leaving out 'thou' ('tu' in French), as this is used only in a family or very friendly environment.

First, then, to the regular verbs. There are three main types (or conjugations) of verbs: those whose infinitive form (to do something) ends in -er, -ir or -re. Thus:

parl**er**   to speak
fin**ir**   to finish
vend**re**   to sell

Note that we speak of the first part of the verb as the

French

'stem' (parl-) and the ending as -er. The endings are shown in bold type in the text.

Present Tense

The present tense (I speak/finish/sell) is conjugated as follows:

	speak -er	*finish* -ir	*sell* -re
je	parl**e**	fin**is**	vend**s**
il/elle/on	parl**e**	fin**it**	vend
nous	parl**ons**	fin**issons**	vend**ons**
vous	parl**ez**	fin**issez**	vend**ez**
ils/elles	parl**ent**	fin**issent**	vend**ent**

Imperfect Tense

The imperfect tense (I was speaking/finishing/selling, or I used to speak/finish/sell) is conjugated as follows:

	speak -er	*finish* -ir	*sell* -re
je	parl**ais**	fin**issais**	vend**ais**
il/elle/on	parl**ait**	fin**issait**	vend**ait**
nous	parl**ions**	fin**issions**	vend**ions**
vous	parl**iez**	fin**issiez**	vend**iez**
ils/elles	parl**aient**	fin**issaient**	vend**aient**

Future Tense

The future tense (I will speak/finish/sell) interposes an -er, -ir or just an -r after the stem, as follows:

	speak	*finish*	*sell*
je	parl**erai**	fin**irai**	vend**rai**
il/elle/on	parl**era**	fin**ira**	vend**ra**
nous	parl**erons**	fin**irons**	vend**rons**
vous	parl**erez**	fin**irez**	vend**rez**
ils/elles	parl**eront**	fin**iront**	vend**ront**

All the common regular verbs are shown in the word list. The irregular verbs are dealt with in Sections 10B and 10C (pp. 49 and 51).

Present Participle

In French, 'I am speaking' is translated as 'I speak'. But the word 'speaking' or any other verb in English ending in -ing can also be used like an adjective. In this case, you would use what is called the present participle thus:

Parl*ant* du roi (Speaking of the king) or
Les étudiants, finiss*ant* **leur leçons** (The students, finishing their lessons)

The present participle is formed by adding -ant to the stem of the verb, or -issant to the stem of any verb ending in -ir, thus:

parlant (speaking), **finissant** (finishing), **vendant** (selling)

However, if you wish to say 'in speaking' or 'in finishing' or 'in selling', you use the little word **'en'** plus the present participle, thus:

En parlant aux étudiants (In speaking to the students)

SESSION EIGHT
To Be and To Have

8   Avoir, Etre and the Perfect Tense

The perfect tense ('I have done' something) is used far more frequently than the historic ('I did' something). It is built up in the same way as in English, using either the verb 'to have' or the verb 'to be', together with what is called the past participle.

The past participle of the three conjugations of regular verbs adds -é, -i or -u to the stem, thus:

parlé (spoken), **fini** (finished), **vendu** (sold)

So if we put the verb 'to have' with the past participle, we get:

I have spoken	– **J'ai parlé**
I have finished	– **J'ai fini**
I have sold	– **J'ai vendu**

French

To build up the perfect tense, you first need to know how to conjugate the two verbs 'to be' (**être**) and 'to have' (**avoir**). These two verbs are thoroughly irregular and are conjugated as follows:

je suis	I am
il/elle/on est	he/she/it/one is
nous sommes	we are
vous êtes	you are
ils/elles sont	they are

j'ai	I have
il/elle/on a	he/she/it/one has
nous avons	we have
nous avez	you have
ils/elles ont	they have

Those words which use '**être**' rather than '**avoir**' in the perfect tense are marked *E in the word list. They include:

aller (to go)	**entrer** (to enter)	**revenir** (to
arriver (to	**monter** (to climb)	return)
arrive)	**mourir** (to die)	**sortir** (to go out)
descendre (to	**partir** (to leave)	**venir** (to come)
go down)	**rester** (to stay)	

It is possible to turn some verbs which normally take '**avoir**' in the perfect tense, into the passive tense, e.g.

'I have finished' can be translated '**j'ai terminé**' but 'the meal is finished' would be '**le repas est terminé**'.

Sometimes we use the past participle just like an adjective, after the verb 'to be':

Je suis fatigué (I am tired)
Elle est fatiguée (She is tired)
Elles sont fatiguées (They – females – are tired)

Whenever we use '**être**', the past participle has to agree with the subject.

Whereas some verbs use '**être**' in French when the English use 'have', there are conversely one or two expressions in which the French use '**avoir**' when we use 'to be'. For example,

J'*ai* froid/chaud (I am cold/hot)
J'*ai* faim/soif (I am hungry/thirsty)
Il *a* raison/tort (He is right/wrong)
J'*ai* vingt ans (I am twenty [years old])

Other Tenses of 'Avoir' and 'Etre'

The imperfect and future tenses of **'avoir'** and
shown below:

	Avoir		*Etre*	
	Imperfect	*Future*	*Imperfect*	*Future*
j'	avais	aurai	étais	serai
il/elle/on	avait	aura	était	sera
nous	avions	aurons	étions	serons
vous	aviez	aurez	étiez	serez
ils/elles	avaient	auront	étaient	seront

SESSION NINE
Object Pronouns

9 Object and Emphatic Pronouns

In French, as in English, the spelling of a pronoun
changes when it becomes the object in a sentence. To take
a simple case:

He hits *him* is translated **Il le frappe**
He changes to *him* in English, **il** changes to **le** in French.

As we saw in Section 5 (p. 40), the object pronoun comes
before the verb in French, except after an imperative (but
not a negative imperative).

Donnez-le-moi (Give it to me)
Ne me le donnez pas (Don't give it to me)

The object pronouns are set out below in two columns,
the first where the pronoun is the direct object of the
verb, the second where the pronoun is the indirect object
– i.e. where in English we would say *'to me'*, *'to him'* or *'to'*
any other pronoun.

Note that **'me'**, **'le'** and **'la'** drop the vowel and take an
apostrophe before a word starting with another vowel.
As, for example, in **'je l'ai'** (I have it).

Direct		Indirect		Emphatic	
me	**me**	to me	**me**	me!	**moi**
him/it	**le**	to him/it	**lui**	him/it!	**lui**
her/it	**la**	to her/it	**lui**	her/it!	**elle**
us	**nous**	to us	**nous**	us!	**nous**
you	**vous**	to you	**vous**	you!	**vous**
them (m)	**les**	to them (m)	**leur**	them! (m)	**eux**
them (f)	**les**	to them (f)	**leur**	them! (f)	**elles**

Where there are two pronouns, the following order should be observed:

$$\left.\begin{matrix} \textbf{me} \\ \textbf{nous} \\ \textbf{vous} \end{matrix}\right\} \quad before \quad \left.\begin{matrix} \textbf{le} \\ \textbf{la} \\ \textbf{les} \end{matrix}\right\} \quad before \quad \left.\begin{matrix} \textbf{lui} \\ \textbf{leur} \end{matrix}\right.$$

I have sent *it to them* – **Je le leur ai envoyé**
You have given *it to me* – **Vous me l'avez donné**

Emphatic Pronouns

Finally, we come to *emphatic* pronouns which are used more in French than in English. If you want to emphasize *'me'* in the sentence 'As for me, I am king', you could translate this either as:

Moi, je suis roi *or* **C'est moi le roi**

'Moi' or **'nous'** are also used after an imperative:

Donnez-moi l'argent (Give me the money)

The emphatic pronoun is sometimes used after the prepositions 'to' (**à**), 'for' (**pour**), 'with' (**avec**) and 'of' (**de**), e.g.

La maison, c'est à moi (The house, it's mine!)

SESSION TEN
Imperatives, Reflexives and Irregular Verbs

10A The Imperative and Reflexive Verbs

We spend a lot of time asking people to do something, or ordering them about. There are only two forms of the imperative in French:

You must (do something)
We must or let us (do something)

It is simple to translate into French. Just use the first or second person plural of the present tense, and drop the **'nous'** or **'vous'**, thus:

Allez (You must go)
Allons (We must go or Let's go)

If a pronoun is the object of an imperative, use the object pronoun, and tack it on to the end of the verb, e.g.

Portez-le à la maison (Carry it to the house)

Except in the case of 'me', when you use the emphatic pronoun (**moi**):

Conduisez-moi au théâtre (Drive me to the theatre)

Reflexive Verbs

Some verbs are 'reflexive' and have to be used with the reflexive pronouns **'me'**, **'se'** (singular), **'nous'**, **'vous'**, **'se'** (plural), as well as the personal pronouns, e.g.

'I dress' is translated as 'I dress myself' (**je m'habille**)
'I sit down' becomes 'I sit myself down' (**je m'assieds**)

The French do not drop the reflexive pronoun, as we do. So, whenever you use the reflexive verb, you must use the pronoun, thus:

	Subject pronoun	*Reflexive pronoun*
I/me	**je**	**me**
he/him	**il**	**se** (or **s'**)
she/her	**elle**	**se** (or **s'**)
we/us	**nous**	**nous**
you/you	**vous**	**vous**
they/them (m)	**ils**	**se** (or **s'**)
they/them (f)	**elles**	**se** (or **s'**)

In the word list, the reflexive verbs are shown with (se) before the infinitive. They all take **'être'** not **'avoir'** in the perfect tense.

10B   Irregular Verbs

There are fewer than 100 irregular verbs in French but many are in common usage. Indeed there are 44 in our word list. In the next section, for each of the 44 verbs, we show the infinitive, the present and past participles, and the present and future tenses. For the perfect tense, use

French

the past participle and build up with **'avoir'** or **'être'**, just as with regular verbs.

If you look through the verbs, you will find a certain pattern emerges. They fall roughly into groups according to their infinitive form:

> those ending in -ire, such as **dire** (to say), **lire** (to read), **rire** (to laugh), **écrire** (to write)

> those ending in -ir, such as **sortir** (to go out), **courir** (to run), **servir** (to serve)

> those ending in -oir, such as **savoir** (to know), **voir** (to see), **recevoir** (to receive)

> those ending in -oire, such as **croire** (to believe), **boire** (to drink)

In nearly all cases, the singular of the present tense uses a short stem; for example:

> **je lis** (I read), **il boit** (he drinks), **je sors** (I go out), **il voit** (he sees)

whereas the plural of the present tense often uses a longer stem, changing, deleting or adding another letter to make it sound better, thus:

> nous **lisons** (we read) *not* nous lirons
> vous **buvez** (you drink) *not* vous boirez
> ils **sortent** (they go out) regular
> nous **voyons** (we see) *not* nous voions
> vous **recevez** (you receive) *not* vous recevoiez
> elles **boivent** (they drink) *not* elles boirent

Conjugating irregular verbs becomes habitual after a time, because the verbs nearly all sound easier to pronounce than if they had been perfectly regular.

So much for the present tense. The endings of the future tense are regular (-ai, -a, -ons, -ez and -ont) and you only need to add them to the final -r of the infinitive, thus:

> **je boirai** (I will drink)
> **je sortirai** (I will go out)
> **je mettrai** (I will put)
> **je lirai** (I will read)

but one or two, such as **'courir'** and **'mourir'**, drop the intermediate i to make them easier to pronounce, thus:

> ils mourront (they will die) *not* ils mouriront
> il courra (he will run) *not* il courira

A few of the 44 irregular verbs crop up all the time, particularly:

aller (to go)	**pouvoir** (to be able)
conduire (to drive)	**venir** (to come)
devoir (to owe)	**voir** (to see)
faire (to make)	**vouloir** (to want/wish)

'**Devoir**' (to owe) and '**pouvoir**' (to be able) are particularly useful as they can be used to make up tenses of other verbs, e.g.

Je dois aller à Paris (I *must* go to Paris)
Je peux venir à Paris (I *can* come to Paris)

You can also use '**pouvoir**' when you would use 'may' or 'might' in English, e.g.

Je peux venir (I *am able* to come)

which is sufficiently close for the beginner to use for 'I may/might come' even though the meaning is slightly different.

10C Irregular Verbs Conjugated

Below we list 44 common verbs (other than '**avoir**' and '**être**'), included in our word list which are irregular in one form or another. Don't try to learn them in one go but read them through two or three times so that you become familiar with them and can recognize them in their written form.

Each verb is shown first in the infinitive, followed by the present and past participles. On the next two lines we show the present and future tenses, without repeating the subject pronouns (**je**, **il**, **nous**, **vous**, **ils**).

We have not shown the imperatives, as these can be picked up from the 1st and 2nd person plural of the present tense.

The endings of the imperfect tense are quite standard (**-ais**, **-ait**, **-ions**, **-iez**, **-aient**) and follow on the stem of the 1st person plural of the present tense, e.g. '**j'allais**' (I was going).

aller (*to go*), allant (*going*), allé (*gone*)
vais, va, allons, allez, vont
irai, ira, irons, irez, iront

French

apprendre (*to learn*), apprenant (*learning*), appris (*learnt*)
apprends, apprend, apprenons, apprenez, apprennent
apprendrai, apprendra, apprendrons, apprendrez,
  apprendront

boire (*to drink*), buvant (*drinking*), bu (*drunk*)
bois, boit, buvons, buvez, boivent
boirai, boira, boirons, boirez, boiront

comprendre (*to understand*), comprenant (*understanding*),
  compris (*understood*)
comprends, comprend, comprenons, comprenez,
  comprennent
comprendrai, comprendra, comprendrons,
  comprendrez, comprendront

conduire (*to conduct, drive*), conduisant (*conducting*),
  conduit (*conducted*)
conduis, conduit, conduisons, conduisez, conduisent
conduirai, conduira, conduirons, conduirez, conduiront

connaître (*to know*), connaissant (*knowing*), connu
  (*known*)
connais, connaît, connaissons, connaissez, connaissent
connaîtrai, connaîtra, connaîtrons, connaîtrez,
  connaîtront

courir (*to run*), courant (*running*), couru (*ran*)
cours, court, courons, courez, courent
courrai, courra, courrons, courrez, courront

couvrir (*to cover*), couvrant (*covering*), couvert (*covered*)
couvre, couvre, couvrons, couvrez, couvrent
couvrirai, couvrira, couvrirons, couvrirez, couvriront

croire (*to believe*), croyant (*believing*), cru (*believed*)
crois, croit, croyons, croyez, croient
croirai, croira, croirons, croirez, croiront

cuire (*to cook*), cuisant (*cooking*), cuit (*cooked*)
cuis, cuit, cuisons, cuisez, cuisent
cuirai, cuira, cuirons, cuirez, cuiront

devenir (*to become*), devenant (*becoming*), devenu
  (*became*)
deviens, devient, devenons, devenez, deviennent
deviendrai, deviendra, deviendrons, deviendrez,
  deviendront

devoir (*to owe, have to*), devant (*owing*), dû (*owed*)
dois, doit, devons, devez, doivent
devrai, devra, devrons, devrez, devront

dire (*to say, tell*), disant (*saying*), dit (*said*)
dis, dit, disons, dites, disent
dirai, dira, dirons, direz, diront

dormir (*to sleep*), dormant (*sleeping*), dormi (*slept*)
dors, dort, dormons, dormez, dorment
dormirai, dormira, dormirons, dormirez, dormiront

écrire (*to write*), écrivant (*writing*), écrit (*wrote*)
écris, écrit, écrivons, écrivez, écrivent
écrirai, écrira, écrirons, écrirez, écriront

envoyer (*to send*), envoyant (*sending*), envoyé (*sent*)
envoie, envoie, envoyons, envoyez, envoient
enverrai, enverra, enverrons, enverrez, enverront

faire (*to make, do*), faisant (*making*), fait (*made*)
fais, fait, faisons, faites, font
ferai, fera, ferons, ferez, feront

lire (*to read*), lisant (*reading*), lu (*read*)
lis, lit, lisons, lisez, lisent
lirai, lira, lirons, lirez, liront

mettre (*to put*), mettant (*putting*), mis (*put*)
mets, met, mettons, mettez, mettent
mettrai, mettra, mettrons, mettrez, mettront

mourir (*to die*), mourant (*dying*), mort (*died*)
meurs, meurt, mourons, mourez, meurent
mourrai, mourra, mourrons, mourrez, mourront

mouvoir (*to move*), mouvant (*moving*), mû (*moved*)
meus, meut, mouvons, mouvez, meuvent
mouvrai, mouvra, mouvrons, mouvrez, mouvront

obtenir (*to obtain*), obtenant (*obtaining*), obtenu (*obtained*)
obtiens, obtient, obtenons, obtenez, obtiennent
obtiendrai, obtiendra, obtiendrons, obtiendrez, obtiendront

offrir (*to offer*), offrant (*offering*), offert (*offered*)
offre, offre, offrons, offrez, offrent
offrirai, offrira, offrirons, offrirez, offriront

ouvrir (*to open*), ouvrant (*opening*), ouvert (*opened*)
ouvre, ouvre, ouvrons, ouvrez, ouvrent
ouvrirai, ouvrira, ouvrirons, ouvrirez, ouvriront

partir (*to leave, go away*), partant (*leaving*), parti (*left*)
pars, part, partons, partez, partent
partirai, partira, partirons, partirez, partiront

French

permettre (*to allow*), permettant (*allowing*), permis
(*allowed*)
permets, permet, permettons, permettez, permettent
permettrai, permettra, permettrons, permettrez,
permettront

pouvoir (*to be able*), pouvant (*being able to*), pu (*could*)
peux, peut, pouvons, pouvez, peuvent
pourrai, pourra, pourrons, pourrez, pourront

prendre (*to take*), prenant (*taking*), pris (*took*)
prends, prend, prenons, prenez, prennent
prendrai, prendra, prendrons, prendrez, prendront

promettre (*to promise*), promettant (*promising*), promis
(*promised*)
promets, promet, promettons, promettez, promettent
promettrai, promettra, promettrons, promettrez,
promettront

recevoir (*to receive*), recevant (*receiving*), reçu (*received*)
reçois, reçoit, recevons, recevez, reçoivent
recevrai, recevra, recevrons, recevrez, recevront

revenir (*to return, come back*), revenant (*coming back*),
revenu (*came back*)
reviens, revient, revenons, revenez, reviennent
reviendrai, reviendra, reviendrons, reviendrez,
reviendront

rire (*to laugh*), riant (*laughing*), ri (*laughed*)
ris, rit, rions, riez, rient
rirai, rira, rirons, rirez, riront

rompre (*to break*), rompant (*breaking*), rompu (*broken*)
romps, rompt, rompons, rompez, rompent
romprai, rompra, romprons, romprez, rompront

savoir (*to know*), savant (*knowing*), su (*known*)
sais, sait, savons, savez, savent
saurai, saura, saurons, saurez, sauront

sortir (*to go out*), sortant (*going out*), sorti (*gone out*)
sors, sort, sortons, sortez, sortent
sortirai, sortira, sortirons, sortirez, sortiront

souvenir (*to remember*), souvenant (*remembering*),
souvenu (*remembered*)
souviens, souvient, souvenons, souvenez, souviennent
souviendrai, souviendra, souviendrons, souviendrez,
souviendront

suivre (*to follow*), suivant (*following*), suivi (*followed*)
suis, suit, suivons, suivez, suivent
suivrai, suivra, suivrons, suivrez, suivront

tenir (*to hold*), tenant (*holding*), tenu (*held*)
tiens, tient, tenons, tenez, tiennent
tiendrai, tiendra, tiendrons, tiendrez, tiendront

traduire (*to translate*), traduisant (*translating*), traduit
  (*translated*)
traduis, traduit, traduisons, traduisez, traduisent
traduirai, traduira, traduirons, traduirez, traduiront

valoir (*to be worth*), valant (*being worth*), valu (*was worth*)
vaux, vaut, valons, valez, valent
vaudrai, vaudra, vaudrons, vaudrez, vaudront

venir (*to come*), venant (*coming*), venu (*came*)
viens, vient, venons, venez, viennent
viendrai, viendra, viendrons, viendrez, viendront

vivre (*to live*), vivant (*living*), vécu (*lived*)
vis, vit, vivons, vivez, vivent
vivrai, vivra, vivrons, vivrez, vivront

voir (*to see*), voyant (*seeing*), vu (*saw*)
vois, voit, voyons, voyez, voient
verrai, verra, verrons, verrez, verront

vouloir (*to want, be willing*), voulant (*wanting*), voulu
  (*wanted*)
veux, veut, voulons, voulez, veulent
voudrai, voudra, voudrons, voudrez, voudront

SESSION ELEVEN
Questions and Negatives

11A   Questions

There are several ways of asking a question in French.
The first just reverses the verb and personal pronoun,
inserting a hyphen in between the two, for example:

Il est anglais (He is English)
Est-il anglais? (Is he English?)

The second, often used, is to start the sentence with the

French

little phrase, **'est-ce que'** (is it that), e.g.

Est-ce qu'il est anglais? (Is it that he is English?)

The English word 'do' or 'does' is not translated. There is no exact equivalent for 'Does she love Frederick?' You translate this by reversing the verb and pronoun as before:

Aime-t-elle Frederick? (literally, Loves-she Frederick?)

Notice that the French insert t in between the two e vowels of **'aime'** and **'elle'** on the basis that the two e vowels together would sound rather unpleasant.

If a noun, rather than a pronoun, is used, the rule is different. You can *not* say **'Est-Martha anglaise?'** (Is Martha English?). You either single out Martha at the beginning of the sentence and ask if she is English, thus:

Martha, est-elle anglaise? (Martha, is she English?)

or you fall back on the tried and trusted phrase, **'est-ce que'** (is it that):

Est-ce que Martha est anglaise? (Is it that Martha is English?)

If, as part of the question, you have to refer to the object pronoun (him, her, them, etc), remember that these come *before* the verb, even in the interrogative form, e.g.

Elle l'aime (She loves him)
L'aime-t-elle? (Does she love him?)

Finally, there is one other way of asking a question without altering either the verb or word order at all. You merely raise your voice at the end of the sentence and make it sound like a question, or add **'hein?'** at the end.

Le garçon a six ans, hein?' (The boy is [has] six [years], eh?)

Remember that **'avoir'**, not **'être'**, is used for expressing age (Section 8, p. 46).

11B   Interrogatives

Most interrogatives in French are straightforward:

où (where) – **Où est mon stylo?** (Where is my pen?)
quand (when) – **Quand arriverez-vous?** (When will you arrive?)
pourquoi (why) – **Pourquoi êtes-vous en retard?** (Why are you late?)

comment (how) – **Comment ça va?** (literally, How goes it, or How are you?)
combien de (how many, how much) – **Combien d'argent avez-vous?** (How much money do you have?)
que (what) – **Que pensez-vous?** (What do you think?)
qui (who) – **Qui va là?** (Who goes there?)

Sometimes the French emphasize the noun or pronoun first, when asking a question, e.g.

Mon stylo, où est-il? (My pen, where is it?)
Frederick, quand arrivera-t-il? (Frederick, when will he arrive?)
Moi, suis-je en retard? (Me, am I late?)

'Who', 'What' and 'Which'

There is no exact translation for 'whose', the English genitive of 'who'. You must be more precise and say **'de qui'** (of whom) or, more commonly, **'à qui'** (to whom), thus:

À qui sont les crayons? (Whose are these pencils?)

'Qui' (who or whom) and **'que'** (what, which, that or whom) can be used as relative pronouns to join two phrases together; for example:

L'homme qui va là (The man who goes there)
Les cours que nous avons eus aujourd'hui (The lessons which we have had today)
L'homme que nous avons rencontré (The man whom we met)
L'homme de qui j'ai parlé (The man of whom I spoke)
La maison que je me rappelle (The house that I remember)

'Of which' or 'of whom' is often translated by the little word **'dont'**:

La maison dont j'ai parlé (The house of which I spoke)

'Quel' is used for 'what' or 'which' when it directly refers to a noun:

Quel cours avons-nous aujourd'hui? (What lesson do we have today?)
Quel dommage! (What a pity!)

Like other adjectives, **'quel'** has a feminine **'quelle'** and a plural **'quels'** (m) or **'quelles'** (f), which have to agree with the noun.

If **'quel'** is used as a relative pronoun together with a

preposition, such as 'with', 'by', 'to' or 'of', it needs to be stressed by adding the definite article as a prefix.

La cuillère avec *la*quelle je mange (The spoon with which I eat)

Le bureau dans *le*quel je travaille (The office in which I work)

11C Negatives

The French emphasize their negatives using two words (**'ne . . . pas'**), not one, rather as we would say 'not at all'.

The **'ne'** follows the noun or personal pronoun and **'pas'** follows the verb, e.g.

Je ne parle pas anglais (I do not speak English)

In the case of the perfect tense, **'pas'** comes before the past participle, e.g.

Je n'ai pas parlé (I have not spoken)

Note that **'ne'** drops the e before a verb starting with a vowel. If you are also using an object pronoun (him, it, us, etc), it follows *after* the **'ne'** and just before the verb, e.g.

Je ne lui parle pas (I do not speak to him)

In the interrogative or imperative form, the word order for **'ne'** and **'pas'** is just the same. But you may remember from Section 11A (p. 55) that there are several ways of asking a question.

N'est-il pas heureux? (Is he not happy?)
Martha, n'est-elle pas anglaise? (Martha, is she not English?)
or **Est-ce que Martha n'est pas anglaise?** (Is it that Martha is not English?)
and **Ne marchez pas là!** (Do not walk there!)

As you can see, the word order does get a little tricky when you combine a negative interrogative with object pronouns, but you will soon get used to it! For example:

Ne le lui a-t-il pas donné (Has he not given it to him?)

Only when 'no' or 'not' is used *without* a verb, do you use **'pas'** on its own, as in

Pas beaucoup (Not much)
Pas encore (Not yet)

SESSION TWELVE
More Adjectives

12A Adjectives and Comparatives

There are 80 adjectives in the 500 word list, but there is no
need to learn them all at once. Some indefinite adjectives
are in common use and you should try to remember
these:

all (**tout**)
another (**un/e autre**)
each (**chaque**)
enough (**assez de**)
less (**moins de**)
many/much (**beaucoup de**)
more (**plus de**)
next (**prochain**)
other (**autre**)
some, unspecified (**quelque**)
too much (**trop de**)

'**Assez**' (enough), '**beaucoup**' (much), '**tout**' (all), '**moins**'
(less), '**plus**' (more) and '**trop**' (too) can also be used as
adverbs but without the '**de**'.

Normally all adjectives have to agree with the noun,
but apart from '**tout**' (all) and '**prochain**' (next) these
adjectives do not have a feminine and a plural form.
'**Autre**' and '**quelque**' do add -s in the plural, but have no
feminine.

As we saw in Section 6B (p. 41), most adjectives add
-e for the feminine and -s for the plural. Those ending in
-l, -n and -t double the consonant and add e in the feminine form. Those ending in -x and -f change to -se and -ve.
However, there are a few adjectives in the list which do
not follow the rules, and these are as follows:

	Singular		Plural	
	M	F	M	F
beautiful	*beau/bel	belle	beaux	belles
complete	complet	complète	complets	complètes
dear	cher	chère	chers	chères
dry	sec	sèche	secs	sèches
fresh	frais	fraîche	frais	fraîches

* '*Bel*', '*nouvel*' and '*vieil*' are used before a vowel or silent h, e.g. **un
bel homme**

French

long	long	longue	longs	longues
mad	fou	folle	foux	folles
new	*nouveau/ nouvel	nouvelle	nouveaux	nouvelles
old	*vieux/ vieil	vieille	vieux	vieilles
soft	doux	douce	doux	douces
white	blanc	blanche	blancs	blanches

Two adjectives in our list, **'gros'** (big) and **'gras'** (fat), also double up the final -s and add -e, thus **'grosse'** and **'grasse'** in the feminine form, and add another -s in the plural, **'grosses'** and **'grasses'**.

One or two English adjectives/adverbs do not have a single word French equivalent, e.g.

> early (**de bonne heure**); literally, in good time
> cheap (**à bon marché**); literally, at a good market

Comparatives

The French use **'plus'** (more) or **'moins'** (less) with another adjective to indicate comparison. Where we say 'whiter', they say **'plus blanc'** (more white), but **'moins blanc'** (less white) is expressed in the same way in both languages.

So much for whit*er*, or *less* white; how do we show whit*est*, or *least* white? Just by inserting **'le'** or **'la'** before **'plus'** or **'moins'**:

> **La neige, la plus blanche** (The whitest snow)
> **Le soleil, le moins rouge** (The least red sun)

Two notable exceptions are 'good' and 'bad', which go as follows:

bon (good)	**meilleur** (better)	**le/la meilleur/e** (best)
mauvais (bad)	**pire** (worse)	**le/la pire** (worst)

12B   Possessive Adjectives

The possessive adjectives – my, your, his, her, its, our and their – behave just like any other adjectives. They have to agree with the noun, not with the owner. It doesn't matter whether you are male or female, the possessive adjective has to agree with the object it refers to, thus:

Mon frère aimable (My friendly brother)
Ma belle fille (My beautiful daughter)

The list is short and easily memorable.

	M	F	Pl
my	**mon**	**ma**	**mes**
his, her, its	**son**	**sa**	**ses**
our	**notre**	**notre**	**nos**
your	**votre**	**votre**	**vos**
their	**leur**	**leur**	**leurs**

If the object is omitted, as in the phrase 'It's mine!' (**C'est à moi!'**), we use **'à'** + the 'emphatic' pronoun:

mine	**à moi**
his/its/hers	**à lui/elle**
ours	**à nous**
yours	**à vous**
theirs	**à eux/elles**

SESSION THIRTEEN
Adverbs, Prepositions and Conjunctions

13A   Common Adverbs

In changing adjectives to adverbs some French words just add -ment to the feminine singular of the adjective, as we would add -ly to the adjective in English, thus:

lent (slow) becomes **lentement** (slowly)
heureux (fortunate) becomes **heureusement** (fortunately)

but some are irregular like 'good' and 'bad':

bon (good) becomes **bien** (well)
mauvais (bad) becomes **mal** (badly)

There are 35 other adverbs in our word list and as you can see from the list below, many are in everyday use.

after (**après**)	already (**déjà**)
again (**encore**)	also/too (**aussi**)
ago (**il y a**)	always (**toujours**)
almost (**presque**)	because (**parce que**)
alone (**seul**)	before (**avant**)

French

enough (**assez**)	quickly (**vite**)
far (**loin**)	so, thus (**ainsi**)
here (**ici**)	sometimes (**quelquefois**)
immediately	soon (**bientôt**)
(**immédiatement**)	suddenly (**soudain**)
inside (**dedans**)	then (**puis**)
late (**en retard**)	there (**là**)
near (**près**)	therefore (**donc**)
never (**jamais**)	today (**aujourd'hui**)
no (**non**)	unfortunately
now (**maintenant**)	(**malheureusement**)
often (**souvent**)	very (**très**)
once (**une fois**)	yes (**oui**)
perhaps (**peut-être**)	

When used with a verb, the word 'never' (**jamais**) behaves just like the negative 'not'. Instead of '**ne . . . pas**', you use the words '**ne . . . jamais**', thus:

> **Je ne l'ai jamais vu** (I have never seen him)

Note also that the adverb 'ago' has no single word French equivalent. You have to use the phrase '**il y a**' which precedes the subject, e.g.

> **Il y a trois années** (Three years ago)

13B Prepositions and Conjunctions

The classification of English words into adjectives and adverbs, prepositions and conjunctions can become very confusing. Many English words have two or three different uses, like the word 'after', which can be an adverb, a preposition or a conjunction. The simplest advice, to forget about their uses and just remember the French, is unfortunately not the best, as the French often employ different words for each use.

What we have tried to show is the common use of the word in English, and then the French translation. Where two or more uses are common, they are indicated in the text.

Conjunctions

These are words used to link up other words, phrases or sentences. There are 10 in our word list.

after (**après que**)	but (**mais**)
and (**et**)	if (**si**)
as (**comme**)	or (**ou**)
because (**parce que**)	since (**depuis que**)
before (**avant que**)	therefore, thus, so (**donc**)

'Donc' (thus), 'après' (after), 'avant' (before) and 'depuis' (since) are also adverbs, the last three without 'de' or 'que'.

Prepositions

These are words indicating position or some other relationship and there are a surprising number in our word list, some of them in constant use.

according to (**selon**)	in (**dans**)
after (**après**)	in order to (**afin de, pour**)
against (**contre**)	
at (**à**)	near (**près de**)
before (**avant**)	of (**de**)
before . . . ing (**avant de + infinitive**)	on (**sur**)
	opposite (**en face de**)
behind (**derrière**)	through (**par**)
between (**entre**)	towards (**vers**)
by (**par** or **à**)	under (**sous**)
during (**pendant**)	with (**avec**)
far from (**loin de**)	without (**sans**)
for (**pour**)	

'Après' (after), 'derrière' (behind), 'près' (near) and 'loin' (far) are also adverbs, the last two dropping the 'de' of the preposition.

SESSION FOURTEEN
Prepositions and Link Words

14A   Here and There, This and That

As you can see below, some words are compounded from others. For example:

ici (here) becomes **vo***ici* (here is/here are)
là (there) becomes **voi***là* (there is/there are)
ce (this) becomes *ce***ci** (this one here)
            or *ce***la** (that one there)

French

'**Ce**', being an adjective, has to agree with the noun:

> **ce soldat** (this soldier), **cette fille** (this girl) and **ces soldats** (these soldiers) but **cet argent**, inserting t before another vowel.

'**Ce**' crops up all the time in '**est-ce que**' (is it that), where '**ce**' is used to translate *'it'* in place of '**il**'.

'It is' can either be translated '**Il est**' or '**C'est**', with '**ce**' dropping the e.

> **C'est à moi!** (It is mine!)

'**Ce que**' can also be used for 'that which' or 'what', thus:

> **Ce que je bois est du vin!** (That which I drink is wine!)

'This' and 'that', 'these' and 'those' take a different form when the noun to which they refer is omitted. In this case you cannot use '**ce**', '**cette**' or '**ces**'. You have to use '**celui**' (m) and '**celle**' (f) in the singular, and '**ceux**' (m) or '**celles**' (f) in the plural, e.g.

> *Cet* **arbre et** *ceux* **que je vois** (This tree and those trees which I see)
> **Cette maison est plus grande que** *celle* **en face** (This house is bigger than that one opposite)

14B   'A', 'De' and Word Contractions

To, At or In

'**A**' means 'to', 'at' or 'in', for example:

> **J'habite à Paris** (I live *in* Paris)
> **Je vais à Paris** (I go *to* Paris)
> **Je prends le train à Paris** (I take the train *at* Paris)
> or **Je prendrai le menu à six francs** (I will take the menu *at* six francs)

But '**à**' is *not* used when it means 'inside'. In this case we use '**dans**', e.g.

> **J'habite dans une grande maison** (I live in a big house)

When '**à**' is used with a definite article (**le** or **les**), the two words are rolled together. '**A**' + '**le**' becomes '**au**'. '**A**' + '**les**' becomes '**aux**'. But '**à la**' and '**à l'**' remain unchanged.

> **Mon fils va à l'école** (My son goes to school)
> **Le soldat marche à l'armée** (The soldier marches to the army)

but **Je vais au supermarché** (I am going to the super-market)

Je vais aux bois (I am going to the woods)

Normally in French the word 'to' in front of a verb is included in the infinitive, thus:

Je veux aller à Paris (I wish to go to Paris)

but a few verbs take **'à'** after them, and these are shown in the word list, e.g.

Je commence à travailler (I am starting to work)

Of

'Of' is translated by **'de'**. It is used widely in French as they do not use the genitive 's which we use in English. For example, it is not possible to translate 'the girl's father' in exactly the same form. You would have to say

Le père de la fille (literally, The father of the girl)

Likewise there is no exact translation for the English word 'whose'. You would need to use **'à qui'** (to whom), **'de qui'** (of whom), **'de quoi'** (of what) or **'dont'** (of which/of whom).

When **'de'** is used with the definite article **'le'** and **'les'**, the two words are contracted, just as they are with **'à'**. **'De le'** becomes **'du'**. **'De les'** becomes **'des'**, but **'de la'** and **'de l''** remain unchanged.

Le fils du soldat (The soldier's son)
L'auteur des livres (The author of the books)

From

'De' also means 'from'.

J'ai voyagé de Paris (I have travelled from Paris)

However, if you want to say 'I have just travelled from Paris', you use the verb **'venir de'** (literally, to come from) plus the infinitive of the verb.

Je viens de voyager de Paris (I have just travelled from Paris)
Je viens de finir mon examen (I have just finished my examination)

'De' after Verbs and Prepositions

A few verbs are automatically followed by **'de'** and these

French

include 'essayer de' (to try to), 'décider de' (to decide), and 'avoir besoin de' (to need to). These are shown with 'de' in the word list.

There are also a number of prepositions, indicating place or position, which are followed by 'de'. These include 'à côté de' (beside/next to), 'en face de' (opposite), 'près de' (near) and 'loin de' (far). Likewise three other common words, 'combien de' (how much, how many), 'beaucoup de' (much, a lot of, many) and 'un peu de' (a little) where 'de' is used in French, and 'of' is omitted in English.

Some/any

'De' also means 'some of', or 'any' and is usually followed by the definite article. Whereas we would just say 'I would like some wine', the French would say:

> **Je voudrais** *du* **vin** (I would like some [of the] wine)
> or **Je voudrais** *des* **pommes** (I would like some [of the] apples)
> but **Je n'ai pas d'argent** (I do not have any money)

However, if you want to replace the nouns 'wine' or 'apples' with the pronouns 'it' or 'them', for example, I would like some *of it*, or some *of them*, you would use the little word 'en' instead of 'de', thus:

> **J'en voudrais** (I would like [some] *of it*)
> **J'en prendrai trois** (I will take three *of them*)

Note that 'en' precedes the verb, just like a personal pronoun.

Other Contractions

In previous sections, we have shown several instances where e or a is dropped when followed by another word starting with a vowel or with a mute h. This applies to 'le' and 'la'; to the pronouns 'je', 'me', 'se'; to the negative 'ne'; to the preposition 'de'; and to 'si' in front of 'il/ils'.

'Ce' also drops its e when followed by 'est', whereas a t would normally be inserted in between to make the sound right, as in 'cet homme' (this man).

SESSION FIFTEEN
Numbers and Time

15A Numbers and Measures

Key numbers are shown below. Build up the long numbers as in English but only use 'et' before one, as in 'vingt *et* un' (21) up to 71. 'Un million' (million) and 'un milliard' (thousand million) have a plural form; so does 'cent' (hundred) if not followed by another number. Note the build-up of seventy (sixty plus ten), eighty (four times twenty) and ninety (plus another ten).

Cardinal Numbers

0	**zéro**	31	**trente et un**
1	**un/une**	32	**trente-deux**
2	**deux**	40	**quarante**
3	**trois**	50	**cinquante**
4	**quatre**	60	**soixante**
5	**cinq**	70	**soixante-dix**
6	**six**	71	**soixante et onze**
7	**sept**		(60 + 11)
8	**huit**	80	**quatre vingts**
9	**neuf**		(four twenties)
10	**dix**	81	**quatre-vingt-un**
11	**onze**	90	**quatre-vingt-dix**
12	**douze**		(4 × 20 + 10)
13	**treize**	100	**cent**
14	**quatorze**	101	**cent un**
15	**quinze**	157	**cent cinquante-sept**
16	**seize**		
17	**dix-sept**	200	**deux cents**
18	**dix-huit**	220	**deux cent vingt**
19	**dix-neuf**	300	**trois cents**
20	**vingt**	1,000	**mille**
21	**vingt et un**	10,000	**dix mille**
22	**vingt-deux**	100,000	**cent mille**
30	**trente**		

157,643 – **cent cinquante-sept mille, six cent quarante-trois**

1,000,000 – **un million**

1,576,432 – **un million, cinq cent soixante-dix-six, quatre cent trente-deux**

1,000,000,000 – **un milliard**

French

Numbers showing order, e.g. first, second, third and so on, add -ième to the stem of the number, as we would add -th to the stem of ours. Except for **'premier/première'** (first).

first	**premier**	eighth	**huitième**
second	**deuxième**	ninth	**neuvième**
third	**troisième**	tenth	**dixième**
fourth	**quatrième**	twentieth	**vingtième**
fifth	**cinquième**	twenty-first	**vingt et unième**
sixth	**sixième**	one hundredth	**centième**
seventh	**septième**	one thousandth	**millième**

The only fractions you are likely to need at this stage are:

one quarter	**un quart**
one third	**un tiers**
one half	**un demi/une moitié**
two thirds	**deux tiers**
three quarters	**trois quarts**
one	**un/e**

There is no equivalent to the English words 'once', 'twice', 'thrice'. The French say **'une fois'** (one time), **'deux fois'** (two times), **'trois fois'** (three times), and so on.

Weights are in kilos (1000 grammes).

un kilo = 35 ounces or just under 2¼ lb
un demi-kilo = just over 1 lb

If you purchase cheese from a delicatessen, for example, you would ask for 350 grammes, not a third of a kilo.

Liquid measures are shown in litres.

one litre = 100 centilitres = 35 fluid ounces = 1¾ pints
one pint = approximately 0.6 litre or 60 centilitres

Distances are in kilometres (1000 metres).

one kilometre or km = 0.6 of one mile
one mile = 1.6 kilometres, ten miles = 16 km

15B   Dates and Time

Une année (a year) is split into four seasons:

spring	**le printemps**
summer	**l'été**
autumn	**l'automne**
winter	**l'hiver**

Two (or more) years is usually written **'deux ans'**, *not* **'deux années'**. **Les mois** (the months) are mostly recognisable from the English.

January	**janvier**	July	**juillet**
February	**février**	August	**août**
March	**mars**	September	**septembre**
April	**avril**	October	**octobre**
May	**mai**	November	**novembre**
June	**juin**	December	**décembre**

Chaque mois (each month) **a quatre semaines** (four weeks) **et chaque jour** (each day) **s'appelle** (calls itself):

Monday	**lundi**	Friday	**vendredi**
Tuesday	**mardi**	Saturday	**samedi**
Wednesday	**mercredi**	Sunday	**dimanche**
Thursday	**jeudi**		

Note that one week, Saturday to Saturday, counts as eight days in France!

The word 'on' is not translated.

J'arriverai mardi (I will arrive *on* Tuesday)

Chaque jour est compris (is comprised) **du matin** (of the morning), **de l'après-midi** (afternoon), **du soir** (evening) **et de la nuit** (night), **et il a vingt-quatre heures** (hours).

Chaque heure a soixante minutes (minutes)
Chaque minute a soixante secondes (seconds)

Quel jour sommes-nous? (What day is it?)

Aujourd'hui c'est mardi, le dix-huit mars (Today, it is Tuesday, 18th March)
Demain matin sera mercredi (Tomorrow morning, it will be Wednesday)
Le lendemain sera jeudi (The morning after will be Thursday)

Quelle heure est-il? (What hour/time is it?)

Il est cinq heures et demie (It is five hours and a half, in other words, half past five)

'A quarter to six' is translated thus:

six heures moins le quart (six hours less quarter)

For minutes past the hour, say

six heures et quart (quarter past six)
cinq heures vingt-sept (five twenty-seven)

French

but for twenty-seven minutes to six, you can either say

cinq heures trente-trois (five thirty-three)
or **six heures moins vingt-sept** (six hours less twenty-seven)

Remember, however, that published times on the Continent work to a 24-hour clock. Up to 12 noon, say

six heures du matin (six hours of the morning)

After **'midi'** (midday) and up to 5 p.m., say

quatre heures de l'après-midi (four o'clock in the afternoon)

After six o'clock, use **'du soir'** (of the evening)

Finally, the weather.

Quel temps fait-il? (What is the weather like?)
Il fait chaud (literally, It makes hot)
Il pleut (It is raining)
Il neige (It is snowing)

Note that **'temps'** also means length of time.

Il n'y a pas beaucoup de temps! (There is not much time!)
Il y a **longtemps** (A long time *ago*)

APPENDIX

Subjunctives

The subjunctive tenses have been left out of the main text as they can be confusing to those learning French. Subjunctives are little used, even less recognized in English, but they are used much more frequently in French. They usually occur in subordinate clauses after the conjunction 'que', following verbs of ordering, wanting, expressing fear, doubt or emotion, or after impersonal verbs, e.g.

Je doute *que* **vous** *ayez* **assez d'argent**
(I doubt that you have enough money)
Je reviendrai afin *que* **vous** *puissiez* **sortir**
(I will come back so that you can go out)

The present and imperfect subjunctive tense endings are set out below for regular verbs, and also for '**avoir**' and '**être**'. The present subjunctive, which is used the most, is the same as the present indicative for -er and -re regular verbs, except that the letter i is inserted in the 1st and 2nd person plural. Regular -ir verbs insert a double s throughout. The imperfect subjunctive is quite different from the indicative, but it is used much less frequently. The perfect subjunctive is built up by using an auxiliary verb plus the past participle.

Present Tense

Regular Verbs

	-er verb endings	*-re verb endings*	*-ir verb endings*	*avoir*	*être*
1st sing	-e	-e	-isse	aie	sois
3rd sing	-e	-e	-isse	ait	soit
1st pl	-ions	-ions	-issions	ayons	soyons
2nd pl	-iez	-iez	-issiez	ayez	soyez
3rd pl	-ent	-ent	-issent	aient	soient

Imperfect Tense

	-er verb endings	*-re verb endings*	*-ir verb endings*	*avoir*	*être*
1st sing	-asse	-isse	-isse	eusse	fusse
3rd sing	-ât	-ît	-ît	eût	fût
1st pl	-assions	-issions	-issions	eussions	fussions
2nd pl	-assiez	-issiez	-issiez	eussiez	fussiez
3rd pl	-assent	-issent	-issent	eussent	fussent

French

Many irregular verbs change their stem (but not their endings) in the subjunctive, just as they do in the indicative tenses.

When speaking French, it is suggested that you start by keeping the sentences fairly simple and avoid too many subordinate clauses, which require the use of the subjunctive. If you want to avoid using the conjunction **'que'** you can often change the sentence and use a simple infinitive instead e.g. **'avant de partir'** (before leaving) instead of **'avant que je parte'** (before I leave).

SPANISH

CONTENTS

FIFTEEN　　　　　**NUMBERS AND TIME**

APPENDIX　　　Subjunctives　　128

Spanish

SESSION ONE
Your Word List

1A 500 Word Vocabulary

a/an **un** (m)/**una** (f)
able, to be **poder**
accept, to **aceptar**
accident **accidente** (m)
according to **según**
account **cuenta** (f)
address **dirección** (f)
advise, to **aconsejar**
aeroplane **avión** (m)
after **después de (que)**
afternoon **tarde** (f)
again **de nuevo**
against **contra**
age **edad** (f)
ago **hace**
agree, to (accept) **acordar**
agree, to (be of same
  opinion) **estar de
  acuerdo**
air **aire** (m)
airmail, by **por avión**
airport **aeropuerto** (m)
all **todo**
allow (let), to **permitir**
almost **casi**
alone **solo**
already **ya**
also (too) **también**
always **siempre**
amuse, to **divertir**
animal **animal** (m)
and **y**
angry **enfadado**
another **otro**
answer, to **responder**
anyone **alguno**
arrive, to **llegar**
art **arte** (m)
as . . . as **tan . . . como**
ask, to **preguntar**

at **a**
attention **atención** (f)
avenue **avenida** (f)

bad/worse **malo/peor**
bag **saco** (m)
baggage (luggage) **equipaje**
  (m)
bank **banco** (m)
bath **baño** (m)
be, to **ser** or **estar**
beach **playa** (f)
beautiful **hermoso**
because **porque**
become, to **hacerse**
bed **cama** (f)
before **antes de (que)**
begin, to (start/commence)
  comenzar (a)
behind **detrás (de)**
believe, to **creer**
between **entre**
bicycle **bicicleta** (f)
big **grande**
bill (account) **cuenta** (f)
black **negro**
blue **azul**
boat **barco** (m)
book **libro** (m)
born, to be **nacer**
bottle **botella** (f)
box **caja** (f)
boy **muchacho** (m)
break, to **romper**
bridge **puente** (m)
bring, to **traer**
brother **hermano** (m)
brown **moreno**
building **edificio** (m)
bus **autobus** (m)

business **negocio** (m)
but **pero**
buy, to **comprar**

cafe/bar **café** (m)
call **llamar**
camera **máquina**
  (fotográfica) (f)
can (verb: be able) **poder**
car **coche** (m)
car park
  aparcamiento (m)
caravan **roulotte** (f)
careful, be! **cuidado!**
carry, to **llevar**
castle **castillo** (m)
cat **gato/a** (m/f)
certain **seguro**
chair **silla** (f)
change, to **cambiar**
cheap **barato**
cheque **cheque** (m)
chemist's (pharmacy)
  farmacia (f)
child **niño/a** (m/f)
choose, to **escoger**
church **iglesia** (f)
cigarette **cigarillo** (m)
class **clase** (f)
clean, to **limpiar**
clear **claro**
clock **reloj** (m)
close, to **cerrar**
clothes **ropa** (f. pl)
coat **chaqueta** (f)
cold **frío**
colour **color** (m)
come, to **venir (a)**
comfortable **cómodo**
complete **completo**
concert **concierto** (m)
continue, to **continuar (a)**
conversation
  conversación (f)
cook, to **cocer**
corner **esquina** (f)
correct **correcto**

cost, to **costar**
cotton **algodón** (m)
count, to **contar**
country **país** (m)
cover, to **cubrir**
cry, to **llorar**
customs **aduana** (f)
cut, to **cortar**

damage **daño** (m)
dance, to **bailar**
dangerous **peligroso**
dark **oscuro**
date **fecha** (f)
daughter **hija** (f)
day **día** (m)
dear (expensive) **caro**
decide, to **decidir**
defend, to **defender**
dentist **dentista** (m, f)
depart, to (leave) **irse**
descend, to (go down)
  descender
desire, to (want) **desear**
die, to **morir**
different **diferente**
difficult **difícil**
direction (way)
  dirección (f)
dirty **sucio**
distance **distancia** (f)
do, to **hacer**
doctor **médico** (m)
door **puerta** (f)
dress **vestido** (m)
drink, to **beber**
drive, to (a car) **conducir**
dry **seco**
during **durante**
duty **deber** (m)

each (every) **cada**
early **temprano**
eat, to **comer**
empty **vacío**
end **fin** (m)
engine **motor** (m)

Spanish

English **inglés**
enough **bastante (de)**
enter, to **entrar**
equal **igual**
evening **tarde** (f)
every (all) **todo**
everything **todo**
excellent **excelente**
exchange, to **cambiar**
excuse, to **excusar**
exit **salida** (f)
expensive (dear) **caro**
eye **ojo** (m)

face **cara** (f)
fall, to **caer**
family **familia** (f)
far **lejos (de)**
fast (quick) **rápido**
fat **gordo**
father **padre** (m)
feel, to **sentir**
field **campo** (m)
film **film** (m)
fight, to **luchar**
fill, to **llenar**
find, to **encontrar**
finish, to **terminar**
fire **incendio** (m)
fix, to **fijar**
floor **piso** (m)
flight (by air) **vuelo** (m)
fly, to **volar**
follow, to **seguir**
food **alimentos** (m. pl)
foot **pie** (m)
football **fútbol** (m)
for (in order to) **para**
for (because of) **por**
forget, to **olvidar**
free **libre**
French **francés**
fresh **fresco**
friend **amigo/a** (m/f)
from **de**
fruit **fruta** (f)
full **lleno**

garage **garaje** (m)
garden **jardín** (m)
German **alemán/a** (m/f)
gift **regalo** (m)
girl **muchacha** (f)
give, to **dar**
glasses **gafas** (f. pl)
glove **guante** (m)
go, to **ir (a)**
go down, to **descender**
go out, to **salir**
go up/climb, to **subir**
gold **oro** (m)
good **bueno**
great **gran/grande**
ground **tierra** (f)
group **grupo** (m)

hairdresser
  peluquero/a (m/f)
hand **mano** (f)
handbag **bolso** (m)
handkerchief **pañuelo** (m)
happen, to **pasar**
happy **feliz**
hard **duro**
hat **sombrero** (m)
have (possession of), to
  tener
have, to (auxiliary) **haber**
hear, to **oír**
heavy **pesado**
healthy **sano**
help, to **ayudar**
here **aquí**
high **alto**
hill **colina** (f)
hold, to **tener**
holiday (vacation)
  vacaciones (f. pl)
hope, to **esperar**
hospital **hospital** (m)
hot **caliente**
hotel **hotel** (m)
hour **hora** (f)
house **casa** (f)
how **como**

how much/how many?
 ¿cuanto?
husband **marido** (m)

ice **hielo** (m)
if **si**
ill **enfermo**
immediately
 inmediatamente
important **importante**
in **en**
include, to **incluir**
industry **industria** (f)
information
 información (f)
inside **dentro de**
intelligent **inteligente**
interesting **interesante**
is (verb: to be) **es, está**
Italian **italiano**

join, to (be part of)
 unirse (a)
journey **viaje** (m)

keep, to **tener**
key **llave** (f)
kind **amable**
king **rey** (m)
kiss, to **besar**
know, to (something)
 saber
know, to (somebody)
 conocer

lady **señora** (f)
language **lengua** (f)
last **último**
late **tarde**
lawyer **abogado** (m)
learn, to **aprender (a)**
leave, to (go out) **salir (a)**
leave, to (depart) **irse**
left (direction) **a la
 izquierda**
lend, to **prestar**
less **menos**

let, to (permit) **permitir**
letter **carta** (f)
lift **ascensor** (m)
light **luz** (f)
like, to **querer/gustar se**
liquid **liquido** (m)
list **lista** (f)
little (small) **pequeño**
little (a) **poco** (m)
live, to **vivir**
live in, to **vivir**
long **largo**
look at, to **mirar**
lorry **camión** (m)
lose, to **perder**
loud **alto**
love, to **amar**
luggage (baggage)
 equipaje (m)

mad **loco**
make, to **hacer**
man **hombre** (m)
manner **manera** (f)
many **muchos**
map **mapa** (m)
market **mercado** (m)
match **fósforo** (m)
medicine **medicina** (f)
meet, to **encontrar**
meeting **reunión** (f)
middle **medio** (m)
million **millón** (m)
minute **minuto** (m)
mirror **espejo** (m)
mistake **error** (m)
money **dinero** (m)
more **más**
morning **mañana** (f)
motorway **autopista** (f)
mother **madre** (f)
mountain **montaña** (f)
mouth **boca** (f)
move, to **mover**
much **mucho**
museum **museo** (m)
music **música** (f)

Spanish

must (verb: to be obliged)
  deber

name **nombre** (m)
near **cerca de**
necessary **necesario**
need, to **necesitar**
never **nunca**
new **nuevo**
newspaper **diario** (m)
next **próximo**
night **noche** (f)
no **no**
noise **ruido** (m)
nothing **nada**
now **ahora**
number (figure)
  número (m)

obtain, to **obtener**
of **de**
offer, to **ofrecer**
office **oficina** (f)
often **a menudo**
oil **aceite** (m)
old **viejo**
on **encima de**
once **una vez**
only (adv.) **solamente**
open, to **abrir**
opposite **enfrente de**
or **o**
ordinary **ordinario**
other **otro**
over **sobre**
owe, to (be obliged)
  deber

package **paquete** (m)
pain **dolor** (m)
paper **papel** (m)
park **parque** (m)
part **parte** (f)
pass, to **pasar**
passenger
  pasajero/a (m/f)
passport **pasaporte** (m)

path **sendero** (m)
pay, to **pagar**
pen **pluma** (f)
pencil **lápiz** (m)
perhaps **quizá**
permit (let) **permitir**
persuade, to **persuadir (a)**
person/people
  persona/s (f)
petrol **gasolina** (f)
pharmacy **farmacia** (f)
photograph **fotografía** (f)
piece **pedazo** (m)
place **sitio** (m)
play, to **jugar**
please **por favor**
police **policía** (m)
point out, to **indicar**
poor **pobre**
port (harbour) **puerto** (m)
porter (hotel) **portero** (m)
possible **posible**
postcard **tarjeta postal** (f)
post office **correos** (m. pl)
prefer, to **preferir**
prepare, to **preparar**
price **precio** (m)
private (not public)
  particular
probable **probable**
profession **profesión** (f)
programme **programa** (m)
promise, to **prometer**
put, to (place) **poner**

quality **calidad** (f)
quantity **cantidad** (f)
question **pregunta** (f)
quick (fast) **rápido**
quiet **silencioso**

rain, to **llover**
read, to **leer**
ready **listo**
receive, to **recibir**
reception (hotel)
  recepción (f)

red **rojo**
regret, to (be sorry)
  lamentar
remember, to **recordar**
repeat, to **repetir**
reply, to **responder**
report, to **informar**
responsible **responsable**
restaurant **restaurante** (m)
return, to **volver (a)**
rich **rico**
right (direction) **a la
  derecha**
right, to be **tener razón**
river **río** (m)
road **carretera** (f)
room **habitación** (m)
run, to **correr (a)**

sad **triste**
same **mismo**
save, to **salvar**
say, to **decir**
school **escuela** (f)
sea **mar** (m, f)
see, to **ver**
seem, to **parecer**
sell, to **vender**
send, to **enviar**
serve, to **servir**
service **servicio** (m)
shoe **zapato** (m)
shop **tienda** (f)
short **corto**
show, to **mostrar**
shower **ducha** (f)
shut, to **cerrar**
sign **señal** (f)
silver **de plata** (f)
since **desde (que)**
sing, to **cantar**
sister **hermana** (f)
sit down, to **sentarse**
ski, to **esquiar**
sky **cielo** (m)
sleep, to **dormir**
slowly **despacio**

small **pequeño**
snow **nieve** (f)
so, thus **así (que)**
soap **jabón** (m)
soft **blando**
some **alguno**
someone **alguién**
sometimes **a veces**
son **hijo** (m)
soon **pronto**
speak, to **hablar**
square (town) **plaza** (f)
stairs **escalera** (f)
stamp **sello** (m)
start, to (begin)
  comenzar
station (railway)
  estación (f)
stay, remain, to **quedar**
step (pace) **paso** (m)
stop, to **parar**
street **calle** (f)
strong **fuerte**
student **estudiante** (m, f)
study, to **estudiar**
suddenly **de repente**
suitcase **maleta** (f)
summer **verano** (m)
sun **sol** (m)
suntan **bronceado** (m)
sweet **dulce**
swim, to **nadar**
swimming pool
  piscina (f)

table **mesa** (f)
take, to **tomar**
tariff (customs)
  arancel (m)
taste, to **probar**
taxi **taxi** (m)
tea **té** (m)
teach, to **enseñar (a)**
teacher **profesor** (m)
telegram **telegrama** (m)
telephone, to **telefonear**
television **televisión** (f)

81

tell, to **decir**
tennis **tenis** (m)
thank you **gracias**
theatre **teatro** (m)
then **entonces**
there **allí**
there is/are **hay**
therefore **por eso**
thing **cosa** (f)
think, to **pensar**
this **este**
through **por**
ticket **billete** (m)
time **tiempo** (m)
time (what time?) **¿que hora?**
time (one or more) **vez** (f)
tip **propina** (f)
tired **cansado**
to (towards) **a**
to (in order to) **para**
too (also) **también**
too much/many **demasiado**
today **hoy**
toilet **servicio** (m)
tomorrow **mañana**
tourist **turista** (m, f)
towards **hacia**
towel **toalla** (f)
town **pueblo** (m)
traffic **circulación** (f)
train (express) **tren** (m)/ **rápido** (m)
translate, to **traducir**
travel, to **viajar**
travel agent **agente de viajes** (f)
tree **árbol** (m)
true **verdadero**
try, to **probar**
typical **típico**
tyre **neumático** (m)

umbrella **paraguas** (m)
under **debajo de**

underground (railway) **metro** (m)
understand, to **entender**
unfortunately **desgraciadamente**
university **universidad** (f)
use, to **emplear**
useful **útil**

vacation (holiday) **vacaciones** (f. pl)
very **muy**
village **aldea** (f)
visit, to (a place) **visitar**
voice **voz** (f)

wait for, to **aguardar**
waiter **camarero** (m)
walk, to **andar (a)**
wall **pared** (m)
want/wish for, to **querer**
wash, to (oneself) **lavar (se)**
watch **reloj** (m)
water **agua** (f)
way (direction) **dirección** (f)
wedding **boda** (f)
week **semana** (f)
weekend **fin de semana** (m)
well **bien**
what! **qué!**
when? **¿cuando?**
where? **¿donde?**
which? **¿cuál?**
which **que**
white **blanco**
who? **¿quién?**
why? **¿por qué?**
wide **ancho**
wife **esposa** (f)
wind **viento** (m)
window **ventana** (f)
wine **vino** (m)
winter **invierno** (m)
wish/want, to **querer**

with **con**

without **sin**

wood **madera** (f)

word **palabra** (f)

work, to **trabajar**

world **mundo** (m)

write, to **escribir**

year **año** (m)

yellow **amarillo**

yes **sí**

yesterday **ayer**

young **joven**

1B   100 Words for Buying Food and Eating Out

Shops

bakery   **panadería** (f)
butcher's   **carnicería** (f)
fishmonger's
  pescadería (f)
grocer's   **tienda de
  comestibles** (f)
market   **mercado** (m)
self service   **autoservicio**
shop   **tienda** (f)
supermarket
  supermercado (m)
tobacconist's   **estanco** (m)

Meals

breakfast   **desayuno** (m)
dining room   **comedor** (m)
dinner   **cena** (f)
drink   **bebida** (f)
food   **comida** (f)
lunch   **comida** (f)
meal   **comida** (f)

Table setting

bottle   **botella** (f)
chair   **silla** (f)
cup   **taza** (f)
fork   **tenedor** (m)
glass   **vaso** (m)
jug   **jarra** (f)
knife   **cuchillo** (m)
menu   **carta** (f)
oil   **aceite** (m)
pepper   **pimienta** (f)
plate   **plato** (m)
salt   **sal** (f)
spoon   **cuchara** (f)
sugar   **azúcar** (m)
table   **mesa** (f)
tip   **propina** (f)
vinegar   **vinagre** (m)
waiter   **camarero** (m)

Drinks

I'm thirsty   **tengo sed**
beer   **cerveza** (f)
brandy   **coñac** (m)
cider   **sidra** (f)
coffee   **café** (m)
cream   **crema** (f)
lemonade   **limonada** (f)
milk   **leche** (f)
orangeade   **naranjada** (f)
tea   **té** (m)
tomato juice   **zumo de
  tomate** (m)
water/sparkling
  water   **agua mineral** (f)/
  con gas
whisky   **whisky** (m)
wine   **vino** (m)

Food

I'm hungry   **tengo hambre**
apple   **manzana** (f)
asparagus   **espárrago** (m)
aubergine   **berenjena** (f)
bacon   **tocino** (m)
banana   **plátano** (m)
bean (French)   **judía
  verde** (f)
bean (haricot)   **judía** (f)
beef   **carne de vaca** (f)
bread   **pan** (m)
broccoli   **bróculi** (m)
butter   **mantequilla** (f)
cabbage   **col** (f)
cake   **pastel** (m)
cauliflower   **coliflor** (m)
celery   **apio** (m)
cheese   **queso** (m)
chicken   **pollo** (m)
chocolate   **chocolate** (m)
coffee   **café** (m)
cucumber   **pepino** (m)
curry   **curry** (m)

egg **huevo** (m)
fish **pescado** (m)
flour **harina** (f)
fruit **fruta** (f)
ham **jamón** (m)
hors d'oeuvre
  entremeses (m. pl)
ice cream **helado** (m)
jam **mermelada** (m)
lemon **limón** (m)
meat **carne** (f)
melon **melón** (m)
milk **leche** (f)
mushroom **seta** (f)
nectarine **nectarina** (f)
oil **aceite** (m)
omelette **tortilla** (f)
onion **cebolla** (f)
orange **naranja** (f)
pancake **crepa** (f)
pâté **paté** (m)
peach **melocotón** (m)
pear **pera** (f)
peas **guisantes** (m. pl)
pepper **pimienta** (f)
pork **cerdo** (m)
potato **patata** (f)
  chipped potatoes
    patatas fritas (f. pl.)
prawns **gambas** (f. pl)
ravioli **raviolis** (m. pl)
rice **arroz** (m)
salad **ensalada** (f)
sauce **salsa** (f)

sausage **salchicha** (f)
soup **sopa** (f)
spaghetti
  espaguetis (m. pl)
spinach **espinaca** (f)
tart **tarta** (f)
tea **té** (m)
toast **pan tostado** (m)
tomato **tomate** (m)
vegetables **verduras** (f. pl)
vinegar **vinagre** (m)

Cooking

boiled **hervido**
fresh **fresco**
fried **frito**
grilled **asado a la parrilla**
rare **poco hecho**
raw **crudo**
sour **ácido**
sweet **dulce**
well cooked **muy hecho**

Containers

bag **bolsa** (f)
bottle **botella** (f)
bottle opener
  abrebotellas (m)
can **lata** (f)
can opener **abrelatas** (m)
corkscrew
  sacacorchos (m)

1C   150 Words for Business Use

interpreter
 intérprete (m, f)
translate, to **traducir**

Organization
 Organización (f)

accountant **contable** (m)
authority **autoridad** (f)
chairman **presidente** (m)
company **compañiá** (f)
company secretary
 secretario
director **consejero** (m)
employee
 empleado/a (m/f)
executive **ejecutivo** (m)
management
 dirección (m)
manager **director** (m)
managing director
 director-gerente (m)
responsible **responsable**
secretary
 secretario/a (m/f)

Office   *Oficina* (f)

agreement **contrato** (m)
airmail **por correo aéreo**
authorize, to **autorizar**
bank **banco** (m)
business **negocio** (m)
computer **ordenador** (m)
contract **contrato** (m)
copy **copia** (f)
data processing **proceso
 de datos** (m)
documentation
 documentación (f)
fax **telefax** (m)
invoice **factura** (f)
lease **arrendamiento** (m)
legal **legal**
official **oficial**

post **correos** (m. pl)
private, confidential
 privado
receipt **recibo** (m)
regulations **normas** (f. pl)
rent **alquiler** (m)
report **informe** (m)
requisition **demanda** (f)
shares (in a company)
 acciones (m. pl)
sign, to **firmar**
signatory **firmante** (m, f)
tariff (customs)
 arancel (m)

Works/factory   *Fábrica* (f)

chemical **producto
 químico** (m)
development
 desarrollo (m)
electrician
 electricista (m, f)
electricity **electricidad** (f)
engineer **ingeniero** (m)
foreman **capataz** (m)
fuel **combustible** (m)
gas **gas** (m)
laboratory **laboratorio** (m)
machinery **maquinaria** (f)
maintenance
 mantenimiento (m)
manual worker
 obrero (m)
metal **metal** (m)
oil (lubricating)
 aceite (m)
raw materials **materias
 primas** (f. pl)
research **investigación** (f)
services (works)
 servicios (m. pl)
site **sitio** (m)
stores (warehouse) **cuarto
 de almacén** (m)

tool room
  herramientas (m)
warehouse **almacén** (m)

Production **Producción** (f)

automation
  automatización (f)
batch **lote** (m)
budget **presupuesto** (m)
construction
  construcción (f)
consumption
  consumo (m)
control, to **controlar**
effluent **efluente** (m)
increase, to **aumentar**
invest, to **invertir**
job (to be done)
  trabajo (m)
new product **producto
  nuevo** (m)
output **producción** (f)
performance
  rendimiento (f)
plan **plan** (m)
productivity
  productividad (f)
quantity **cantidad** (f)
reduce, to **reducir**
schedule **programa** (m)
timetable **horario** (m)
ton **tonelada** (f)
utilization **utilización** (f)
volume **volumen** (m)
waste **desechos** (m. pl)
works order **pedido**

Marketing
  Comercialización (m)

achieve, to **conseguir**
advertise, to **anunciar**
agent (sales) **agente** (m)
agree/accept, to **acordar**
assess, to **evaluar**
brand **marca** (f)

commission (payment)
  comisión (f)
competition
  competición (f)
customer **cliente** (m, f)
delivery **entrega** (f)
demand **demanda** (f)
distribution
  distribución (f)
economic **económico**
forecast, to **pronosticar**
market objective **objetivo
  de mercado** (m)
market research **estudio
  de mercados** (m)
opportunity
  oportunidad (f)
packaging **embalaje** (m)
presentation
  presentación (f)
price **precio** (m)
product test **ensayo** (m)
promote, to **promocionar**
quality **calidad** (f)
representative
  representante (m, f)
sales **ventas** (f. pl)
sales force
  vendedores (m. pl)
service (customer)
  servicio (m)
share (of market) **porción
  de mercado** (f)
target **objetivo** (m)

Employment **Empleo** (m)

assessment **valoración** (f)
benefit **beneficio** (m)
bonus **paga extra** (f)
canteen **comedor** (m)
job (for person)
  trabajo (m)
pension **pensión** (f)
personnel **personal** (m)
salary **sueldo** (m)
skill **habilidad** (m)

social security **seguridad social** (f)
training **formación** (f)
unemployed **parado**
vacancy **vacante** (f)
wage **salario** (m)

Accounts ***Cuentas*** (f. pl)

actual **real**
asset, net **activo neto** (m)
bad debt **deuda irrecuperable** (f)
balance sheet **balance** (m)
borrow, to **tomar prestado**
capital **capital** (m)
capital expenditure **desembolso de capital** (m)
cash **dinero en efectivo** (m)
cash flow **cash-flow** (m)
cost of sales **costo de ventas**
credit control **control de créditos** (m)
creditor **acreedor/a** (m/f)
debtor **deudor/a** (m/f)

depreciation **depreciación** (f)
dividend **dividendo** (m)
expenditure **gastos** (m. pl)
grant **subvención** (f)
interest (bank) **interés** (m)
labour cost **costo de mano de obra** (m)
liability (balance sheet) **pasivo** (m)
liability (damages) **responsabilidad** (f)
loan (bank) **empréstito** (m)
margin, gross **margen bruto** (m)
profit, net **beneficio neto** (m)
share capital **capital en acciones** (m)
stocks **reservas** (f. pl)
taxation **impuestos** (m. pl)
variance **variación** (f)
working capital **capital de trabajo** (m)

SESSION TWO
Pronunciation

2A Letters and Sounds

Spanish	Sounds like	Example
a	**a** in p**a**r	p**a**dre
b	**b** in **b**at lightly sounded	**b**año
c	**c** in **c**at *but* **th** in **th**in before e and i	**c**asi nego**c**io

ch	ch in church	fecha
d	d in dog *but* th in then between vowels or at word end	difícil marido
e	ay in may	fecha
f	f in fix	familia
g	g in got *but* ch in loch before e and i	guante general
h	not sounded	–
i	ee in feet *but* y before another vowel	igual invierno
j	ch in loch	hijo
k	k in kit (used only in foreign words)	kilo
l	l in lit	lista
ll	ll in million *but* many Spanish treat it like y in yes	millón
m	m in man	mano
n	n in not *but* nasal n in wing before k and g	no engañar
ñ	ni in onion	baño
o	o in polo	poco
p	p in pin	persona
qu	c in cat	qué
r	r in rat *but* trilled slightly (except at word end)	río
rr	trilled more strongly	correr

Spanish

s	s in **s**ave	**t**riste
	but z in bla**z**e before b, d and m	a**s**besto
t	t in **t**in	**t**eatro
u	**oo** in p**oo**l	**ú**til
	but silent after g and q	g**u**erra
	and sounds like w when placed	
	before another vowel	p**u**eblo
v	**b** in **b**ath	**v**iaje
	lightly sounded (not an	
	explosive b)	
w	not used	–
x	**x** in e**x**it	e**x**aminar
y	**y** in **y**es, at the beginning of a	**y**o
	syllable	
	but **ee** in f**ee**t on its own, or at	
	word end	re**y**
z	**th** in **th**in	ra**z**ón

2B   Accents and Stress

Spanish pronunciation is clear, precise and regular, although travellers will find differences in pronunciation in certain regions of Spain – as one would in England.

As a general rule, vowels are sounded rather more strongly than consonants.

Unlike French, in which all syllables are evenly stressed, the Spanish lay stress on:

The *last* syllable – for words ending in a consonant (except n and s)

The *last but one* syllable – for words ending in a vowel, or n or s

S usually indicates the plural form of a word, so the stress carries on as though the word remained in its singular form.

The only exception to these rules is where a stress mark like an acute accent (´) is placed over a different syllable, as in 'décimo' (tenth), which means that this syllable must be stressed.

Where two vowels are placed together, they are still sounded separately. However, i and u are *weak* vowels and get rolled into the next vowel, sounding more like an English y or w, as in 'Rioja' or 'después' (after). (Note the stress mark on the final e in 'después' to show that normal stress rules have been broken.)

There are no accents, as such, but the stress mark is also used to differentiate between words which are spelt the same but have different meanings, or to indicate an interrogative, such as 'por qué' (why). 'Porque' *without* an accent means 'because'.

SESSION THREE
Absorbing the Language

This is a practice session, for you to try in your own time.

Go through the main vocabulary in Section 1A and read all the words aloud.

Go through a second time, covering up the English and see how many words you can translate.

Now go through a third time, this time covering up the Spanish and see how many words you can translate from the English. Don't worry if there are only a few. Your vocabulary will develop with regular practice.

SESSION FOUR
Message Builders

4A Message Builders

The 80 or so *'message builders'* shown below comprise part-phrases, interrogatives or verbs in everyday use, which you can use to build up questions and messages. You can use these *'message builders'* with your own list of key words to find your way round and to give yourself practice in speaking the language. There are no nouns shown in the list below; you get these from your own word list, or the main vocabulary. (Note that the nouns in the vocabulary are shown only in the singular, and the

Spanish

adjectives are shown in their masculine form, but you will find out in Session Six how to deal with the word endings.)

In Section 4B (p. 94) you will find the commonest forms of address and greetings which will 'top and tail' your messages. Liberal use of 'please' and 'thank you' will add considerably to your communication skills!

English	Spanish
Today is	**Hoy estamos a . . . . .**
I speak	**Hablo . . . . .**
Do you speak	**¿Habla . . . . .**
Yes . . . . . no	**Sí . . . . . no**
My name is	**Me llamo . . . . .**
My number is	**Mi número es . . . . .**
I live in	**Vivo en . . . . .**
This is my	**Este es mi* . . . . .**
Who is/who are	**¿Quién es/quiénes son . . . . .**
I am/we are	**Soy/somos . . . . .**
Why are we	**¿Por qué somos** (or **estamos) . . . . .**
Are you	**¿Está . . . . .**
Where is/where are	**¿Dónde está/dónde están . . . .**
a	**un (m), una (f) . . . . .**
the	**el (m), la (f), los/las (pl) . . . . .**
my	**mi (sing), mis (pl) . . . . .**
Where can I find	**¿Dónde se encuentra . . . . .**
I have lost	**He perdido . . . . .**
I have broken	**He roto . . . . .**
I have forgotten	**He olvidado . . . . .**
When does . . . . . open	**¿A qué hora abre . . . . .**
When does . . . . . start	**¿A qué hora comienza . . . . .**
When does . . . . . close	**¿A qué hora cierra . . . . .**
Excuse me	**Perdón . . . . .**
What is the way to	**¿Por dónde se va a . . . . .**
I want to go to	**Quiero ir a . . . . .**
Is it far to	**¿Queda lejos . . . . .**
Is it	**¿Está** (or **es) . . . . .**
It is	**Está** (or **es) . . . . .**
It is not	**No está** (or **no es) . . . . .**
Here is/here are	**Aquí está/aquí están . . . . .**

Is there.....	¿Hay.....
There is/there are.....	Hay.....
Is there..... near here	¿Hay..... por aquí.....
Do you have/have you got.....	¿Tiene usted.....
I have reserved.....	He reservado.....
It's for.....	Es para.....
Does it have.....	¿Tiene.....
I have/we have.....	Tengo/tenemos.....
Can I have.....	¿Déme.....
Can you.....	¿Puede (+ infinitive)
Would you like.....	¿Le gustaría.....
I would like/we would like.....	Quisiera (or quiero)/ quisiéramos (or queremos).....
Another.....	Otro.....
I am sorry that.....	Siento que.....
There is no.....	No hay.....
What..... do you have	¿Qué..... tiene
How many..... do you have	¿Cuánto*..... tiene
Anything else.....	¿Algo más.....
I would prefer.....	Preferiría.....
It is too.....	Es (or está) demasiado.....
I need/we need.....	Necesito/necesitamos.....
I will take/we will take.....	llevaré/llevaremos.....
I like..... very much	Me gusta mucho.....
Give me.....	Déme.....
How much is.....	¿Cuánto vale.....
More/less.....	Más/menos.....
One/two/three/four/five.....	Uno/dos/tres/cuatro/cinco.....
Ten/twenty/fifty.....	Diez/veinte/cincuenta.....
One hundred/one thousand.....	Cien/mil.....
Tell me.....	Dígame.....
What time is it?	¿Qué hora es?
When does..... leave	¿A qué hora sale.....
When does..... arrive	¿A qué hora llega.....
When do we.....	¿Cuándo (+ verb).....
How do we.....	¿Cómo (+ verb).....
I am going to.....	Voy (+ infinitive).....
I have just.....	Acabo de (+ infinitive).....

* *masculine only*

Spanish

Don't go!	**No vaya!**
Let's go to	**Vamos a . . . . .**
Meet me at	**Reúnase commigo en . . . . .**
Telephone me at	**Telefonéeme a . . . . .**
I ought to/we must	**Tengo/tenemos que (+ infinitive)**
I can/we can	**Puedo/podemos (+ infinitive)**
Take care!	**Tenga cuidado!**
I will come back on	**Volveré . . . . .**
I can't understand	**No entiendo**
Speak more slowly	**Hable más despacio por favor**
Could you repeat that!	**Repita, por favor!**

4B Addressing Friends and Strangers

Spanish is more formal and polite than English. So:
● Shake hands when you meet and part company every day.
● Address adult strangers as **'señor'** (sir) or **'señora'** (madam), and girls as **'señorita'** (miss), thus:

Perdón, señor, puedo hallar . . . (Excuse me, sir, can I find . . .)

● **'Por favor'** (please) and **'gracias'** (thank you) or **'muchas gracias'** (many thanks) should be used liberally.

Sí, por favor (yes, please)
No, gracias (no, thank you)

● The time of day to the Spanish is like the weather to the English, so:

Good morning	**Buenos días**
Good afternoon	**Buenas tardes**
Good evening	**Buenas tardes**
Good night	**Buenas noches**
Goodbye	**Adiós**

● Useful words of greeting include **'Hóla!'** (Hello!), **'Cómo está usted'** (How are you). You could reply **'Muy bien, gracias'** (Very well, thank you).
● Other useful expressions which you are likely to need include:

Salud! (Good health!)
Buen apetito (Enjoy your meal)
Me gusta mucho (I like it very much)
Hasta mañana (See you tomorrow)

SESSION FIVE
Language Structure

5   Word Order

Similar to English, but with a few principal differences:

1   Longer adjectives usually follow the nouns. Thus **'un libro difícil'** is literally translated as 'a book difficult'. But certain very common or short adjectives precede the noun, thus:

> **un buen hombre** (a good man)
> **un gran general** (a great general)

2   Object pronouns and reflexive pronouns are positioned *before* the verb, except where an infinitive or imperative is used. Where there are two pronouns the indirect precedes the direct.

> **(Yo)** *le lo* **doy** means literally, 'I *to him it* give'

3   The negative **'no'** comes before the object pronoun and verb:

> **(Yo) no le he visto** means literally 'I *not* him have seen'

Note that the verb **'he'** (have) and the past participle **'visto'** are not separated, thus:

> **¿Ha visto usted mi padre?** means literally, 'Have seen you my father?'

4   In asking a question the verb and subject (noun or pronoun) are usually reversed, but when an interrogative word such as 'who' or 'when' is used, the word order remains similar to English, except of course for the negative and object pronouns.

SESSION SIX
Nouns, Adjectives and The Two Articles

6A   Nouns and Adjectives

Every noun in Spanish is either masculine (m) or feminine (f), and so are the definite and indefinite articles:

the = **el** (m) or **la** (f)
a   = **un** (m) or **una** (f)

Examples are:

the boy   – **el muchacho**
the girl   – **la muchacha**
a man   – **un hombre**
a woman – **una mujer**

The only exception is when the noun describes a thing or an idea which has no gender, and the Spanish use the neuter form of the definite article, **'lo'**. Thus, **'lo mismo'** (the same thing).

There are no easy rules for determining whether a noun is masculine or feminine, except that masculine objects and those ending in -o, -or and -al are usually masculine, whilst nouns ending in -a, -d, -z and -ión are usually feminine. So try to learn the gender at the same time as you learn the word. Once you have heard the word in Spanish or used it a few times, the gender can be memorized automatically with the word itself.

Note that a few words beginning with a- or ha- remain feminine, but use the masculine article **'el'** in order to prevent two a's following one another.

Adjectives

One principal difference between our two languages is that in Spanish, the adjective always has to agree with the noun*. If the noun is feminine, so is the adjective, thus:

Vino tinto (Red wine)
La casa tinta (The red house)

Those adjectives ending in -o change to -a when they become feminine. A few which end in -on, -or and -an just add an a, whilst most other adjectives do not change, thus:

---

* *Further information on adjectives follows in Section 12A (p. 116).*

bueno (good) changes to **buena**
marrón (brown) changes to **marróna**
feliz (happy) does not change
libre (free) does not change

As we saw in Section 5 (p. 95), adjectives usually follow the noun. But some common or short adjectives like 'good' (**bueno**) and 'bad' (**malo**) precede the noun. Where this occurs, the masculine adjectives drop their final -o, and '**grande**' (great) drops its final -de, thus:

Un buen muchacho (A good boy)
Gran Bretaña (Great Britain)

6B   Plurals

Nouns ending in a vowel add -s in the plural, just as in English. Those ending in a consonant (and y) add -es. The adjectives have a plural form too, which must agree with the noun. But the rules for the endings are the same as for the nouns. Very logical, but easy to forget.

The definite article also changes from '**el**' to '**los**', and '**la**' to '**las**'

Singular	*Plural*
el hermano (brother)	**los hermanos**
la casa bonita (beautiful house)	**las casas bonitas**
el primer soldado (first soldier)	**los primeros soldados**

There is one exception to the rule. Words ending in -z change to -ces in the plural, thus:

'**feliz**' (happy) becomes '**felices**'.

The indefinite article '**un**' or '**una**' changes to '**unos**' (some or any) and '**unas**' in the plural. But it can be omitted (whether singular or plural) if its meaning is clearly understood:

Veo unos árboles (I see some trees)
No tengo dinero (I don't have any money)

But don't drop the definite article as we do in English. This should be repeated before each noun.

Los hermanos y *las* hermanas (The brothers and [the] sisters)

If there are two nouns, one masculine and one feminine, an adjective which has to agree with them both should be shown as masculine plural, thus:

Spanish

La casa y el jardín son bellos (The house and the garden are beautiful)

SESSION SEVEN
Personal Pronouns and Verbs

7A Subject Pronouns

Before moving on to verbs, we should run through the personal pronouns – I, he, we, you and they – which are the *subject* of the verb. We usually describe the subject pronouns as being in the 1st, 2nd or 3rd person singular, or plural, and modify the verb endings accordingly. The subject pronouns are as follows:

1st person singular	I	**Yo**
2nd person singular	you	–
3rd person singular	he/it (m)	**el**
	she/it (f)	**ella**
	your honour	**usted**
1st person plural	we (m)	**nosostros**
	we (f)	**nosostras**
2nd person plural	you	–
3rd person plural	they (m)	**ellos**
	they (f)	**ellas**

In everyday speech, for 'you' the Spanish use the old-fashioned word **'usted'** or **'ustedes'** (plural) which literally means 'your honour', and this requires the use of the 3rd person, *not* the 2nd person singular. The words for 'you' in Spanish – **'tú'** (singular) and **'vosotros'** (plural) – are used only in a family environment and can be left out of this grammar. In the text we abbreviate **'usted'** to **'vd'** and **'ustedes'** (plural) to **'vds'**.

However, as we shall see in Section 7B (below), the subject pronouns are often omitted when the verb endings make the meaning clear.

7B Regular Verbs

Present, Imperfect and Future Tenses

In this section we start with the regular verbs, then move on to some of the irregular verbs. To make it easier, we have restricted the tenses to the present (I am doing), the imperfect (I was doing), the future (I will or shall do) and the past (I have done). We shall therefore leave out the tenses which mean 'I did' (historic), 'I would or could do' (conditional), 'I may or might do' (subjunctive) and a few other tenses less frequently used, even though their use in many sentences would be grammatically correct. However, a note does appear on the use of the subjunctive in the Appendix, which we have left right to the end (p. 128).

In Spanish, as in English, the verb endings change, both with the pronouns used and the tense. However, the Spanish do not use different words to indicate tense, such as 'am', 'was', 'will', 'shall', 'had', 'have', 'should', 'could', 'may' or 'might'. These are all incorporated in the verb itself, and indicated by the verb ending.

We saw the subject pronouns in Section 7A (facing page). These require only four verb endings: I, he/she/it/your honour, we, they/your honours. Remember, we are leaving out 'thou' and 'you' (**'tú'/'vosostros'** in Spanish) as these are only used in a family context.

First, then, to the regular verbs. There are three main types (or conjugations) of verbs: those whose infinitive form (to do something) ends in -ar, -er, or -ir. Thus:

hablar   to speak
vender   to sell
vivir   to live

Note that we refer to the first part of the verb as the 'stem', (habl-) and the ending as -ar. The endings are in bold type in the text.

Present Tense

The present tense (I speak/sell/live) is conjugated as follows:

	speak	*sell*	*live*
	-ar	-er	-ir
yo	hablo	vendo	vivo
el/ella/vd	habla	vende	vive
nosostros/as	hablamos	vendemos	vivimos
ellos/ellas/vds	hablan	venden	viven

As the verb endings are different, their meaning is clear, so you don't need to use the personal pronoun as well, thus:

Vivo en Gran Bretaña (I live in Britain)

Spanish

Imperfect Tense

The imperfect tense (I was speaking/selling/living, or I used to speak/sell/live) is conjugated as follows:

	speak -ar	*sell* -er	*live* -ir
yo	habl**aba**	vend**ía**	viv**ía**
el/ella/vd	habl**aba**	vend**ía**	viv**ía**
nosostros/as	habl**ábamos**	vend**íamos**	viv**íamos**
ellos/ellas/vds	habl**aban**	vend**ían**	viv**ían**

Future Tense

The future tense (I will or shall speak/sell/live) merely adds different endings onto the infinitive (**'hablar'**, **'vender'**, **'vivir'**), thus:

	speak -ar	*sell* -er	*live* -ir
yo	hablar**é**	vender**é**	vivir**é**
el/ella/vd	hablar**á**	vender**á**	vivir**á**
nosostros/as	hablar**emos**	vender**emos**	vivir**emos**
ellos/ellas/vds	hablar**án**	vender**án**	vivir**án**

If you are going to do something, and not doing it already, translate exactly as in English:

(Yo) voy a (I am going to) + infinitive

All the common regular verbs are shown in the word list. The irregular verbs are dealt with in Sections 10B and 10C (pp. 107 and 111).

Present Participle

In Spanish, 'I am speaking' can be translated as 'I speak' (**Yo hablo**). But if 'speaking' is still continuing, it can be translated just as in English. In this case, you would use what is called the present participle for 'speaking' (**hablando**) together with the verb 'to be', thus:

Estoy (I am) **hablando** (speaking)

The present participle is formed by adding -ando to the stem of the verbs ending in -ar, and -iendo to all others:

hablando (speaking),   **vendiendo** (selling),
viviendo (living)

Not all English verbs ending in -ing are translated by the present participle in Spanish. If the Spanish word used is an adjective, it will use a different ending, either -ante or -ente, thus:

Es muy interesante (It is very interesting)

SESSION EIGHT
To Be and To Have

8A   Haber and the Perfect Tense

The perfect tense ('I have done' something) is built up in exactly the same way as in English, using the auxiliary verb **'haber'** (to have), together with what is called the past participle.

The past participle of the three conjugations of regular verbs adds -ado or -ido to the stem, thus:

hablado (spoken),   **vendido** (sold),   **vivido** (lived)

So if we put the verb 'to have' together with the past participle, we get:

I have spoken/I spoke – **He hablado**
I have sold/I sold   – **He vendido**
I have lived/I lived – **He vivido**

In order to build up the perfect tense, you need to know how to conjugate **'haber'**. Its present and future tenses are conjugated as follows:

Present Tense

I have	**he**
he/she has/you have	**ha**
we have	**hemos**
they have	**han**

Future Tense

I will/shall have	**habré**
he/she/you will/shall have	**habrá**
we will/shall have	**habremos**
they will/shall have	**habrán**

The imperfect tense (I was having etc) is perfectly regular, following all verbs with an -er infinitive ending (i.e. **había, había, habíamos, habían**).

'Haber' is *only* used as an auxiliary verb together with

Spanish

the past participle. The Spanish verb 'to have', meaning 'to own' or 'to hold', is **'tener'**.

Note that we have not shown the personal pronouns – yo, el, nosostros, ellos or vds – as the meaning is usually clear without using them.

Irregular Past Participles

Some -er or -ir verbs have irregular past participles. In most cases they are abbreviated or altered to improve the sound. There are 10 in our word list, as follows:

abierto	(opened)	*not* abrido
cubierto	(covered)	*not* cubrido
dicho	(said)	*not* decido
escrito	(written)	*not* escribido
hecho	(done)	*not* hacido
muerto	(died)	*not* morido
puesto	(put)	*not* ponido
roto	(broken)	*not* rompido
visto	(seen)	*not* vido
vuelto	(returned)	*not* volvido

Past Participles as Adjectives

Words like 'completed', 'closed', 'dried', 'fixed', 'situated' or 'written' can be used as adjectives, usually in conjunction with the verb 'to be'.

Es concluido (It is completed)
Estoy cansado (I am tired)
La vía es cerrada (The road is closed)

When the past participle is used as an adjective, it has to agree with the noun.

A number of past participles are shortened when they are used as adjectives. There are seven in our word list.

Past participle			*Adjective*
experimentado	(tried)	*becomes*	**experto**
faltado	(wanted)	*becomes*	**falto**
fijado	(fixed)	*becomes*	**fijo**
juntado	(joined)	*becomes*	**junto**
limpiado	(cleaned)	*becomes*	**limpio**
nacido	(born)	*becomes*	**nato**
salvado	(saved)	*becomes*	**salvo**

8B To Be – Ser or Estar

There are two words for the verb 'to be' in Spanish: **'ser'** and **'estar'**. **'Ser'** is used to indicate a settled or permanent state of affairs, **'estar'** a temporary condition.

For example, 'he is my brother', 'he is English', 'he is young', 'he is tall', 'he is from London', 'he lives in a house but the house is mine', all describe a relatively permanent state of affairs. While 'he' will grow old eventually and might move house, we would say that he was settled for the time being, and so you should use **'ser'** in every case, thus:

Es mi hermano	– He is my brother
Es inglés	– He is English
Es joven	– He is young
Es alto	– He is tall
Es de Londres	– He is from London
La casa es mía	– The house is mine
La casa será mía	– The house will be mine

'Ser' is also used where we would say 'it's' or 'it is' plus an adjective in a completely impersonal context.

Es verdad (It is true)
Es difícil (It is difficult)
Es fácil (It is easy)
Es barato (It is cheap)

'Ser' is conjugated as follows:

I am	**soy**
he/she/it is	**es**
we are	**somos**
they are	**son**
I was	**era**
he/she/it was	**era**
we were	**éramos**
they were	**eran**
I will/shall be	**seré**
he/she/it will/shall be	**será**
we will/shall be	**seremos**
they will/shall be	**serán**

However, if you are describing something which is happening today, or right now, you use **'estar'**, thus:

¿Como está?	– How are you?
Estoy bien	– I am well

Spanish

¿Donde está?	– Where are you?
Estoy aquí	– I am here
Estoy en los correos	– I am in the post office
Los correos están abiertos	– The post office is open
Estoy escribiendo a mi amigo	– I am writing to my friend
Estaré allí en dos minutos	– I will be there in two minutes

'Estar' is conjugated as follows:

I am	**estoy**	I will/shall	**estaré**
he/she/it is	**está**	he/she/it will	**estará**
we are	**estamos**	we will	**estaremos**
they are	**están**	they will	**estarán**
I was	**estaba**		
he/she/it was	**estaba**		
we were	**estábamos**		
they were	**estaban**		

In one or two English expressions which use the verb 'to be', you do not use **'ser'** or **'estar'** in Spanish, but **'tener'** (to have) just as in French.

Tengo calor (I am hot; literally, I have heat)
Tengo sed (I am thirsty)
Tengo razón (I am right)

SESSION NINE
Object Pronouns

9   Object Pronouns

In Spanish, as in English, the spelling of a pronoun changes when it becomes the object in a sentence. To take a simple case:

He hits *him* is translated **(El) lo pega**
He changes to *him* in English, **el** changes to **lo** in Spanish

As we saw in Section 5 (p. 95), the object pronoun comes *before* the verb in Spanish except where an infinitive or imperative is used; in this case the pronoun is actually tacked on to the end of the verb.

No quiero pegarlo (I do not wish to hit *him*)
Démelo (Give *it to me*)

The object pronouns are set out below in two columns, the first where the pronoun is the direct object of the verb, the second where the pronoun is the indirect object – i.e. where in English we would say 'to me', 'to him' or 'to' any other pronoun. As you can see from the table, the only distinction between the two lies in the 3rd person singular and plural.

	Direct		*Indirect*	
me	**me**	to me	**me**
him/you (m. sing)	**lo** or **le***	to him/you	**le**
it	**lo**	to it	**le**
her/you/it (f. sing)	**la**	to her/you/it	**le**
us	**nos**	to us	**nos**
them (people)/you (m. pl)	**les**	to them	**les**
them (things) (m)	**los**	to them	**les**
them/you (f. pl)	**las**	to them/you	**les**

* *'le'* *is used in central and northern Spain.*

Where two pronouns precede the verb, the *indirect* pronoun goes first, and the direct pronoun second, e.g.

(Vd) me le ha dado (You have given it to me)

If however two pronouns both start with l- the first changes to **'se'** to make it sound better.

(Yo) se lo he tomado (I have taken it to him)

Pronouns which Clarify

In the table above, you can see that the use of one word **'le'** for 'to him', 'to it', 'to her' and 'to you' can be a bit confusing! So the Spanish clarify this by using the pronouns shown above and then repeating 'to her' or 'to you' afterwards in a more clear form. This is also to give a pronoun more emphasis. Thus:

Le **hablo** *a usted* – (To you) I am speaking to *you*

Pronouns after Prepositions

After the preposition **'a'** (to), you use the subject pronouns – el, ella, usted, nosostros, ellos, ellas and ustedes – shown in Section 7A, p. 98. However, in the 1st person singular, you use the pronoun **'mí'** instead of **'yo'**. Note that **'el'** takes an accent (**él**) when used in this way, thus:

Le hablo a *él* (I am speaking to *him*)

105

The subject pronouns can be used with any preposition, such as 'by' (**por**), 'with' (**con**), 'to' (**a**), or 'of' (**de**), but if the pronoun 'me' (**mí**) is used with the preposition 'with' (**con**) it changes its form and gets rolled up with the preposition, e.g.

Habla *conmigo* (He talks *with me*)

SESSION TEN
Imperatives, Reflexives and Irregular Verbs

10A The Imperative and Reflexive Verbs

If you instruct someone to do something, you use the imperative – and the Spanish use it quite a lot. There are only two forms which you need:

You must (do something)
We must, or let us (do something)

Remember that 'you', singular or plural, takes the 3rd person, **'usted'** or **'ustedes'**. The imperative is formed by changing the verb ending in the present tense, either from -a to -e, or from -e to -a, thus:

	-ar verbs end in	-er/-ir verbs end in
you must (singular)	**-e**	**-a**
we must, or let us	**-emos**	**-amos**
you must (plural)	**-en**	**-an**

For example:

(You, singular, must) speak, sell, live – **Hable, venda, viva (vd)**
(We must/let us) speak, sell, live – **Hablemos, vendamos, vivamos (nosostros)**
(You, plural, must) speak, sell, live – **Hablen, vendan, vivan (vds)**

Remember to add the pronouns on to the end of the imperative, as we saw in the last section, p. 104.

Démelo (Give it to me)

However, this rule does not apply in the negative:

No me lo dé (Don't give it to me)

Reflexive Verbs

Many verbs become 'reflexive' just by changing the pronouns:

(El) le pega (He hits him)
(El) se pega (He hits himself) is reflexive

The reflexive pronouns are very simple:

myself	**me**
him/her/it/yourself	**se**
ourselves	**nos**
them/yourselves	**se**

As the pronoun **'se'** can have so many meanings, you will sometimes see or hear the pronoun repeated after the verb, in order to make the meaning absolutely clear, e.g.

(El) se pega á el (He hits himself)

The Spanish use the reflexive form more than we do. Where we would say 'I get dressed', the Spanish would say 'I dress myself'. Examples are:

(Yo) me levanto (I get up)
(El) se lava (He washes himself)
(Nosostros) nos vestímos (We get dressed)
(Vds) se sientan (You sit down)

The reflexive verbs are shown in the word list with -se added to the infinitive.

The reflexive verb is also used where the subject matter is impersonal or you are being polite, and it is used to translate the English passive e.g.:

Se dice (It is said that, or one says that)
Se prohibe (It is forbidden)
Se habla inglés (English is spoken; literally, 'speaks itself')
Se sierve almuerzo aquí (Lunch is served here)

10B Slightly Irregular Verbs

In the next two sections we show 'Slightly Irregular Verbs' and 'Really Irregular Verbs'. Read through both sections, but don't try to memorize any but the most common verbs. Just refer to the text when you see a word which you cannot understand. In time, you will assimilate most of the irregularities and will recognize the words when you see them in print.

Spanish

In this section we show those categories of verbs which are only slightly irregular. Those with irregular participles have already been shown in previous sections and do not need repeating. The three categories shown here are those:

(a) Verbs which change their stem (present and imperative)
(b) Verbs which change their stem (future tense)
(c) Verbs which change their spelling

There are several words in all three categories which appear in our word list. But don't be put off. The changes are fairly slight, and they are all designed either to make them easier to pronounce, or to retain the original sound of the stem when the endings change. For example, a verb with a stem ending in -c would have two different sounds if the verb ending changed from -e to -a or -o. In the first case it would sound like th in *thin*, the second like c in *cat*. The Spanish overcome this problem by changing the c to z which also has a th sound so the stem can keep its original sound. There are a few others like it.

Verbs which change their stem (present and imperative)

Eight words in our list change the middle vowel in their stem from o to ue in the present tense (except for the 1st person plural) and also in the imperative. Nine change the middle vowel from e to ie, and two change from e to i as follows:

Verbs changing from o to ue

cocer	– to cook
costar	– to cost
encontrar	– to meet
jugar	– to play
mostrar	– to show
mover	– to move
volar	– to fly
volver	– to return

Example – **volar** (to fly)

Present tense

v**ue**lo	– I fly
v**ue**la	– he/she/you fly
volamos	– we fly
v**ue**lan	– they/you fly

Imperative

vuele!   – Fly! (you [sing])
volemos – Let us fly
vuelen!   – Fly! (you [pl])

Verbs changing from e to ie

cerrar	– to shut
comenzar	– to begin
defender	– to defend
descender	– to descend
entender	– to understand
pensar	– to think
perder	– to lose
preferir	– to prefer
sentarse	– to sit down
sentir	– to feel

Example – **perder** (to lose)

Present tense

pierdo   – I lose
pierde   – he/she/you lose
perdemos – we lose
pierden   – they/you lose

Imperative

pierda!   – Lose! (you [sing])
perdamos – Let us lose
pierdan!   – Lose! (you [pl])

Verbs changing from e to i

pedir	– to ask
repetir	– to repeat

Example – **pedir** (to ask)

Present tense

pido   – I ask
pide   – he/she/you ask
pedimos – we ask
piden   – they/you ask

Imperative

pida!   – Ask! (you [sing])
pidamos – Let us ask
pidan!   – Ask! (you [pl])

Spanish

Verbs which change their stem (future tense)

Regular verbs form the future tense by adding the ending to the infinitive -ar, -er or -ir. But 10 common -er and -ir verbs modify the stem. The endings themselves are perfectly regular:

decir (to say)	**diré** (I will say)	*not* deciré
haber (to have)	**habré** (I will have)	*not* haberé
hacer (to make)	**haré** (I will make)	*not* haceré
poder (to be able)	**podré** (I will be able)	*not* poderé
poner (to put)	**pondré** (I will put)	*not* poneré
querer (to like/wish)	**querré** (I will like)	*not* quereré
saber (to know)	**sabré** (I will know)	*not* saberé
salir (to go out)	**saldré** (I will go out)	*not* saliré
tener (to have/own)	**tendré** (I will have)	*not* teneré
venir (to come)	**vendré** (I will come)	*not* veniré

In the grammar we have only shown the future tense, that is to say 'I will' or 'I shall' (do something). However, it is worth showing one word which will be useful for travellers in its *conditional* tense:

Querría (I *would* like)

Verbs which change their spelling

Verbs with a stem ending in -c, -z, -g or -gu change whether they are followed by -e or by -a or -o. There are not many words in our word list which do this, but here are all the spelling changes in case you come across them in your reading. We suggest that you don't learn them, only make yourself aware that these changes occur.

Verb ending:

    -cer/-cir (after a *consonant*)

c changes to z before a and o, thus:
vencer (to conquer), **venzo** (I conquer), vence (he conquers)

    -cer/-cir (after a *vowel*)

c changes to zc before a and o, thus:
conocer (to know), cono**zc**o (I know), conoce (he knows)

    -ger/-gir

g changes to j before a or o, thus:
dirigir (to direct), diri**j**o (I direct), dirige (he directs)

-guir

gu drops the u before a or o
seguir (to follow), sigo (I follow), sigue (he follows)

-quir

qu changes to c before a or o, thus:
delinquir (to sin), delinco (I sin), delinque (he sins)

10C   Irregular Verbs

There are not many really irregular verbs in Spanish, but there are 18 in our 500 word list (apart from **'haber'**, **'ser'** and **'estar'**), all of them in everyday use, which are shown below. Note that the endings are almost always regular; only the stem changes.

Each verb is shown first in the infinitive, followed by the present and past participle. On the next two lines we show the present and future tenses, without repeating the subject pronouns. On the fourth line we show the imperative for 'you must' (singular), 'we must' or 'let us' and 'you must' (plural).

Two verbs, **'ir'** (to go) and **'ver'** (to see), have an irregular imperfect tense which is shown on an additional line.

The verbs for 'to be' and 'to have' (auxiliary) are shown in Sections 8A and 8B (pp. 101 and 103).

caer (*to fall*), cayendo (*falling*), caído (*fallen*)
Present: caigo, cae, caemos, caen
Imperfect: caía, caía, caíamos, caían
Future: caeré, caerá, caeremos, caerán
Imperative: caiga, caigamos, caigan

dar (*to give*), dando (*giving*), dado (*given*)
Present: Doy, da, damos, dan
Future: daré, dará, daremos, darán
Imperative: dé, demos, den

decir (*to say, tell*), diciendo (*saying*), dicho (*said*)
Present: digo, dice, decimos, dicen
Future: diré, dirá, diremos, dirán
Imperative: diga, digamos, digan

dormir (*to sleep*), durmiendo (*sleeping*), dormido (*slept*)
Present: duermo, duerme, dormimos, duermen
Future: dormiré, dormirá, dormiremos, dormirán
Imperative: duerma, durmamos, duerman

Spanish

hacer (*to do, make*), ha**c**iendo (*doing*), **hech**o (*done*)
Present: ha**g**o, hace, hacemos, hacen
Future: ha**r**é, ha**r**á, ha**r**emos, ha**r**án
Imperative: ha**g**a, ha**g**amos, ha**g**an

ir (*to go*), **y**endo (*going*), ido (*gone*)
Present: **voy**, **va**, **va**mos, **va**n
Imperfect: iba, iba, íbamos, iban
Future: iré, irá, iremos, irán
Imperative: **vaya**, **va**mos (or **vaya**mos), **vay**an

jugar (*to play*), ju**g**ando (*playing*), ju**g**ado (*played*)
Present: j**ue**go, j**ue**ga, jugamos, j**ue**gan
Future: jugaré, jugará, jugaremos, jugarán
Imperative: j**ue**ge, j**ue**gemos, j**ue**gen

morir (*to die*), m**u**riendo (*dying*), m**uert**o (*died*)
Present: m**u**ero, m**u**ere, morimos, m**u**eren
Future: moriré, morirá, moriremos, morirán
Imperative: m**u**ere, m**u**ramos, m**u**eran

oir (*to hear*), o**y**endo (*hearing*), o**í**do (*heard*)
Present: o**ig**o, o**y**e, o**í**mos, o**y**en
Future: oiré, oirá, oiremos, oirán
Imperative: o**ig**a, o**ig**amos, o**ig**an

poder (*to be able to*), p**u**diendo (*being able to*), podido
(*could*)
Present: p**ue**do, p**ue**de, podemos, p**ue**den
Future: po**dr**é, po**dr**á, po**dr**emos, po**dr**án

poner (*to put*), po**n**iendo (*putting*), p**uest**o (*put*)
Present: pon**g**o, pone, ponemos, ponen
Future: pon**dr**é, pon**dr**á, pon**dr**emos, pon**dr**án
Imperative: pon**g**a, pon**g**amos, pon**g**an

querer (*to like, wish, want*), queriendo (*wanting*), querido
(*wanted*)
Present: qu**i**ero, qu**i**ere, queremos, qu**i**eren
Future: que**rr**é, que**rr**á, que**rr**emos, que**rr**án
Imperative: qu**i**era, queramos, qu**i**eran

saber (*to know*), sabiendo (*knowing*), sabido (*knew*)
Present: **sé**, sabe, sabemos, saben
Future: sa**br**é, sa**br**á, sa**br**emos, sa**br**án
Imperative: s**ep**a, s**ep**amos, s**ep**an

salir (*to go out*), saliendo (*going out*), salido (*gone out*)
Present: salgo, sale, salimos, salen
Future: saldré, saldrá, saldremos, saldrán
Imperative: salga, salgamos, salgan

tener (*to have, hold*), teniendo (*having*), tenido (*had*)
Present: tengo, tiene, tenemos, tienen
Future: tendré, tendrá, tendremos, tendrán
Imperative: tenga, tengamos, tengan

traer (*to bring*), trayendo (*bringing*), traído (*brought*)
Present: traigo, trae, traemos, traen
Future: traeré, traerá, traeremos, traerán
Imperative: traiga, traigamos, traigan

venir (*to come*), viniendo (*coming*), venido (*came*)
Present: vengo, viene, venimos, vienen
Future: vendré, vendrá, vendremos, vendrán
Imperative: venga, vengamos, vengan

ver (*to see*), viendo (*seeing*), visto (*saw*)
Present: veo, ve, vemos, ven
Imperfect: veía, veía, veíamos, veían
Future: veré, verá, veremos, verán
Imperative: vea, veamos, vean

'**Poder**' (to be able) shown above is particularly useful in Spanish, as it can be used to make up tenses of other verbs, e.g.

> **No puedo cocinar muy bien** (I can't cook very well)
> **Puedo venir** (I can come)

You can also use '**poder**' when you would use 'may' or 'might' in English. '**Puedo venir**' is sufficiently close for the beginner to use for 'I may/might come', even though the meaning is slightly different.

SESSION ELEVEN
Questions and Negatives

11A   Questions

One way to ask a question in Spanish is to reverse the subject and the verb:

Spanish

Los estudiantes trabajan bien (The students work well)
¿Trabajan bien los estudiantes? (Do the students work well?)

Note that the word does (or do) in English is *not* translated into Spanish at all.

Notice also the inverted question mark before the sentence begins, as well as the normal question mark at the end.

In the perfect tense the auxiliary verb **'haber'** should be kept together with the past participle, and should not be split up as it is in English, e.g.

¿Han terminado los estudiantes? (*Have* the students *finished?*)

A slight problem arises over personal pronouns, which are usually omitted in Spanish, so the sentence is often the same for a question as for a statement, e.g.

Habla inglés (He speaks English)
¿Habla inglés? (Does he speak English?)

In reading Spanish you can pick this up by the question mark at the beginning of the sentence. When you are speaking Spanish you get round it quite simply by raising your voice at the end of the question, or by adding an exclamation such as **'verdad'** (truly), **'no'** (isn't it) or just **'eh!'**

11B   Interrogatives

Most of the interrogatives in Spanish are quite straightforward, and they all bear an accent to show what they are.

dónde (where) – **¿Dónde está mi bolígrafo?** (Where is my pen?)
cuándo (when) – **¿Cuándo llega (vd)?** (When will you arrive?)
por qué (why) – **¿Por qué está (vd) tarde?** (Why are you late?)
cómo (how) – **¿Cómo está?** (How are you?)
cuánto (how many, how much) – **¿Cuánto dinero ha (vd)?** (How much money do you have?)
Note that **cuánto** is an adjective and must agree with the noun.
qué (what) – **¿Qué piensa (vd)?** (What are you thinking?) **¿Qué quiere?** (What do you want?)

quién (who/which) – **¿Quién va allí?** (Who goes there?)

'Who', 'What' and 'Which'

In English the genitive of 'who' is 'whose'. The Spanish are more likely to say **'de quién'** (of whom), in asking a question, e.g.

¿De quién es esta casa? (literally, Of whom is this house?)

but they do have a pronoun **'cuyo'** for 'whose', which has to agree with the noun.

El hombre cuyo casa es en Madrid (The man whose house is in Madrid)

Both **'quien'** (who) and **'que'** (who, whom, what, which or that) can be used as relative pronouns to join two phrases together. But in this case neither **'que'** nor **'quien'** has an accent.

El hombre que vive allí (The man who lives there)
La lección que (nosostros) tenemos hoy (The lesson which we have today)
La casa que (yo) recuerdo (The home that I remember)

Both **'que'** and **'quien'** are widely used in Spanish after prepositions such as 'of', 'for', 'with', 'by' or 'to'. The plural of **'quien'** is **'quienes'**, which has to agree with the subject.

Los muchachos *con quienes* **estudio** (The boys with whom I study)
La casa *a que* **voy** (The house to which I am going)

'Cual' is used for 'what or which?' where it directly refers to a noun.

¿Cual lección tenemos hoy? (What lesson do we have today?)

Like other adjectives, **'cual'** has a plural but not a feminine form which has to agree with the noun.

¿Cuales lecciónes tiene (vd)? (What lessons do you have?)

If **'cual'** is used as a relative pronoun together with a preposition such as 'with', 'by', 'to' or 'of', it needs to be stressed by adding the definite article as a prefix.

> **La oficína en** *la* **cual trabajo** (The office in which I work)

11C   Negatives

To form a negative in Spanish, just put **'no'** in front of the verb, even if you have just answered 'No!' to a question.

> **No, no hablo inglés** (No, I do not speak English)

Remember, in the perfect tense the auxiliary verb and the past participle stick together.

> **No** *he vivido* **en España** (I have not lived in Spain)

Only the object pronoun can come between 'no' and the verb.

> **No** *me* **ha hablado** (He has not spoken to me)

'Neither . . . nor' is translated **'no . . . ni'**.

> **No me gusta esta casa ni esa** (I don't like this house or that one)

'**No**' plus '**nunca**' means never.

> **No le he amado nunca!** (I never loved him!)

Finally:

> **No importa!** (It doesn't matter!)

SESSION TWELVE
More Adjectives

12A   Adjectives and Comparatives

There are 80 adjectives in the word list. There is no need to remember them all here, but some indefinite adjectives are in common use and you should try to remember these:

all (**todo**)	more (**más**)
each (**cada**)	next (**próximo**)
enough (**bastante**)	other/another (**otro**)
less (**menos**)	some (**algún**)
many/much (**mucho**)	too, too much (**demasiado**)

'**Bastante**' (enough), '**mucho**' (much), '**todo**' (all), '**menos**' (less), '**más**' (more) and '**demasiado**' (too much) can also be used as adverbs.

Normally all adjectives have to agree with the noun, but a few such as '**bastante**' (enough), '**cada**' (each), '**menos**' (less) and '**más**' (more) do not have a feminine and a plural form.

As we saw in Section 6 (p. 96), all other adjectives ending in -o change to -a in the feminine, those ending in -on, -or and -an add an -a, whilst the other adjectives do not change at all. Most adjectives add -s in the plural but those ending in a consonant (or -y) add -es and those ending in -z change to -ces in the plural.

Remember that all except the very short or very common adjectives follow the noun in word order.

Comparatives

The Spanish use '**más**' (more) or '**menos**' (less) with another adjective to indicate comparison. Where we say 'whiter', they say '**más blanco**' (more white) but '**menos blanco**' (less white) is expressed in the same way in both languages.

Two notable exceptions are 'good' and 'bad', which go as follows:

bueno (good)   **mejor** (better)   **el mejor** (best)
malo (bad)   **peor** (worse)   **el peor** (worst)
(Ella) es mejor que él (She is better than him)
Es más difícil que (vd) piensa (It's more difficult than you think)

Note the use of '**que**' for 'than' after a comparative.

So much for whit*er*, or *less* white; how do we show whit*est*, or *least* white? Just by inserting the definite article (which has to agree) before '**más**' or '**menos**'.

La nieve, la más blanca (The whitest snow)
El sol, el menos rojo (The least red sun)

However, the definite article is omitted where a possessive pronoun is used:

mi mejor amigo (my *best* friend)

12B   Possessive Adjectives and Pronouns

The possessive adjectives – my, your, his, her, its, our and their – are very simple in Spanish and they are set out

Spanish

below. They have only one singular and plural form, except for **'nuestro'** which changes to **'nuestra/as'** in the feminine.

	Sing	*Pl*
my	**mi**	**mis**
his, her, its, your (sing)	**su**	**sus**
our	**nuestro/a**	**nuestros/as**
their, your (pl)	**su**	**sus**

In each case they have to agree with the object they refer to, thus:

Mi hermano simpático (My friendly brother)
Mis hijas bonitas (My beautiful daughters)
Su casa (Their house)

As you can see in the example **'su casa'**, the adjective **'su'** agrees with 'the house' which is singular, not with 'them' who are plural. Like the object pronoun **'le'**, **'su'** has so many possible interpretations that you may need to clarify it by changing the phrase to:

La casa de ellos (literally, The house of them)

If the object is inferred rather than stated, and you are just referring to 'mine' rather than 'my house', you use a possessive pronoun. This has to agree with the inferred object.

Su casa y la mía (Your house and mine)

The possessive pronouns run as follows; each with a masculine, feminine and plural form.

	Sing	*Pl*
mine	**el/la mío/a**	**los/las míos/as**
his, hers, yours (sing)	**el/la suyo/a**	**los/las suyos/as**
ours	**el/la nuestro/a**	**los/las nuestros/as**
theirs, yours (pl)	**el/la suyo/a**	**los/las suyos/as**

The definite article is only omitted before the possessive pronoun when the verb **'ser'** (to be) is used.

El sombrero es mío (The hat is mine)

SESSION THIRTEEN
Adverbs, Prepositions and Conjunctions

13A   Common Adverbs

In changing adjectives to adverbs many Spanish words add -mente to the feminine singular, just as we would add -ly to the adjective in English, thus:

rápido (quick) becomes **rápidamente** (quickly)

but some are irregular like 'good' and 'bad':

bueno (good) becomes **bien** (well)
malo (bad) becomes **mal** (badly)

If the word gets too long with -mente added, the Spanish will often change the sentence round to achieve the same meaning. For example, instead of **'frecuentamente'** (frequently) one might use **'a menudo'** (often).

There are 36 other adverbs in our word list and as you can see from the list below, many are in everyday use.

after (**después**)
again (**de nuevo**)
ago (**hace**)
almost (**casi**)
already (**ya**)
also/too (**también**)
always (**siempre**)
before (**antes**)
enough (**bastante**)
far (**lejos**)
here (**aquí**)
immediately
   (**inmediatamente**)
inside (**dentro**)
late (**tarde**)
much (**mucho**)
near (**cerca**)
never (**nunca**)
no (**no**)

now (**ahora**)
often (**a menudo**)
once (**una vez**)
only, alone (**solamente**)
perhaps (**tal vez**)
slowly (**despacio**)
so, thus (**así**)
sometimes (**a veces**)
soon (**pronto**)
suddenly (**subito**)
then (**entonces**)
there (**allí**)
therefore (**por lo tanto**)
today (**hoy**)
too much (**demasiado**)
unfortunately
   (**desgraciadamente**)
very (**muy**)
yes (**sí**)

Note that the adverb 'ago' usually precedes the subject:

Hace tres años (Three years ago)

Spanish

13B Prepositions and Conjunctions

The classification of English words into adjectives and adverbs, prepositions and conjunctions can become very confusing. Many English words have two or three different uses, like the word 'after', which can be an adverb, a preposition or a conjunction. The simplest advice, to forget about their uses and just remember the Spanish, is unfortunately not the best, as the Spanish often employ different words for each use.

What we have tried to show is the most common use of the word in English, and then the Spanish translation. Where two or three uses are common they are indicated in the text.

Conjunctions

These are words used to link up other words, phrases or sentences. There are only a handful in our word list.

after (**después que**)	if (**si**)
and (**y**)	or (**o**)
as (**como**)	since (**desde que**)
because (**porque**)	so (**así que**)
before (**antes que**)	when (**cuando**)
but (**pero**)	

'**Después**', '**desde**', '**antes**' and '**así**' are also adverbs, but without the '**que**'.

Prepositions

These are words indicating position or some other relationship and there are a surprising number in our vocabulary, some of them in constant use.

according to (**según**)	in order to (**para**)
after (**después de**)	inside (**dentro de**)
against (**contra**)	near (**cerca de**)
at, to, towards (**a**)	of, from (**de**)
before (time) (**antes**)	on (**sobre**)
behind (**detrás de**)	opposite (**enfrente de**)
between (**entre**)	over (**sobre**)
during (**durante**)	under (**debajo de**)
for, by, through (**por**)	with (**con**)
in (**en**)	without (**sin**)

'**Después**' (after), '**detrás**' (behind), '**cerca**' (near), '**debajo**' (underneath) and '**dentro**' (inside) are also adverbs, each dropping the '**de**' of the preposition.

120

Note that you use an infinitive in place of the present participle after a preposition.

He venido sin com*er*! (I have come without eat*ing*!)

SESSION FOURTEEN
Prepositions and Link Words

14A   This and That, 'Para' and 'Por'

'Este' (this) and **'ese'** (that) have to agree with the nouns they refer to, whether stated or not.

Their feminine and plural forms are:

	Singular		Plural	
	m	f	m	f
this/these	**este**	**esta**	**estos**	**estas**
that/those	**ese**	**esa**	**esos**	**esas**

Esta maleta o esa maleta (This suitcase or that suitcase)
¿Estos sombreros o ésos? (These hats or those?)
Esta es mi maleta (This is my suitcase)

Note that when the noun is omitted, the written form for 'those' (**ésos**) carries an accent, but the pronunciation does not change.

The Spanish also have another word for 'that' (**aquel**) when the object referred to is distant.

Esta casa y aquella (This house and that one – i.e. that one right over there)

The feminine of **'aquel'** is **'aquella'** and the plural, **'aquellos'** (m) or **'aquellas'** (f).

If 'that' or 'those' is followed by 'which' (**que**), you should use the definite article instead of **'este'**.

Esta casa y *las que* (yo) puedo ver (This house and those which I can see)

Por and Para (For)

'Por' is used in Spanish for most but not all uses of the prepositions 'for', 'by' and 'through'.

Vendré por ocho dias (I will come for a week [eight days])
Viajaré por Paris en coche (I will travel through Paris by car)

Spanish

But if 'for' indicates intention, use **'para'** instead.

Salgo para Londres (I leave for London)
La vida es para vivir (Life is for living)
El sombrero es para mí (The hat is for me)

'Para' also means 'in order to'.

(Yo) trabajo para ganar dinero (I work in order to earn money)

14B   To and From, Some and More

To, At or On

In Spanish **'a'** means 'to', 'towards', or 'at'. It can sometimes mean 'on' as in 'on a journey'.

Voy a Paris (I am going to Paris)
Tomo el tren a Paris (I take the train at Paris)
Paris es a mi viaje a Madrid (Paris is on my journey to Madrid)
En el restaurante, tomaré la carta a sesenta pesetas (In the restaurant, I will take the menu at sixty pesetas)

Normally the word 'to' in front of a verb is included in the infinitive, thus:

Quiero ir a Paris (I wish to go to Paris)

but some verbs take **'a'** after them, such as **'aprender a'** (to learn), **'empezar a'** (to begin), **'persuadir a'** (to persuade), and these are indicated in the word list followed by **'a'**, and it is a good habit to try to remember the two words together.

'A' is also used before a person or personal pronoun when that person is the object of a verb. This is peculiar to Spanish, and may be rather hard to remember.

(Yo) pego *a* Pedro (I hit Pedro)
(Yo) le veo a usted (I see you) – note repetition of 'you' to make it clearly understood

When **'a'** is used before the definite article **'el'** the two words are rolled into **'al'**, but **'a la'**, **'a los'** and **'a las'** remain unchanged, e.g.

Voy al restaurante (I'm going to the restaurant)

Of and From

In Spanish **'de'** means 'of' or 'from'. It is used more widely than in English as the Spanish do not use the genitive *'s* and so you can't say 'the girl's father'. You have to say

El padre de la chica (The father of the girl)

'De' also means 'from', as in:

He viajado de Madrid (I have travelled from Madrid)

When **'de'** is used before the definite article **'el'**, the two words are rolled into **'del'**, but **'de la'**, **'de los'** and **'de las'** remain unchanged, e.g.

La fotografía del hombre (The photo of the man)

There are also a number of prepositions which are always followed by **'de'**, including **'enfrente de'** (opposite), **'a lado de'** (by the side of), **'debajo de'** (under), **'después de'** (after), **'cerca de'** (near), **'dentro de'** (inside), **'detrás de'** (behind). These are shown with **'de'** in the word list.

Some, Any and None

The simplest form of 'some' is **'unos'**, or **'unas'**, but you can also use **'algún'** which has to agree with the noun. If the word 'some' or 'any' is obvious, the Spanish sometimes omit it altogether, which we never do in English. So you have three alternatives:

Tengo algunas manzanas
Tengo unas manzanas } (I have some apples)
Tengo manzanas

Similarly if you ask a question:

¿Tiene (vd) manzanas? (Do you have any apples?)

'No' or 'none' in Spanish is **'ningún'**, so:

Tengo ningunas manzanas (I have no apples)

but you could use a negative instead:

No tengo manzanas (I don't have any apples)

Spanish

SESSION FIFTEEN
Numbers and Time

15A Numbers and Measures

Cardinal Numbers

0	cero	30	treinta
1	un/uno/una	31	treinta y uno
2	dos	32	treinta y dos
3	tres	40	cuarenta
4	cuatro	50	cincuenta
5	cinco	60	sesenta
6	seis	70	setenta
7	siete	80	ochenta
8	ocho	90	noventa
9	nueve	100	cien (no un if exact)
10	diez	101	ciento uno
11	once	157	ciento cincuenta y siete
12	doce	200	doscientos
13	trece	300	trescientos
14	catorce	400	cuatrocientos
15	quince	500	quinientos
16	dieciséis	600	seiscientos
17	diecisiete	700	setecientos
18	dieciocho	800	ochocientos
19	diecinueve	900	novecientos
20	veinte	1,000	mil (no un)
21	veintiuno	10,000	diez mil
22	veintidos	100,000	cien mil

157,643 – **ciento cincuenta siete mil, seiscientos/as cuarenta y tres**
1,000,000 – **un millón**
2,000,000 – **dos millones**
1,576,432 – **un millón, quinientos/as setenta y seis mil, cuatrocientos/as treinta y dos**
1,000,000,000 – **un billón**

Note the use of **'y'** (and) to link all but the round numbers (40, 50 etc) between 31 and 99.

'Uno' has to agree with the noun, but drops the o before a masculine singular noun, e.g. **'un soldado'**. **'Un'** is not needed in front of 100 (**cien**) or 1000 (**mil**).

'Cien' drops the ending -to when it is 100 or 100,000 exactly. **'Ciento'** (plural) has to agree with the noun, e.g. **'doscientos soldados'**.

Numbers showing order are as follows:

first	**primero**	sixth	**sexto**
second	**segundo**	seventh	**séptimo**
third	**tercero**	eighth	**octavo**
fourth	**cuarto**	ninth	**noveno**
fifth	**quinto**	tenth	**décimo**

As adjectives, they have to agree with the noun. **'Primero'** drops the -o before a masculine noun, e.g. **'el primer hombre'** (the first man). Ordinal numbers over 10, **'vigésimo'** (20), **'trigesimo'** (30) etc, are seldom used and you can use the ordinary numbers.

The only fractions you are likely to need at this stage are:

one quarter	**un cuarto**
one third	**un tercio**
one half	**un medio**
two thirds	**dos tercios**
three quarters	**tres cuartos**
one	**un/uno/una**

There is no equivalent to the English words 'once', 'twice', 'thrice'. The Spanish say **'una vez'** (one time), **'dos veces'** (two times), **'tres veces'** (three times), and so on.

Weights are in kilos (literally, *1000* gramos [grammes])

un kilo = 35 ounces or just under 2¼ lb
un medio kilo = just over 1 lb

If you purchase cheese from a delicatessen, for example, you would ask for 350 gramos, *not* 'un tercio kilo' (one third of a kilo).

Liquid measures are in litros (litres)

un litro (one litre) = cien (100) centilitros = 35 fluid ounces = 1¾ pints
one pint = approximately 0.6 litro or 60 centilitros

Distances are in kilómetros (1000 metres)

un kilómetro or km = 0.6 of one mile
one mile = 1.6 kilómetros, ten miles = 16 km

15B Dates and Time

Un año (a year) is split into four seasons:

spring	**la primavera**
summer	**el verano**
autumn	**el otoño**
winter	**el invierno**

Los meses (the months) are mostly recognizable from the English.

January	**enero**	July	**julio**
February	**febrero**	August	**agosto**
March	**marzo**	September	**septiembre**
April	**abríl**	October	**octubre**
May	**mayo**	November	**noviembre**
June	**junio**	December	**diciembre**

Cada mes (each month) **tiene cuatro semanas** (four weeks) **y cada día** (each day) **se llama** (calls itself):

Monday	**lunes**	Friday	**viernes**
Tuesday	**martes**	Saturday	**sábado**
Wednesday	**miércoles**	Sunday	**domingo**
Thursday	**jueves**		

Note that one week, Saturday to Saturday, counts as eight days in Spain!

The Spanish use the definite article before the day of the week and do not translate the word 'on', e.g.

Llegaré el martes (I will arrive on Tuesday)

Cada día consta (is comprised) **de la mañana** (of the morning), **de la tarde** (afternoon and evening) **y de la noche** (night) **y hay** (there are) **veinticuatro horas** (24 hours) **todos los días** (every day).

Cada hora tiene sesenta minutos (minutes)
Cada minuto tiene sesenta segundos (seconds)
¿A cuántos estamos? (What is the date?; literally, at how many are we?)
Hoy, estamos al lunes, el dieciocho de mayo (Today we are at/(it is) Monday 18th May)

Note that cardinal numbers are used to show dates, except **'el primero'** (the first).

Mañana por la mañana (tomorrow morning) **será martes** (will be Tuesday)
El próximo día será miércoles (The next day will be Wednesday)

¿Que hora es? (What hour/time is it?)
Son las cinco y media (It is five hours and a half; in other words, half past five)

Note that '**son**' *not* '**es**' has to be used for more than one hour.

The word '**horas**' (hours) is omitted, as in English, but the definite article is always used and has to agree with '**horas**'.

'A quarter to six' is translated as:

las seis menos cuarto (*the* six less quarter)

For minutes past the hour, say

las cinco y veinte y siete (*the* five *and* twenty-seven)

and for minutes before the hour, just use the word **menos** (less)

las seis menos veinte y siete (*the* six *less* twenty-seven)

Don't bother to say 'minutes' so long as this is understood. Up to 12 noon, say

las seis de la mañana (the six of the morning)

but remember that published times on the Continent work to a 24-hour clock.

After '**mediodía**' (midday) and up to '**medianoche**' (midnight) we would say '**las cinco de la tarde**' (five in the afternoon) or '**las diez de la noche**' (ten at night).

Finally, the weather.

¿Qué tiempo hace? (What is the weather like?)
Hace calor (It is hot; literally, it makes hot)
Hace frío (It is cold)
Nieva (It is snowing)

Note that '**tiempo**' also means length of time.

No hay mucho tiempo! (There is not much time!)
Hace mucho tiempo (A long time ago)

Spanish

APPENDIX

Subjunctives

The subjunctive tenses have been left out of the main text as they can be confusing to those learning Spanish. Subjunctives are little used, even less recognized in English, but they are used much more frequently in Spanish. They usually occur in subordinate clauses after the conjunctive 'que', following verbs of ordering, wanting, expressing fear or doubt or emotion, or after impersonal verbs e.g.

Dudo *que* **(vd) haya bastante dinero** (I doubt you have enough money)

Volveré para *que* **(vd) pueda salir** (I will come back so that you can go out)

The present and imperfect subjunctive tense endings are set out below for the regular verbs and also for **'haber'**, **'ser'** and **'estar'**. The imperfect subjunctive should be used when the verb in the main sentence is in the past tense, also in conditional sentences starting with **'si'** (if) where the answer is likely to be negative. The perfect subjunctive can be built up from **'haber'** and the past participle.

Present Tense

Regular Verbs

	-ar verb endings	*-er/-ir verb endings*	*haber*	*ser*	*estar*
1st sing	-e	-a	haya	sea	esté
3rd sing	-e	-a	haya	sea	esté
1st pl	-emos	-amos	hayamos	semos	estemos
3rd pl	-en	-an	hayan	sean	estén

Imperfect Tense

	-ar verb endings	*-er/-ir verb endings*	*haber*	*ser*	*estar*
1st sing	-ara	-iera	hubiera	fuera	estuviera
3rd sing	-ara	-iera	hubiera	fuera	estuviera
1st pl	-áramos	-iéramos	hubiéramos	fuéramos	estuviéramos
3rd pl	-aran	-ieran	hubieran	fueran	estuvieran

There is an alternative ending for the imperfect subjunctive, substituting the letters -se for -ra, which is used less frequently.

Many irregular verbs change their stem, but not their

endings in the subjunctive, just as they do in the indicative tenses.

When speaking Spanish, it is suggested that you start by keeping the sentences fairly simple and avoid too many subordinate clauses, which require the use of the subjunctive.

ITALIAN

CONTENTS

SESSION ONE
Your Word List

1A 500 Word Vocabulary

a/an **un/uno/una**
able, to be **potere**
accept, to **accettare**
accident **incidente** (m)
according to **secondo**
account (bill) **conto** (m)
address **indirizzo** (m)
advise, to **consigliare**
aeroplane **aereo** (m)
after **dopo**
afternoon **pomeriggio** (m)
again **di nuovo**
against **contro**
age **età** (f)
ago **fa**
agree with, to **essere
d'accordo**
air **aria** (f)
airmail **posta aerea**
airport **aeroporto** (m)
all **tutto**
allow (let), to **permettere
(di + verb)**
almost **quasi**
alone **solo**
already **già**
also (too) **anche**
always **sempre**
amuse, to **divertire**
animal **animale** (m)
and **e**
angry **arrabbiato**
another **un altro**
answer, to **rispondere**
anyone **qualcuno**
arrive, to **arrivare** *E

art **arte** (f)
as . . . as **così . . . come**
ask (question), to
domandare
at **a**
attention **attenzione** (f)
avenue **viale** (m)

bad **cattivo**
bag **sacco** (m)
baggage (luggage)
bagaglio (m)
bank **banca** (f)
bath **bagno** (m)
be, to **essere**
beach **spiaggia** (f)
beautiful **bello**
because **perché**
become, to **divenire** *E
bed **letto** (m)
before **prima**
begin, to (start/
commence)
cominciare (a)
behind **dietro**
believe, to **credere (di +
verb)**
between **in mezzo**
bicycle **bicicletta** (f)
big **grande**
bill (account) **conto** (m)
black **nero**
blue **azzurro**
boat **barco** (m)
book **libro** (m)
born, to be **nascere** *E

*E indicates verbs which use 'essere': see p. 163

(No) indicates -ire verbs which do not add -isc to the stem in the present
tense: see p. 160

bottle **bottiglia** (f)
box **scatola** (f)
boy **ragazzo** (m)
break, to **rompere**
bridge **ponte** (m)
bring, to **portare**
brother **fratello** (m)
brown **bruno**
building **edificio** (m)
bus **autobus** (m)
business **affari** (m. pl)
but **ma**
buy, to **comprare**

cafe/bar **caffè** (m)
camera **macchina fotografica** (f)
can (verb: be able) **potere**
car **macchina** (f)
car park **parcheggio** (m)
caravan **roulotte** (f)
carry, to **portare**
careful, be! **attento!**
castle **castello** (m)
cat **gatto/a** (m/f)
certain **certo**
chair **sedia** (f)
change, to (alter) **cambiare**
cheap **economico**
cheque **assegno** (m)
chemist's (pharmacy) **farmacista** (m/f)
child **bambino/a** (m/f)
choose, to **scegliere**
church **chiesa** (f)
cigarette **sigaretta** (f)
class **classe** (f)
clean, to **pulire**
clear **chiaro**
clock **orologio** (m)
close, to **chiudere**
clothes **vestiti** (m.pl)
coat (over) **soprabito** (m)
cold **freddo**
colour **colore** (m)
come, to **venire** (No) *E

comfortable **confortevole**
complete **completo**
concert **concerto** (m)
continue, to **continuare (a + verb)**
conversation **conversazione** (f)
cook, to **cuocere**
corner **angolo** (m)
correct **corretto**
cost, to **costare**
cotton **cotone** (m)
count, to **contare**
country **paese** (m)
cover, to **coprire** (No)
cry, to **piangere**
customs (border) **dogana** (f)
cut, to **tagliare**

damage **danno** (m)
dance, to **ballare**
dangerous **pericoloso**
dark **buio**
date **data** (f)
daughter **figlia** (f)
day **giorno** (m)
dear (expensive) **caro**
decide, to **decidere (di + verb)**
defend, to **difendere**
dentist **dentista** (m)
depart, to (leave) **partire**
descend, to (go down) **scendere**
desire, to (want) **desiderare**
die, to **morire** (No) *E
different **differente**
difficult **difficile**
direction (way) **direzione** (f)
dirty **sporco**
distance **distanza** (f)
do, to **fare**
doctor (medical) **dottore/essa** (m/f)

Italian

dog **cane** (m)
door **porta** (f)
dress **abito** (m)
drink, to **bere**
drive, to (a car) **guidare**
dry **secco**
during **durante**
duty (customs) **dazio**
 doganale (m)
duty (obligation)
 dovere (m)

each (every) **ogni**
early **presto**
eat, to **mangiare**
empty **vuoto**
end **fine** (f)
engine **motore** (m)
English **inglese**
enough **abbastanza**
enter, to **entrare (in)** *E
equal **uguale**
evening **sera** (f)
every **ogni**
everything **tutto**
excellent **eccellente**
exchange, to (money)
 cambiare
excuse, to **scusare**
exit **uscita** (f)
expensive (dear) **caro**
eye **occhio** (m)

face **faccia** (f)
fall, to **cadere** *E
family **famiglia** (f)
far **lontano**
fast (quick) **rapido**
fat **grasso**
father **padre** (m)
feel, to **sentire**
field **campo** (m)
film **film** (m)
fight, to **combattere**
fill, to **riempire**
find, to **scoprire**
finish, to **finire (di)**

fire **fuoco** (m)
fix, to **fissare**
floor **pavimento** (m)
flight (by air) **volo** (m)
fly, to **volare**
follow, to **seguire** (No)
food **cibo** (m)
foot **piede** (m)
football (game)
 calcio (m)
for **per**
forget, to **dimenticare**
free **libero**
French **francese**
friend **amico/a** (m/f)
from **da**
fruit **frutto** (m)
full **pieno**

garage **garage** (m)
garden **giardino** (m)
German **tedesco**
gift **dono** (m)
girl **ragazza** (f)
give, to **dare**
glasses **occhiali** (m. pl)
glove **guanto** (m)
go, to **andare (a)** *E
go down, to **scendere** *E
go out, to **uscire** (No) *E
go up/climb, to **salire** *E
god **dio** (m)
gold **oro** (m)
good **buono**
great **grande**
ground **terreno** (m)

hairdresser **parrucchiere/
 a** (m/f)
hand **mano** (f)
handbag **borsetta** (f)
handkerchief
 fazzoletto (m)
happen, to **succedere** *E
happy **felice**
hard **duro**
hat **cappello** (m)

have (possession of), to **avere**
have, to (auxiliary) **avere**
hear, to **sentire**
heavy **pesante**
healthy **sano**
help, to **aiutare (a + verb)**
here **qui**
high **alto**
hill **colle** (m)
hold, to **tenere**
holiday (vacation) **vacanza** (f)
hope, to **sperare (di + verb)**
hospital **ospedale** (m)
hot **caldo**
hotel **albergo** (m)
hour **ora** (f)
house **casa** (f)
how **come**
how much/how many? **quanto/quanti?**
husband **marito** (m)

ice **ghiaccio** (m)
if **se**
ill **malato**
immediately **subito**
important **importante**
in **in**
include **includere**
industry **industria** (f)
information **informazione** (f)
inside **dentro**
intelligent **intelligente**
interesting **interessante**
is (verb: to be) **è**
Italian **italiano/a**

join, to (be part of) **iscriversi (a)**
journey **viaggio** (m)

keep, to **tenere**

key **chiave** (f)
kind **gentile**
king **re** (m)
kiss, to **baciare**
know, to (something) **sapere**
know, to (somebody) **conoscere**

lady **signora** (f)
language **lingua** (f)
last **finale**
late **tardi**
lawyer **avvocato/essa** (m/f)
learn, to **imparare (a + verb)**
leave, to (depart) **partire** *E
leave, to (go out) **uscire di** *E
left (on the) **a sinistra**
lend, to **prestare**
less **meno**
let, to (permit) **permettere (di)**
letter **lettera** (f)
lift **ascensore** (m)
light (noun) **luce** (f)
like, to **piacere**
liquid **liquido** (m)
list **lista** (f)
little (small) **piccolo**
little (a) **un po' di**
live, to **vivere**
live in, to **abitare**
long **lungo**
look at, to **guardare**
lorry **camion** (m)
lose, to **perdere**
loud **forte**
love, to **amare**
luggage (baggage) **bagaglio** (m)

mad **matto**
make, to **fare**

Italian

man **uomo** (m)
manner **modo** (m)
many **molti**
map **mappa** (f)
market **mercato** (m)
match (light)
 fiammifero (m)
medicine **medicina** (f)
meet, to **incontrare**
meeting **incontro** (m)
middle, the **mezzo** (m)
million **milione** (m)
minute **minuto** (m)
mirror **specchio** (m)
mistake **errore** (m)
money **denaro** (m)
month **mese** (m)
more **più**
morning **mattina** (f)
motorway **autostrada** (f)
mother **madre** (f)
mountain **montagna** (f)
mouth **bocca** (f)
move, to **muovere**
much **molto**
museum **museo** (m)
music **musica** (f)
must (verb: to be obliged)
 dovere

name **nome** (m)
near **vicino**
necessary **necessario**
need, to **aver bisogno di**
never **mai**
new **nuovo**
newspaper **giornale** (m)
next **prossimo**
night **notte** (f)
no **no**
noise **rumore** (m)
nothing **niente**
now **ora**
number (figure)
 numero (m)

obtain, to **ottenere**

of **di**
offer, to **offrire**
office **ufficio** (m)
often **spesso**
oil **olio** (m)
old **vecchio**
on **su**
once **una volta**
only **solo**
open, to **aprire** (No)
opposite **opposto**
or **o**
ordinary **ordinario**
other **altro**
over **sopra**
owe, to (be obliged)
 dovere

package **pacco** (m)
pain **dolore** (m)
paper **carta** (f)
park **parco** (m)
part **parte** (f)
pass, to (hand to) **passare**
passenger **viaggiatore/**
 trice (m/f)
passport **passaporto** (m)
path **sentiero** (m)
pay, to **pagare**
pen **penna** (f)
pencil **matita** (f)
perhaps **forse**
permit (let) **permettere**
person/people
 persona (f)
persuade, to **persuadere**
petrol **benzina** (f)
pharmacy **farmacia** (f)
photograph **fotografia** (f)
piece **pezzo** (m)
place **luogo** (m)
play, to **giocare**
please **per favore**
police **polizia** (f)
point out, to **indicare**
poor **povero**
port (harbour) **porto** (m)

porter **facchino** (m)
possible **possibile**
postcard **cartolina** (f)
post office **ufficio postale** (m)
prefer, to **preferire**
prepare, to **preparare**
price **prezzo** (m)
private (not public) **privato**
probable **probabile**
profession **professione** (f)
programme **programma** (m)
promise, to **promettere (di + verb)**
put, to (place) **mettere**

quality **qualità** (f)
quantity **quantità** (f)
question **domanda** (f)
quick (fast) **rapido**
quiet **tranquillo**

rain, to **piovere**
read, to **leggere**
ready **pronto**
receive, to **ricevere**
reception (hotel) **reception** (m)/ **portineria** (f)
red **rosso**
regret, to (be sorry) **rimpiangere**
remember, to **ricordarsi (di)**
repeat, to **ripetere**
reply, to **rispondere**
report, to **riferire**
responsible **responsabile**
restaurant **ristorante** (m)
return, to **tornare** *E
rich **ricco**
right (direction) **destra**
right, to be **avere ragione**
river **fiume** (m)
road **strada** (f)

room **stanza** (f)
run, to **correre**

sad **triste**
same **stesso**
save, to **salvare**
say, to **dire**
school **scuola** (f)
sea **mare** (m)
see, to **vedere**
seem, to **sembrare**
sell, to **vendere**
send, to **mandare**
serve, to **servire** (No)
service **servizio** (m)
shoe **scarpa** (f)
shop **negozio** (m)
short **corto**
show, to **mostrare**
shower **doccia** (f)
shut, to **chiudere**
sign **segno** (m)
silver (adj) **d'argento**
since **da allora**
sing, to **cantare**
sister **sorella** (f)
sit down, to **sedersi** *E
skiing (noun) **sci** (m)
sky **cielo** (m)
sleep, to **dormire**
slowly **piano**
small **piccolo**
snow **neve** (f)
so, thus **così**
soap **sapone** (m)
soft **molle**
some **del**
someone **qualcuno**
sometimes **qualche volta**
son **figlio** (m)
soon **presto**
speak, to **parlare**
square (town) **piazza** (f)
stairs **scale** (f. pl)
stamp **francobollo** (m)
start, to (begin) **iniziare**

Italian

station (railway) **stazione** (f)
stay, remain, to **restare**
step (pace) **passo** (m)
stop, to **finire**
street **strada** (f)
strong **forte**
student **studente/essa** (m/f)
study, to **studiare**
suddenly **improvvisamente**
suitcase **valigia** (f)
summer **estate** (f)
sun **sole** (m)
suntan **abbronzatura** (f)
sweet **dolce**
swim, to **nuotare**
swimming pool **piscina** (f)

table **tavola** (f)
take, to **prendere**
taste, to **assaggiare**
taxi **tassì** (m)
tea **tè** (m)
teach, to **insegnare (a + verb)**
teacher **insegnante** (m, f)
telegram **telegramma** (m)
telephone, to **telefonare**
television **televisione** (f)
tell, to **dire**
tennis **tennis** (m)
thank you! (very much) **grazie! (molte)**
theatre **teatro** (m)
then **allora**
there **là**
there is/are **c'è/ci sono**
therefore **perciò**
thing **cosa** (f)
think, to **pensare**
this/that **questo/quello**
through (train) **diretto** (m)
ticket **biglietto** (m)

time (what time is it?) **tempo** (m) **(che ore sono?)**
time (one or more) **volta** (f)
tip **mancia** (f)
tired **stanco**
to (direction) **verso**
to (in order to) **per**
too (also) **anche**
too much/many **troppo/troppi**
today **oggi**
toilet **servizi** (m. pl)
tomorrow **domani**
tourist **turista** (m, f)
towards **verso**
towel **asciugamano** (m)
town **città** (f)
traffic **traffico** (m)
train (express) **treno (espresso)** (m)
translate, to **tradurre**
travel, to **viaggiare**
travel agent **agenzia di viaggi** (f)
tree **albero** (m)
true **vero**
try, to **tentare**
typical **tipico**
tyres **gomme** (f. pl)

umbrella **ombrello** (m)
under **sotto**
underground (rail) **metropolitana** (f)
understand, to **capire**
unfortunately **purtroppo**
university **università** (f)
use, to **usare**
useful **utile**

vacation (holiday) **vacanza** (f)
very **molto**
village **villaggio** (m)
visit, to (a place) **visitare**

voice **voce** (f)

wait for, to **aspettare**
waiter **cameriere** (m)
walk, to **camminare**
wall **muro** (m)
want/wish for, to **volere**
wash (oneself), to
 lavarsi *E
watch **guardare**
water **acqua** (f)
way (direction) **strada** (f)
wedding **matrimonio** (m)
week **settimana** (f)
weekend **fine
 settimana** (f)
well **bene**
what! **che!**
when? **quando?**
where? **dove?**
which? **quale?**
which **il quale**
white **bianco**

who **chi**
why? **perché**
wide **largo**
wife **moglie** (f)
wind **vento** (m)
window **finestra** (f)
wine **vino** (m)
winter **inverno** (m)
wish/want, to **volere**
with **con**
without **senza**
wood **legno** (m)
word **parola** (f)
work, to **lavorare**
world **mondo** (m)
write, to **scrivere**

year **anno** (m)
yellow **giallo**
yes **sí**
yesterday **ieri**
young **giovane**

1B 100 Words for Buying Food and Eating Out

Shops

baker's **panificio** (m)
butcher's **macelleria** (f)
delicatessen **salumeria** (f)
fishmonger's
  pescivendolo (m)/
  pescheria (f)
grocer's **drogheria** (f)
market **mercato** (m)
self service
  self-service (m)
shop **negozio** (m)
supermarket
  supermercato (m)
tobacconist's
  tabaccheria (f)

Meals

breakfast **prima
  colazione** (f)
dining room **sala da
  pranzo** (f)
dinner **cena** (f)
drink **bibita** (f)
food **cibo** (m)
lunch **colazione** (f)
meal **pasto** (m)

Table setting

bottle **bottiglia** (f)
chair **sedia** (f)
cup **tazza** (f)
fork **forchetta** (f)
glass (table) **bicchiere** (m)
jug **brocca** (f)
knife **coltello** (m)
menu **menu** (m)
oil **olio** (m)
pepper **pepe** (m)
plate **piatto** (m)
salt **sale** (m)
spoon **cucchiaio** (m)

sugar **zucchero** (m)
table **tavola** (f)
tip **mancia** (f)
vinegar **aceto** (m)
waiter **cameriere** (m)

Drinks

I'm thirsty **ho sete**
beer **birra** (f)
brandy **cognac** (m)
cider **sidro** (m)
coffee **caffè** (m)
cream **crema** (f)
lemonade **limonata** (f)
milk **latte** (m)
orangeade **aranciata** (f)
tea **tè** (m)
tomato juice **succo di
  pomodoro** (m)
water/sparkling water
  acqua (f)/**frizzante**
whisky **whisky** (m)
wine **vino** (m)

Food

I'm hungry **ho fame**
apple **mela** (f)
asparagus **asparago** (m)
aubergine **melanzana** (f)
bacon **pancetta** (f)
banana **banana** (f)
bean (French)
  fagiolino (m)
bean (haricot) **fagiolo** (m)
beef **manzo** (m)
bread **pane** (m)
broccoli **broccolo** (m)
butter **burro** (m)
cabbage **cavolo** (m)
cake **torta** (f)
cauliflower **cavolfiore** (m)
celery **sedano** (m)
cheese **formaggio** (m)

chicken **pollo** (m)
chocolate **cioccolato** (m)
cucumber **cetriolo** (m)
curry **curry** (m)
egg **uovo** (m)
fish **pesce** (m)
flour **farina** (f)
fruit **frutto** (m)
ham **prosciutto** (m)
hors d'oeuvre
  antipasto (m)
ice cream **gelato** (m)
jam **marmellata** (f)
lemon **limone** (m)
meat **carne** (f)
melon **melone** (m)
milk **latte** (m)
mushroom **fungo** (m)
nectarine **pesca noce** (f)
oil **olio** (m)
omelette **omelette** (f)
onion **cipolla** (f)
orange **arancia** (f)
pancake **frittella** (f)
pâté **pâté** (m)
peach **pesca** (f)
pear **pera** (f)
peas **piselli** (m. pl)
pepper **pepe** (m)
pork **carne di maiale** (f)
potato **patata** (f)
  chipped potatoes
    patatine fritte (f. pl)
prawns **gamberi** (m. pl)
ravioli **ravioli** (m)
rice **riso** (m)

salad **insalata** (f)
sauce **salsa** (f)
sausage **salsiccia** (f)
soup **minestra** (f)
spaghetti **spaghetti** (m)
spinach **spinaci** (m. pl)
tart **torta** (f)
toast **toast** (m)
tomato **pomodoro** (m)
vegetables **verdura** (f)
vinegar **aceto** (m)

Cooking

boiled **bollito**
fresh **fresco**
fried **fritto**
grilled **alla griglia**
rare **al sangue**
raw **crudo**
sour **acido**
sweet **dolce**
well cooked **cotto a**
  puntino

Containers

bag **sacco** (m)
bottle **bottiglia** (f)
bottle opener
  apribottiglie (m)
can **scatola** (f)
can opener
  apriscatole (m)
corkscrew **cavatappi** (m)

1C 150 Words for Business Use

interpreter
  interprete (m, f)
translate, to **tradurre**

Organization
  Organizzazione (f)

accountant
  contabile (m, f)
authority **autorità** (f)
chairman **presidente** (m)
company **compagnia** (f)
company secretary
  segretario/a
  d'azienda (m, f)
director **direttore** (m)
employee **impiegato** (m)
executive **dirigente** (m)
management
  amministrazione (f)
manager **amministratore**
  delegato (m)
managing director
  consigliere delegato (m)
responsible **responsabile**
secretary
  segretario/a (m/f)

Office **Ufficio** (m)

agreement **accordo** (m)
airmail **posta aerea** (f)
authorize, to **autorizzare**
bank **banca** (f)
business **affari** (m. pl)
computer **computer** (m)
contract **contratto** (m)
copy **copia** (f)
data processing
  elaborazione di dati (f)
document **documento** (m)
fax **facsimile** (m)
invoice **fattura** (f)
lease **affitto** (m)
legal **legale**

official **ufficiale**
post **posta** (f)
private, confidential
  privato
receipt (of goods)
  ricevuta (f)
regulations
  regolamento (m)
rent **affitto** (m)
report **rapporto** (m)
requisition
  requisizione (f)
shares (in a company)
  azioni (f. pl)
sign, to **firmare**
signatory **firmatorio** (m)
tariff (customs) **tariffa** (f)

Works/factory **Fabbrica** (f)

chemicals **prodotti**
  chimici (m. pl)
development
  sviluppo (m)
electrician **elettricista** (m)
electricity **elettricità** (f)
engineer **ingegnere** (m)
foreman **caposquadra** (m)
fuel **combustibile** (m)
gas **gas** (m)
laboratory **laboratorio** (m)
machinery
  macchinario (m)
maintenance
  manutenzione (f)
manual worker
  operaio (m)
metal **metallo** (m)
oil **olio** (m)
raw materials **materie**
  prime (f. pl)
research **ricerca** (f)
site **luogo** (m)
stores (warehouse)
  deposito (m)

tool room **ripostiglio per attrezzi** (m)

warehouse **magazzino** (m)

Production **Produzione** (f)

automation **automazione** (f)

batch **lotto** (m)

budget **bilancio** (m)

construction **costruzione** (f)

consumption **consumo** (m)

control, to **controllare**

effluent **le scorie** (f. pl)

increase, to **aumentare**

invest, to **investire**

job **mestiere** (m)

(new) product **(nuovo) prodotto** (m)

output **rendimento** (m)

performance **esecuzione** (f)

plan **progetto** (m)

productivity **produttività** (f)

quantity **quantità** (f)

reduce, to **ridurre**

schedule **programma** (m)

scrap (waste) **rifiuti** (m. pl)

timetable **orario** (m)

ton **tonellata** (f)

utilization **utilizzazione** (f)

volume **volume** (m)

works order **andamento fabbrica**

Marketing **Marketing** (m)

achieve, to **compiere**

advertise, to **annunziare**

agent (sales) **agente (vendite)** (m)

agree/accept, to **essere d'accordo**

assess, to **valutare**

brand **marchio** (m)

commission (payment) **commissione** (f)

competition **concorrenza** (f)

customer **cliente** (m)

delivery **consegna** (f)

demand **richiesta** (f)

distribution **distribuzione** (f)

economic **economico**

forecast, to **predire**

market objective **obiettivo di mercato** (m)

market research **ricerca di mercato** (f)

opportunity **occasione** (f)

packaging **confezione** (f)

presentation **presentazione** (f)

price **prezzo** (m)

product test **controllo prodotto** (m)

promote, to **promuovere**

quality **qualità** (f)

representative **rappresentante** (m)

sales **vendite** (f. pl)

sales force **venditori** (m)

service (customer) **servizio** (m)

share (of market) **quota (di mercato)** (f)

target **obiettivo** (m)

Employment **Impiego** (m)

assessment **valutazione** (f)

benefit **beneficio** (m)

bonus **incentivo** (m)

canteen **mensa** (f)

job (for person) **impiego** (m)

Italian

pension **pensione** (f)
personnel **personale** (m)
salary **stipendio** (m)
skill **abilità** (f)
social security **previdenza sociale** (f)
training **addestramento** (m)
unemployed **disoccupato**
vacancy **posto libero** (m)
wage **paga** (f)

Accounts **Conti** (m. pl)

actual **reale**
asset, net **attivo, netto** (m)
bad debt **debito, irredimibile** (m)
balance sheet **bilancio** (m)
borrow, to **prendere in prestito**
capital **capitale** (m)
capital expenditure **spese di investimento** (f. pl)
cash **contante** (m)
cash flow **liquido disponibile** (m)
cost of sales **costo di vendita** (m)

credit control **controllo crediti** (m)
creditor **creditore** (m)
debtor **debitore** (m)
depreciation **deprezzamento** (m)
dividend **dividendo** (m)
expenditure **spese** (f. pl)
grant **concessione** (f)
interest (bank) **interesse** (m)
labour cost **costo di produzione** (m)
liability (balance sheet) **passivo** (m)
liability (damages) **responsabilità** (f)
loan **prestito** (m)
margin, gross **reditto, lordo** (m)
profit, net **profitto, netto** (m)
share capital **capitale azionario** (m)
stocks, inventories **riserve** (f. pl)
taxation **imposte** (f. pl)
variance **variazione** (f)
working capital **capitale d'esercizio** (m)

SESSION TWO
Pronunciation

2A Letters and Sounds

Italian	*Sounds like*	*Example*
a	**a** in par	padre
b	**b** in bat	bere

c	c in cat	caro
	but **ch** as in **ch**at before e and i	città
ch	k in kit before e and i	chilo
d	d in dog	dove
e	ay in may	viale
	but **e** as in met usually (but not always) when stress falls on the e (see note on stress p. 148)	eccellente
f	f in fix	faccia
g/gh	g in got	eguale
	but **g** in **G**eorge when g is followed by e or i	giardino
gli	ll in million	famiglia
gn	ni in onion	ogni
gu	gu in language	guardare
h	not sounded	–
i	ee in feet	così
j	not used	–
k	not used	–
l	l in lit	solo
m	m in man	sempre
n	n in not	buono
	but nasal **n** in wi**n**g before c, g and q	includere
o	o as in polo	solo
	but **au** as in **au**to usually (but not always) when the stress falls on the o (see note on stress p. 148)	cotone
p	p in pin	piccolo
qu	qu in quick	acqua

Italian

r	**r** in rat, *but* trilled	strada
s	**s** in save *but* **z** in **z**oo when followed by a consonant or placed between two vowels	settimana turista
sc	**sk** in **sk**ip *but* **sh** in **sh**ip before e and i	scuola sci
t	**t** in tin	tavola
u	**oo** in p**oo**l	duro
v	**v** as in **v**an	viaggio
w	not used	–
x	not used	–
y	not used	–
z	**ds** as in be**ds** *but* **ts** as in be**ts** before ie, io and ia	vacanza informazioni

2B Vowels, Accents and Stress

Italian pronunciation is clear, precise and melodious, although travellers will find differences in pronunciation in certain regions of Italy – as one would in England.

As a general rule, vowels are sounded rather more robustly than consonants.

Unlike French, in which all syllables are evenly stressed, the Italians generally stress the last but one syllable (the ending -ia or -io generally counts as one syllable). If the last syllable is stressed, it carries an accent over the final vowel – either acute (´) over i or u, or grave (`) over a.

Accents are also used, as in Spanish, to differentiate between two single syllable words with the same spelling, but a different meaning. These are indicated in the text and also in the word list.

Where two or more vowels are placed together, they are still sounded separately, but i and u are weak vowels and get rolled into the next vowel. If two weak vowels come together, 'ui' in Italian sounds like 'we' in English, and 'iu' sounds like 'you'.

SESSION THREE
Absorbing the Language

This is a practice session, for you to try in your own time.

Go through the main vocabulary in Section 1A and read all the words aloud.

Go through a second time, covering up the English and see how many words you can translate.

Now go through a third time, this time covering up the Italian and see how many words you can translate from the English. Don't worry if there are only a few. Your vocabulary will develop with regular practice.

SESSION FOUR
Message Builders

4A Message Builders

The 80 or so *'message builders'* shown below comprise part-phrases, interrogatives or verbs in everyday use, which you can use to build up questions and messages. You can use these *'message builders'* with your own list of key words to find your way round and to give yourself practice in speaking the language. There are no nouns shown in the list below; you get these from your own word list, or the main vocabulary. (Note that the nouns in the vocabulary are shown only in the singular, and the adjectives are shown in their masculine form, but you will find out in Session Six how to deal with the word endings.)

In Section 4B (p. 152) you will find the commonest forms of address and greetings which will 'top and tail' your messages. Liberal use of 'please' and 'thank you' will add considerably to your communication skills!

Italian

English	Italian
Today is.....	**Oggi è**.....
I speak.....	**Parlo**.....
Do you speak.....	**Parla**.....
Yes.....no	**Sí**.....**no**
My name is.....	**Mi chiamo**.....
My number is.....	**Il mio numero è**.....
I live in.....	**Vivo a**.....
This is my.....	**Questo è il mio***.....
Who is/who are.....	**Chi è/chi sono**.....
I am/we are.....	**Io sono/noi siamo**.....
Why are we.....	**Perchè siamo**.....
Are you.....	**È**.....
Where is/where are.....	**Dov'è/dove sono**.....
a.....	**un** (m), **una** (f)
the.....	**il** (m), **la** (f)
	i (m. pl), **le** (f. pl)
my.....	**il mio** (m), **i miei** (m. pl)
Where can I find.....	**Dove si trova**.....
I have lost.....	**Ho perso**.....
I have broken.....	**Ho rotto**.....
I have forgotten.....	**Ho dimenticato**.....
When does.....open	**A che ora apre**.....
When does.....start	**A che ora comincia**.....
When does.....close	**A che ora chiude**.....
Excuse me.....	**Scusi**.....
What is the way to.....	**Per andare a**.....
I want to go to.....	**Voglio andare a**.....
Is it far to.....	**È lontano**.....
Is it.....	**È**.....
It is.....	**È**.....
It is not.....	**Non è**.....
Here is/here are.....	**Eccolo!/Eccoli!**.....
Is there.....	**C'è**.....
There is/there are.....	**C'è/ci sono**.....
Is there.....near here	**C'è**.....**qui vicino**
Do you have/have you got.....	**Avete**.....
I have reserved.....	**Ho prenotato**.....
It's for.....	**È per**.....

masculine only

150

Does it have	**Ha .....**
I have/we have	**Ho/abbiamo .....**
Can I have	**Posso avere .....**
Can you	**Può (+ infinitive) .....**
Would you like	**Vuole .....**
I would like/we would like	**Vorrei/vorremmo .....**
Another	**Un altro .....**
I am sorry that	**Mi dispiace .....**
There is no	**Non c'è .....**
What ..... do you have	**Quale* ..... ha**
How many ..... do you have	**Quanti* ..... ha**
Anything else?	**Basta cosí?**
I would prefer	**Preferirei .....**
It is too	**È troppo .....**
I need/we need	**Ho bisogno di/abbiamo bisogno di .....**
I will take/we will take	**Prendo/prendiamo .....**
I like ..... very much	**Mi piace molto .....**
Give me	**Mi dia .....**
How much is	**Quanto costa .....**
More/less	**Più/meno .....**
One/two/three/four/five	**Uno/due/tre/quattro/cinqu**
Ten/twenty/fifty	**Dieci/venti/cinquanta .....**
One hundred/one thousand	**Cento/mille .....**
Tell me	**Mi dica .....**
What time is it?	**Che ora è?**
When does ..... leave	**A che ora parte .....**
When does ..... arrive	**A che ora arriva .....**
When do we	**Quando (+ verb)**
How do we	**Come (+ verb)**
I am going to	**Vado a .....**
I have just	**Ho appena .....**
Don't go!	**Non vada!**
Let's go to	**Andiamo a .....**
Meet me at	**Ci incontriamo a .....**
Telephone me at	**Mi telefoni .....**
I ought to/we must	**Dovrei/dobbiamo (+ infinitive)**
I can/we can	**Posso/possiamo (+ infinitive)**
Take care!	**Faccia attenzione!**

Italian

I will come back on	**Tornerò** . . . . .
I can't understand	**Non capisco**
Speak more slowly	**Può parlare più lentamente, per favore**
Could you repeat that!	**Può ripetere, prego!**

4B   Addressing Friends and Strangers

Italian is more formal and polite than English. So:
● Shake hands when you meet and part company every day.
● When introduced, you can say **'piacere'** (my pleasure).
● Address adult strangers as **'signore'** (sir) or **'signora'** (madam), and girls as **'signorina'** (miss), thus:

Scusi, signore, mi può mostrare . . . ? (Excuse me, sir, can you show . . . ?)

● **'Per favore'** (please) and **'grazie'** (thank you) or **'molte grazie'** (many thanks) should be used liberally.

Sí, per favore (yes, please)
No, grazie (no, thank you)

● The time of the day to the Italians is like the weather to the English, so:

Good morning	**Buongiorno**
Good evening (from about 4 p.m.)	**Buona sera**
Good night	**Buona notte**
Goodbye	**Arrivederci**

● Useful words of greeting include **'Ciao'** (familiar hello or goodbye), and **'Come sta?'** (How are you) or **'Come va?'** (How are things). You could reply **'Va bene, grazie'** (Very well, thank you).
● Other useful expressions which you are likely to need include:

Salute! (Cheers!)
Buon appetito (Enjoy your meal)
Mi piace molto (I like it very much)
Prego (You're welcome)
A domani! (See you tomorrow!)

SESSION FIVE
Language Structure

5   Word Order

Similar to English, but with these main differences:

1   Longer adjectives normally follow the nouns. Thus **'un libro difficile'** is literally translated as 'a book difficult'. But certain very common or short adjectives precede the noun, thus:

> **un buon uomo** (a good man)
> **un gran castello** (a big castle)

2   Object and reflexive pronouns other than 'Loro' (you) and 'loro' (them) are usually placed before the verb, but they can be tacked on to the end of the imperative, the infinitive or the present participle. Exceptions are shown in Section 9 (p. 164).

> **(Io) glielo do** means literally 'I *to him it* give'

Where two pronouns are used, the *indirect* precedes the direct. Note that the two pronouns **'gli'** and **'lo'** have been rolled together into **'glielo'**.

3   The negative **'non'** comes before the object pronoun and the verb:

> **(Io) non lo ho veduto** means literally 'I not him have seen'

Note that the auxiliary verb **'ho'** (have) and the past participle **'veduto'** (seen) stay close together:

> **Ha veduto (Lei) mio padre?** (Have you seen my father?)

4   As you can see from the last example, the verb and the subject (noun or pronoun) are usually inverted in asking a question. However, when an interrogative word such as 'who' or 'when' is used, the word order remains similar to English – except of course for the negative and object pronouns!

SESSION SIX
Nouns, Adjectives and The Two Articles

6A   Nouns and Adjectives

Every noun in Italian is either masculine (m) or feminine (f). Nouns ending in -o are masculine, most of those ending in -a are feminine and a few of those ending in -e can be of either gender. Any exceptions can be seen in the word list.

Both the definite article ('the') and the indefinite article ('a') also have a masculine and feminine form, which have to agree with the noun.

The indefinite article in Italian can be **'un'** or **'uno'** (masculine) or **'un''** or **'una'** (feminine). **'Un''** is only used before a feminine noun starting with a vowel.

The definite article (singular) can be **'il'** or **'lo'** (masculine), **'la'** (feminine) or **'l''** before any single noun starting with a vowel.

'Uno' and **'lo'** are only used in front of a masculine noun starting with z- or s- followed by a consonant.

Examples are

un uomo	– a man	**una donna**	– a woman
il ragazzo	– the boy	**la ragazza**	– the girl
but **lo zio**	– the uncle	**uno zio**	– an uncle
and **l'autunno**	– the autumn	**un' amica**	– a friend (f)

The definite article is nearly always used before nouns in Italian, even before surnames (*The* Mr X) and is not dropped as in English:

Le ragazze italiane parlano chiaro (Italian girls speak clearly)

However, the indefinite article does sometimes get dropped:

Che bella casa! (What *a* beautiful house!)

Adjectives

A principal difference between our two languages is that in Italian, the adjective has to agree with the noun*.
   The majority of adjectives in our word list end in -o and

* *Further information on adjectives follows in Section 12A (p. 177)*

these change to -a if the noun is feminine. Those ending in -e do *not* change in the feminine.

> **Vino rosso** (Red wine)
> **La casa rossa** (The red house)
> but **Una strada difficile** (A difficult road)

As we saw in Section 5 (p. 153) adjectives usually follow the noun. But some common or short adjectives such as **'buono'** (good) and **'grande'** (big) precede the noun and these two in particular drop their endings, thus:

> **Un buon ragazzo** (A good boy)
> **Gran Bretagna** (Great Britain)

6B Plurals

Both nouns and adjectives change their endings in the plural, as does the definite article.

Masculine nouns change their endings to -i in the plural. **'L'uovo'** (the egg) is a rare exception and changes to **'le ouva'** (feminine in the plural).

Most feminine nouns change their endings from -a to -e in the plural, but a handful ending in -e in the singular change to -i in the plural.

Adjectives change their endings in the plural just like the nouns. Those ending in -o change to -i (masculine) and those ending in -a change to -e (feminine). Those ending in -e also change to -i regardless of gender.

The definite article also changes its endings in the plural:

il	(masculine)	changes to **i**
lo and **l'**	(masculine)	change to **gli**
la and **l'**	(feminine)	change to **le**

As you can see, Italian does have rather more forms for the definite article than other European languages, but the noun and adjectival endings are somewhat easier than most. Until you become familiar with the language, just remember that, in the plural, most words change the final letter from:

-o to -i (masculine)
-a to -e (feminine)

and the rest will fall into place. For example:

Italian

Singular	Plural
il ragazzo piccolo (the small boy)	**i ragazzi piccoli**
la casa rossa (the red house)	**le case rosse**
lo zio ricco (the rich uncle)	**gli zii ricchi**
l'albero vecchio (the old tree)	**gli alberi vecchi**

Exceptions

Note that 'gli' drops the -i before any masculine noun starting with i-, thus:

gl' italiani (the Italians)

Also that nouns ending in -io change to -ii *only* when the first i is stressed, otherwise the final -i is dropped. The i also gets dropped in the plural where nouns end in a consonant plus -cia or -gia e.g. **'la faccia'** (the face), **'le facce'** (faces).

Some nouns ending in -co, -go, -ca and -ga insert an h after c or g in the plural, in order to keep the sound hard (otherwise i and e after c or g would soften the sound).

A few nouns ending in -ù, an accented vowel, a consonant or those which only have one syllable, do not change in the plural.

Summary: Gender and Plurals

In the table below we show all the word endings, masculine, feminine, singular and plural, which we covered in Sections 6A and 6B.

	Masculine	
	Singular	*Plural*
Nouns	**-o** (all*)	**-i**
	-a (some)	**-i**
	-e (few)	**-i**
Adjectives	**-o** (most)	**-i**
	-e	**-i**
'A'	**un**	–
	uno (before s † or z)	–
'The'	**il**	**i**
	l' (before vowel)	**gli'** (or gl' ‡)
	lo (before s † or z)	**gli**

Notes: * *except* **'la mano'** *(the hand)*
  † *s followed by consonant*
  ‡ *before a word starting with i-*

	Feminine	
	Singular	*Plural*
Nouns	**-a** (most)	**-e**
	-e (few)	**-i**
Adjectives	**-a** (most)	**-e**
	-e	**-i**
'A'	**una**	–
	un' (before vowel)	–
'The'	**la**	**le**
	l' (before vowel)	**le**

SESSION SEVEN
Personal Pronouns and Verbs

7A   Subject Pronouns

Before moving on to verbs, we should run through the personal pronouns – I, he, we, you and they – which are the *subject* of the verb. We usually describe the subject pronouns as being in the 1st, 2nd or 3rd person singular, or plural, and modify the verb endings accordingly. The subject pronouns are as follows:

1st person singular	I	**io**
2nd person singular	you	**tu**
	he	**lui**
	she	**lei**
3rd person singular	it (m)	**esso**
	it (f)	**essa**
	you (polite)	**Lei**
1st person plural	we	**noi**
2nd person plural	you (business)	**voi**
	they (people)	**loro**
	they (things)	**essi** (m)
3rd person plural		**esse** (f)
	you (polite)	**Loro**

There is no disguising the fact that Italian has more personal pronouns than English, and in one or two cases their usage is changing. There is no problem with **'io'** (I) or **'noi'** (us), the 1st person singular and plural, nor with **'lui'** (he), **'lei'** (she) and **'loro'** (they); whilst the two

Italian

words for 'it' (**'esso'** and **'essa'**) are seldom used. The trouble arises over the use of the word 'you'.

Traditionally, Italians have addressed one another in the 3rd person singular or plural, using either **'lei'** (singular) or **'Loro'** (plural). The familiar word for 'you' (singular), **'tu'**, was reserved for family and close friends. Nowadays, **'tu'** is becoming much more widely used. However, you should stick to **'Lei'**, the polite form of address, until you feel comfortable with the language and local customs. The verb endings for **'tu'** and the pronoun forms are shown in Appendix II, p. 193.

The plural form of 'you' (**voi**) is much more common and is widely used in business. This form is shown throughout the main text.

It is obvious that **'lei'** (she) and **'Lei'** (you, polite) sound the same, as do **'loro'** (they) and **'Loro'** (you, plural, polite), although the polite form is always shown with a capital 'L' in print. In writing or speech, the Italians usually leave out personal pronouns where the meaning is clear, so you need to go by the verb endings.

Don't forget that **'Lei'** and **'Loro'** need 3rd person endings. If you get confused think of **'Lei'** as 'sir' and **'Loro'** as 'gentlemen (or ladies)', and you won't go far wrong.

7B   Regular Verbs

Present, Imperfect and Future Tenses

In this section we start with the regular verbs, then move on to some of the irregular verbs. To make it easier, we have restricted the tenses to the present (I am doing), the imperfect (I was doing or I used to do), the future (I will or shall do) and the past (I have done). We shall therefore leave out the tenses which mean 'I did' (historic), 'I would do' (conditional), 'I may or might do' (subjunctive) and a few other tenses which are less frequently used, even though their use in many sentences would be grammatically correct. However, a note does appear on the use of the subjunctive in Appendix I, which we have left right to the end (p. 192).

In Italian, as in English, the verb endings change, both with the pronoun used and the tense. However, the Italians do not use different words to indicate tense, such as 'am', 'was', 'will', 'shall', 'had', 'have', 'should', 'could', 'may' or 'might'. These are all incorporated in the verb itself, and indicated by the verb ending.

We have seen the subject pronouns in Section 7A (p. 157). These require only four verb endings for the pronouns: I, he/she/it/you, we, they/you. We are leaving out 'thou' or 'you' (singular) from the main text as this is used only in a family context, but we have shown **'voi'** for travellers on business. Once you have mastered the polite form of speech, you can easily pick up the familiar form, which is summarized in Appendix II (p. 193).

First, then, to the regular verbs. There are three main types (or conjugations) of verbs. Those whose infinitive form (to do something) ends in -are, -ere, or -ire. Thus:

parl**are**	to speak	(1st conjugation)
vend**ere**	to sell	(2nd conjugation)
serv**ire**	to serve	} 3rd conjugation
fin**ire**	to finish	}

The first part of the verb we call the 'stem' (parl-) and the ending -are. The endings are in bold type in the text. Those verbs ending in -ire have two types of endings and these are both shown below. Those like **'finire'**, which are the majority, insert -isc after the stem, as we shall see in the present tense and the imperative.

Present Tense

The present tense (I speak/sell/serve/finish) is conjugated as follows:

	speak -are	*sell* -ere	*serve* -ire	*finish* -ire
io	parl**o**	vend**o**	serv**o**	fin**isco**
lui/lei/Lei	parl**a**	vend**e**	serv**e**	fin**isce**
noi	parl**iamo**	vend**iamo**	serv**iamo**	fin**iamo**
voi	parl**ate**	vend**ete**	serv**ite**	fin**ite**
loro/Loro	parl**ano**	vend**ono**	serv**ono**	fin**iscono**

As the verb endings are different, their meaning is clear, so you don't need to use the personal pronoun as well, thus:

Parlo poco italiano (I speak little Italian)

Imperfect Tense

The imperfect tense (I was speaking/selling/serving/finishing, or I used to speak/sell/serve/finish) is conjugated as follows:

Italian

	speak -are	*sell* -ere	*serve* -ire	*finish* -ire
io	parl**avo**	vend**evo**	serv**ivo**	fin**ivo**
lui/lei/Lei	parl**ava**	vend**eva**	serv**iva**	fin**iva**
noi	parl**avamo**	vend**evamo**	serv**ivamo**	fin**ivamo**
voi	parl**avate**	vend**evate**	serv**ivate**	fin**ivate**
loro/Loro	parl**avano**	vend**evano**	serv**ivano**	fin**ivano**

Future Tense

The future tense (I will or shall speak/sell/serve/finish) modifies the infinitive (**'parlare'**, **'vendere'**, **'servire'** and **'finire'**) and just adds different endings.

	speak -are	*sell* -ere	*serve* -ire	*finish* -ire
io	parler**ò**	vender**ò**	servir**ò**	finir**ò**
lui/lei/Lei	parler**à**	vender**à**	servir**à**	finir**à**
noi	parler**emo**	vender**emo**	servir**emo**	finir**emo**
voi	parler**ete**	vender**ete**	servir**ete**	finir**ete**
loro/Loro	parler**anno**	vender**anno**	servir**anno**	finir**anno**

All the common regular verbs are shown in the word list and have endings as shown above. Nearly all -ire verbs add -isc to the stem in the present tense, but those which don't are marked (No) in the word list. The irregular verbs are dealt with in Sections 10B and 10C (pp. 168 and 170).

Present Participle

In Italian, 'I am finishing' can be translated as 'I finish' (**io finisco**). But if 'finishing' is still continuing, it can be translated just as in English. In this case, you would use what is called the present participle for 'finishing' (**finendo**) together with the verb 'to be', thus:

Sto (I am) **finendo** (finishing)

The present participle is formed by adding -ando to the stem of the verbs ending in -are, and -endo to all others.

parlando (speaking),   **vendendo** (selling),
servendo (serving)

Not all English words ending in -ing can be translated by the present participle in Italian. If the word is used as an adjective, it will add -ante or -ente to the stem, instead of -ando or -endo:

È molto interess*ante* (It is very interesting)

SESSION EIGHT
To Be and To Have

8A   Avere and the Perfect Tense

The perfect tense ('I have done' something) is built up in exactly the same way as in English, using the auxiliary verb **'avere'** (to have), together with what is called the past participle.

The past participle of the three conjugations of regular verbs adds -ato, -uto or -ito to the stem, thus:

parl*ato* (spoken),   **vend*uto*** (sold),   **fin*ito*** (finished)

So if we put the verb 'to have' together with the past participle, we get:

I have spoken – **ho parlato**
I have sold   – **ho venduto**
I have finished – **ho finito**

In order to build up the perfect tense, you need to know how to conjugate **'avere'**. The present tense is conjugated as follows:

		Present Tense
I have	(io)	**ho**
he, she, it has	(lui, lei) ⎫	
you have	(Lei) ⎭	**ha**
we have	(noi)	**abbiamo**
you (common)	(voi)	**avete**
they, you have	(loro, Loro)	**hanno**

Many common verbs have irregular past participles. These are shown in Section 10B (p. 168). Fortunately most of them are only abbreviations which Italians are fond of making to improve the flow of the language. For example, the past participle of the verb **'decidere'** (to decide) should be **'deciduto'** (decided). How much more sensible to shorten this to **'deciso'**.

If the object of the verb is a 3rd person pronoun ('him', 'her', 'it' or 'them') which precedes the verb, the past participle behaves like an adjective and has to agree with the object.

(Io) li ho mangiati (literally, them I have eaten)

(See Section 9, p. 164, for details of Object Pronouns.)

Italian

Other Tenses of 'Avere'

The imperfect and future tenses of **'avere'** are conjugated as follows:

	Imperfect
I was having	**avevo**
he/she/it/you was/were having	**aveva**
we were having	**avevamo**
you (bus.) were having	**avevate**
they/you were having	**avevano**

	Future
I will/shall have	**avrò**
he/she/it will/shall have	**avrà**
we will/shall have	**avremo**
you (bus.) will/shall have	**avrete**
they/you will/shall have	**avranno**

Other Uses of 'Avere'

There are some occasions in Italian, as in French and Spanish, where you use the verb 'to have' in place of 'to be' in English. For example,

Ho **ragione** (I am right; literally, I have right)
Ho **fame** (I am hungry; literally, I have hunger)
Ho **sete** (I am thirsty)
Ho **freddo** (I am cold)

Quanti anni ha (Lei)? (How old are you?; literally, how many years have you?)
Ho **trent' anni** (I *am* thirty; i.e. I have thirty years)

8B   Essere – To Be

The present, imperfect and future tenses of **'essere'**, the Italian verb for 'to be', are shown below:

Present	
I am	**sono**
he/she/it is	**è**
you are (sing)	**è**
we are	**siamo**
you (bus.) are	**siete**
they/you are	**sono**

162

Imperfect

I was	**ero**
he/she/it was	**era**
you were (sing)	**era**
we were	**eravamo**
you (bus.) were	**eravate**
they/you were	**erano**

Future

I will/shall be	**sarò**
he/she/it/you will/shall be	**sarà**
we will/shall be	**saremo**
you (bus.) will/shall be	**sarete**
they/you will/shall be	**saranno**

'**Essere**' crops up in nearly every sentence whether indicating state or activity, or in its use as an auxiliary verb (like '**avere**'). It is also frequently used in an impersonal context where we would say 'it's . . .' or 'it is . . .'

> **Sono inglese** (I am English)
> **È necessario parlare italiano** (It is necessary to speak Italian)
> **Non è difficile** (It is not difficult)

However, '**essere**' is not used to describe the weather – in this case you have to use the verb '**fare**' (to make) just as in French.

> **Fa caldo** (It *is* hot; literally, it makes hot)
> **Fa freddo** (It *is* cold; literally, it makes cold)

Nor is it used when the verb 'to be' could also mean 'to stand', 'to stay' or 'to remain'. Then you use the Italian verb '**stare**'. This is particularly true in describing the state of your health, thus:

> **Sto bene, grazie** (I am well, thank you, i.e. I stay well)
> **Sto alla stazione** (I am at the station, i.e. I stand at the station)

With some verbs, '**essere**' is used to make up the perfect tense, in place of '**avere**' (to have), the most common being those which describe motion (i.e. come, go, arrive, leave, climb, fall) and reflexive verbs. These are marked *E in the word list.

> **È venuto** (He has come)
> **Sono partito** (I have left)
> **Siamo tornati** (We have returned)

Whenever you use '**essere**' the past participle has to agree with the subject. Hence **'tornato'** changes its ending to **'tornati'**, as 'we' are plural. If 'we' are feminine, we would say

Siamo arrivate (We have arrived)

'Essere' can also be used to make a verb passive, rather than active:

Ho finito (I *have* finished)
Sono finito (I *am* finished)

Finally, there is one very useful phrase using the verb 'to be' which you will need every day:

C'è (There is)
Ci sono (There are)
C'è ancora da lavorare! (There is more work ahead!)

SESSION NINE
Object Pronouns

9   Object Pronouns

In Italian, as in English, the spelling of a pronoun changes when it becomes the object in a sentence. To take a simple case:

He hits *him* is translated **Lui lo colpisce**
He changes to *him* in English, **lui** changes to **lo** in Italian

The object pronouns are set out below in two columns, the first where the pronoun is the direct object of the verb, the second where the pronoun is the indirect object – i.e. where in English we would say 'to me', 'to him' or '*to*' any other pronoun.

Direct		*Indirect* (i.e. *'to me'*, *'to him'*, *'to you'* etc)
me	**mi**	**mi** (or **me**)
him/it (m)	**lo**	**gli**
her/it (f)	**la**	**le**
you (sing)	**La**	**Le**
us	**ci**	**ci** (or **ce**)
you (bus.)	**vi**	**vi** (or **ve**)
them (m)	**li**	**loro**

them (f)	**le**	**loro**
you (m. pl)	**Li**	**Loro**
you (f. pl)	**Le**	**Loro**

As we have seen before in Section 5 (p. 153), the object pronoun usually comes *before* the verb in Italian. There are some exceptions to this rule. The pronouns **'Loro'** and **'loro'** come after the verb.

Lo darò loro (I will give it to them)

The object pronouns also follow the infinitive or present participle of a verb. With the exception of **'loro/Loro'**, they are tacked on to the end of the verb, the infinitive dropping the final -e, thus:

Non voglio dirlo (I do not wish to say it)

Object pronouns can also be tacked on to the end of the imperative, when the 1st or 2nd person is used in the *affirmative*, thus:

Compriamolo (Let us buy it) (1st person plural)
but, **Non lo mangiamo** (Don't let's eat it) (negative)
Me lo dia (Lei)! (Give it to me!) (3rd person singular)

When two pronouns precede the verb the *indirect* pronoun goes first and the direct pronoun second, e.g.

(Lei) me lo darà (You will give it to me)

'Mi', **'lo'**, **'la'**, **'vi'** and **'ci'** (before -e and -i) drop the vowel and take an apostrophe before a word starting with a vowel (or with h which is not sounded):

(Io) l'amo (I love him/her)

One other change is made to improve the flow of the language. The pronouns **'mi'**, **'ci'** and **'vi'** (to me, to us or to you) change to **'me'**, **'ce'** or **'ve'** before **'lo'**, **'la'** and **'le'** (i.e. him, her, it or them). The first letter of the pronoun is doubled after a single syllable imperative, e.g.

Dammelo! (Give it to me, *not* **damilo!**)

Likewise **'gli'** and **'le'** change to **'glie'** before **'lo'**, **'la'** and **'le'** when the two pronouns are rolled together.

Glielo do (I give it to him)

Most people find the pronouns rather forbidding at first glance but they soon fall into place. A problem sometimes arises when a pronoun has two or three meanings, and you have to judge the meaning from the context. One alternative to using an indirect pronoun is to use the preposition 'a' (to) with the subject pronouns 'lui' (he), 'lei' (she), 'noi' (us), etc.

Io parlo a Lei (I am speaking to you)

This form is often used when you want to emphasize the pronoun, indeed it is sometimes called the 'emphatic' pronoun.

Many prepositions such as 'with' (con), 'of' (di), 'for' (per) and 'to' (a) are used in this way.

Io voglio passeggiare con lei (I want to walk with her)

The only difference between the 'emphatic' and the subject pronoun is that you use 'me' (me) instead of 'io':

Lei vuole passeggiare con *me* (She wants to walk with me)

SESSION TEN
Imperatives, Reflexives and Irregular Verbs

10A The Imperative and Reflexive Verbs

The Italian for 'we must' do something or 'you must' do something (in business use) are exactly the same as the 1st and 2nd person plural of the present tense.

	speak -are	*sell* -ere	*serve* -ire	*finish* -ire
we must/let us	parl**iamo**	vend**iamo**	serv**iamo**	fin**iamo**
you (plural) must	parl**ate**	vend**ete**	serv**ite**	fin**ite**

As we saw in the last section, the object pronoun is tacked on to the end of the imperative verb, when the 1st or 2nd person is used in the affirmative. If the command is negative, the object pronouns precede the verb.

Compriamo questa casa! (Let's buy this house!)
Vendetecelo! (Sell it to us!)

but **Non ce lo vendete!** (Do not sell it to us!)
Remember, the 'ci' changes to 'ce' before 'lo'.

However, the most common use of the imperative is when we ask a 3rd person to do something and the formal 'Lei' (singular) or 'Loro' (plural) is either used or implied. In this case the endings come from the subjunctive shown in Appendix I (p. 192). In Italian, as in other languages, the subjunctive changes a single vowel in the verb ending to differentiate it from the present tense, i.e.

	speak	*sell*	*serve*	*finish*
you (Lei) must	parl**i**	vend**a**	serv**a**	finis**ca**
you (Loro) must	parl**ino**	vend**ano**	serv**ano**	finis**cano**

Here are some examples:

Ci parlino! (Loro) (Speak to us!)
Non lo finiscano! (Loro) (Do not finish it!)
Me lo venda! (Lei) (Sell it to me!)

Some common verbs have irregular imperatives and these are shown in Section 10C (p. 170).

Reflexive Verbs

Many verbs become 'reflexive' just by changing the pronouns:

(Lui) lo colpisce (He hits him)
(Lui) si colpisce (He hits himself) is reflexive

The reflexive pronouns are quite simple and always precede the verb:

myself	**mi**
him/her/it/yourself	**si**
ourselves	**ci**
yourselves (business)	**vi**
them/yourselves	**si**

In the perfect tense the reflexive verbs always use **'essere'** as the auxiliary verb rather than **'avere'**.

(Noi) ci siamo vestiti (We have dressed ourselves)

Note that the past participle **'vestito'** has to agree with the subject.

The negative **'non'** behaves in the normal way, preceding the verb:

(Lui) non si sederà (He will not sit down)

In the imperative, the reflexive pronoun follows the verb:

Vestasi! (Lei)! (Get dressed [you]!)

The Italians use the reflexive form more than we do and they don't leave out the reflexive pronoun. Where we would say 'I get dressed' or 'I get ready', the Italians would say 'I dress myself' or 'I get myself ready'. Examples are:

   (Io) mi alzo (I get up)
   (Lui) si lava (He washes himself)
   (Noi) ci vestiamo (We get dressed)
   (Voi) vi preparate (You prepare yourselves/get ready)
   Loro si sedano (You sit down)

The reflexive verbs are shown in the word list with the final -e dropped from the infinitive and substituted by -si.

   The reflexive verb is also used where the subject matter is impersonal or to express the English passive:

   Si dice (It is said that; or, one says that)
   Si parla inglese (English is spoken; literally, 'speaks itself')
   Qui si serve pranzo (Lunch is served here)
   Si sono scritti molti libri (Many books have been written)

One case where a reflexive pronoun is *not* used is when you use the verb **'piacere'** (to please). The polite form for 'I like' in Italian is **'mi piace'** (it pleases me). In this case you use the *indirect* object pronoun, thus:

   Mi piace (I like; literally, it pleases me)
   Gli piace (he likes; literally, it pleases him)
   Le piace (you like/she likes; literally, it pleases you/her)
   Ci piace (we like; literally, it pleases us) etc.

However, if you want to ask for something you use the conditional tense (not shown in this grammar) of 'volere' (to want), e.g.

   Vorrei del vino, per favore (I would like some wine, please)

10B   Slightly Irregular Verbs

Many of the verbs in our word list are irregular in one form or another. Fortunately many of them are irregular only in the historic and subjunctive tenses which we are not covering in the main text. In this section we deal with those in our word list which only have *one* irregularity. In Section 10C (p. 170) we show those which are more irregular (principally in the present tense).

   We have already seen that nouns ending in -ca or -ga need the inclusion of the letter h before e or i in the plural, otherwise the sound would change. The same occurs with verbs. Those ending in -care or -gare need an h before any -e or -i ending, thus:

Io pago (I pay)
Io pagherò (I will pay)

Verbs ending in -*ci*are or -*gi*are drop the i before e or i, thus:

Io mangio (I eat)
Io mangerò (I will eat)

Other verbs ending in -iare also drop the i before another i in the ending, e.g.:

studiare (to study) – stem (studi-) + ending (-iamo)
'We study' is therefore **'Noi studiamo** (*not* **'Noi studiiamo'**)

There is one verb in our list, **'vivere'** (to live), which is irregular only in the future tense. This verb drops the e, as follows:

vivrà (he lives) *not* **viverà**
vivremo (we live) etc

However, there are a number of verbs which have irregular past participles, which form part of the perfect tense. These irregularities are mainly abbreviations to make the words easier to pronounce, and to improve the flow of the Italian language. Those which are only irregular in this one respect are listed below.

Don't try to learn them in one go. Read them through two or three times so you become familiar with the words and can recognize them in their written form. Out of interest, see how many you can recognize from your knowledge of French or Latin, or from their English derivation.

Infinitive		*Past participle*
aprire	to open	aperto
assidersi	to sit	assiso
chiedere	to choose	chiesto
chiudere	to close	chiuso
condurre	to drive	condotto
conoscere	to know	conosciuto
coprire	to cover	coperto
correre	to run	corso
decidere	to decide	deciso
difendere	to defend	difeso

Italian

frangere	to break	franto
giungere	to arrive	giunto
leggere	to read	letto
mettere	to put	messo
nascere	to be born	nato
offrire	to offer	offerto
parere	to seem	parso
perdere	to lose	perso
persuadere	to persuade	persuaso
piangere	to cry	pianto
prediligere	to prefer	prediletto
prendere	to take	preso
ridere	to laugh	riso
rispondere	to reply	risposto
rompere	to break	rotto
scendere	to descend	sceso
scrivere	to write	scritto
vivere	to live	vissuto
volgere	to turn	volto

10C   Irregular Verbs

Below we list 27 common verbs included in our word list which have more than one irregular feature. Most of these are -ere or -ire verbs but four only – **'andare'** (to go), **'dare'** (to give), **'stare'** (to stay) and **'fare'** (to make) – are 1st conjugation verbs with an **-are** infinitive.

Each verb is shown below, firstly in the infinitive, followed by the present and past participle. On the next two lines we show the present and future tenses, without repeating the subject pronouns. On the fourth line we show the imperatives for 'you must' (singular), 'we must' and 'you must' (plural).

andare (*to go*), andando, (*going*), andato (*gone*)
Present: vado, va, andiamo, andate, vanno
Future: andrò, andrà, andremo, andrete, andranno
Imperative: vada, andiamo, vadano

bere (*to drink*), bevendo (*drinking*), bevuto (*drunk*)
Present: bevo, beve, beviamo, bevete, bevono
Future: berrò, berrà, berremo, berrete, berranno
Imperative: beva, beviamo, bevano

condurre (*to lead, drive*), conducendo (*leading*), condotto (*led*)

Present: conduco, conduce, conduciamo, conducete, conducono
Future: condurrò, condurrà, condurremo, condurrete, condurranno
Imperative: conduca, conduciamo, conducano

cuocere (*to cook*), cuocendo (*cooking*), cotto (*cooked*)
Present: cuocio, cuoce, cociamo, cocete, cuociono
Future: cuocerò, cuocerà, cuoceremo, cuocerete, cuoceranno
Imperative: cuocia, cociamo, cuociano

dare (*to give*), dando (*giving*), dato (*given*)
Present: do, dà, diamo, date, danno
Future: darò, darà, daremo, darete, daranno
Imperative: dia, diamo, diano.

divenire (*to become*), divenendo (*becoming*), divenuto (*became*)
Present: divengo, diviene, diveniamo, divenite, divengono
Future: diverrò, diverrà, diverremo, diverrete, diverranno
Imperative: divenga, diveniamo, divengano

dire (*to say, tell*), dicendo (*saying*), detto (*said*)
Present: dico, dice, diciamo, dite, dicono
Future: dirò, dirà, diremo, direte, diranno
Imperative: dica, diciamo, dicano

dovere (*to have to, must*), dovendo (*having to*), dovuto (*had to*)
Present: devo (debbo), deve, dobbiamo, dovete, devono (debbono)
Future: dovrò, dovrà, dovremo, dovrete, dovranno
Imperative: debba (deva), dobbiamo, debbano (devano)

fare (*to make, do*), facendo (*making*), fatto (*made*)
Present: faccio, fa, facciamo, fate, fanno
Future: farò, farà, faremo, farete, faranno
Imperative: faccia, facciamo, facciano

morire (*to die*), morendo (*dying*), morto (*died*)
Present: muoio, muore, moriamo, morite, muoiono
Future: morirò, morirà, moriremo, morirete, moriranno *or* morrò, morrà, morremo, morrete, morrano

Italian

Imperative: muoia, muoiamo, muoiano

muovere (*to move*), movendo (*moving*), mosso (*moved*)
Present: muovo, muove, moviamo, movete, muovono
Future: muoverò, muoverà, muoveremo,
              muoverete, muoveranno
Imperative: muova, muoviamo, muovano

parere (*to seem*), parendo (*seeming*), parso (*seemed*)
Present: paio, pare, paiamo, parete, paiono
Future: parrò, parrà, parremo, parrete, parrano

piacere (*to like*), piacendo (*liking*), piaciuto (*liked*)
Present: piaccio, piace, piacciamo, piacete, piacciono
Future: piacerò, piacerà, piaceremo, piacerete,
              piaceranno
Imperative: piaccia, piaciamo, piacciano

porre (*to put*), ponendo (*putting*), posto (*put*)
Present: pongo, pone, poniamo, ponete, pongono
Future: porrò, porrà, porremo, porrete, porranno
Imperative: ponga, poniamo, pongano

potere (*to be able – may, can*), potendo (*being able*), potuto
(*was able*)
Present: posso, può, possiamo, potete, possono
Future: potrò, potrà, potremo, potrete, potranno
Imperative: possa, possiamo, possano

rimanere (*to remain*), rimanendo (*remaining*), rimasto
(*remained*)
Present: rimango, rimane, rimaniamo, rimanete,
              rimangono
Future: rimarrò, rimarrà, rimarremo, rimarrete,
              rimarranno
Imperative: rimanga, rimaniamo, rimangano

salire (*to ascend*), salendo (*ascending*), salito (*ascended*)
Present: salgo, sale, saliamo, salite, salgono
Future: salirò, salirà, saliremo, salirete, saliranno
Imperative: salga, saliamo, salgano

sapere (*to know*), sapendo (*knowing*), saputo (*knew*)
Present: so, sa, sappiamo, sapete, sanno
Future: saprò, saprà, sapremo, saprete, sapranno
Imperative: sappia, sappiamo, sappiano

scegliere (*to choose*), scegliendo (*choosing*), scelto (*chosen*)
Present: scelgo, sceglie, scegliamo, scegliete,
              scelgono
Future: sceglierò, sceglierà, scegliremo,
              sceglierete, seglieranno
Imperative: scelga, scegliamo, scelgano

sedere (*to sit*), sedendo (*sitting*), seduto (*sat*)
Present: siedo (seggo), siede, sediamo, sedete,
              siedono (seggono)
Future: sederò, sederà, sederemo, sederete,
              sederanno
Imperative: sieda, sediamo, siedano (seggano)

stare (*to stay*), stando (*staying*), stato (*stayed*)
Present: sto, sta, stiamo, state, stanno
Future: starò, starà, staremo, starete, staranno
Imperative: stia, stiamo, stiano

tenere (*to hold*), tenendo (*holding*), tenuto (*held*)
Present: tengo, tiene, teniamo, tenete, tengono
Future: terrò, terrà, terremo, terrete, terranno
Imperative: tenga, teniamo, tengano

udire (*to hear*), udendo (*hearing*), udito (*heard*)
Present: odo, ode, udiamo, udite, odono
Future: udirò, udirà, udiremo, udirete, udiranno
Imperative: oda, udiamo, odano

uscire (*to go out*), uscendo (*going out*), uscito (*went out*)
Present: esco, esce, usciamo, uscite, escono
Future: uscirò, uscirà, usciremo, uscirete,
              usciranno
Imperative: esca, usciamo, escano

valere (*to be worth*), valendo (*being worth*), valso (*was worth*)
Present: valgo, vale, valiamo, valete, valgono
Future: varrò, varrà, varremo, varrete, varranno
Imperative: valga, valiamo, valgano

venire (*to come*), venendo (*coming*), venuto (*came*)
Present: vengo, viene, veniamo, venite, vengono
Future: verrò, verrà, verremo, verrete, verranno
Imperative: venga, veniamo, vengano

volere (*to want*), volendo (*wanting*), voluto (*wanted*)
Present: voglio, vuole, vogliamo, volete, vogliono
Future: vorrò, vorrà, vorremo, vorrete, vorranno
Imperative: voglia, vogliamo, vogliano
Conditional: vorrei (*I would like*)

We have not set out the imperfect tense as all the endings
are regular i.e. just replace final **-re** of the infinitive with
-vo, -va, -vamo, -vate and **-vano**. But there are a handful of
verbs which modify their stems in the *imperfect* tense:

1st sing of
$$\begin{cases}
\textbf{fare (to do) is facevo (not favo)} \\
\textbf{dire (to say) is dicevo (not divo)} \\
\textbf{porre (to put) is ponevo (not porvo)} \\
\textbf{condurre (to drive) is conducevo (not} \\
\text{condurvo)} \\
\textbf{bere (to drink) is bevevo (not bevo)}
\end{cases}$$

'**Dovere**' (to owe) and '**potere**' (to be able) are particularly useful verbs as they can be used to make up tenses of
other verbs, for example:

Devo andare a Roma (I must go to Rome)
Non posso cuocere molto bene (I can't cook very well)
Posso venire (I can *or* I could come)

You can also use '**potere**' when you would use 'may' or
'might' in English; for example,

Posso venire = I am able to come

which is sufficiently close for the beginner to use for 'I
may or might come' even though the meaning is slightly
different.

SESSION ELEVEN
Questions and Negatives

11A   Questions

One way to ask a question in Italian is to invert the subject
and the verb:

Gli studenti lavorano bene (The students work well)
Lavorano bene gli studenti? (Do the students work
well?)

Note that the word 'does' (or do) in English is *not* translated into Italian at all.

In the perfect tense the auxiliary verb **'avere'** should be kept together with the past participle, and should not be split up as it is in English, e.g.

Hanno finito gli studenti? (*Have* the students *finished*?)

A slight problem arises over personal pronouns, which are usually omitted in Italian, so the sentence is often the same for a question as for a statement, e.g.

Parla inglese (He speaks English)
Parla inglese? (Does he speak English?)

In reading Italian you can pick this up by the question mark at the end, and by the context of the question. When you are speaking Italian, you get round it quite simply by inflecting your voice at the end of the question, or by adding another question, such as **'non è vero?'** (is it not true?) at the end.

11B Interrogatives

Most of the interrogatives in Italian are quite straightforward:

dove (where) – **Dov' è la mia penna?** (Where is my pen?)
quando (when) – **Quando arriverà (Lei)?** (When will you arrive?)
perchè (why) – **Perchè è (Lei) in ritardo?** (Why are you late?)
come (how) – **Come sta?** (How are you?)
quanto (how many, how much) – **Quanto denaro ha (Lei)?** (How much money do you have?)

Note that 'quanto' is an adjective and must agree with the noun, thus: **Quanti libri ha?** (How many books do you have?)
che (what) – **Che pensa (Lei)?** (What do you think?)
or
che cosa (what thing) – **Che cosa vuole?** (What do you want?)
chi (who) – **Chi va là?** (Who goes there?)
quale (which) – **Quale preferisce?** (Which do you prefer?)

Who, What and Which

In English the genitive of 'who' is 'whose'. The Italians are more likely to say **'di chi'** (of whom), in asking a question.

> **Di chi è questa casa?** (literally, of whom is this house?) and
>
> **Con chi arriverà (Lei)?** (With whom will you arrive?)

but they do have a relative pronoun **'il cui'** for 'whose', which has to agree with the noun.

> **La donna la cui casa è a Roma** (The woman whose house is in Rome)

'Che' can also be used as a relative pronoun for 'who', 'what', 'which' and 'that' in joining two phrases together.

> **L'uomo che vive là** (The man who lives there)
> **La lezione che (noi) abbiamo oggi** (The lesson which we have today)
> **La casa che (io) vedo** (The house that I see)

But after a preposition (such as 'of', 'for', 'with', 'by' or 'to') you use **'cui'** instead of **'che'**.

> **I ragazzi con cui studio** (The boys with whom I study)
> **La casa a cui vado** (The house to which I am going)

Note that 'a' (alone amongst prepositions) sometimes gets omitted.

'Quale' is used for 'which' when it refers directly to a noun. It has a plural **'quali'** (but no feminine form) which has to agree with the noun. Before another vowel, **'qual''** takes an apostrophe.

> **Quali lezioni ha (Lei) oggi?** (Which lessons do you have today?)
> **Qual' è la data?** (What is the date?)

If **'quale'** (which) is used as a relative pronoun together with a preposition (such as 'with', 'by', 'to' or 'of') you must add the definite article as a prefix.

> **L'ufficio nel quale lavoro** (The office in which I work)

11C Negatives

To form a negative in Italian, just put **'non'** in front of the verb, even if you have just answered 'No!' to a question.

> **No! non parlo inglese** (No, I do not speak English)

Remember, in the perfect tense the auxiliary verb and the past participle stick together.

Non ho vissuto in Italia (I have not lived in Italy)

Only the object pronoun can come between **'non'** and the verb.

Non mi ha parlato (He has not spoken to me)

'Neither . . . nor' is translated **'non . . . nè'**.

Non voglio questa casa nè quella (I don't want this house or that one)

'Non' plus **'mai'** means never, but in this case **'mai'** does come before the past participle.

Non l' ho mai amato! (I have never loved him!)

'Non' plus **'niente'** means nothing.

Non vedo niente! (I can see nothing!)

Finally:

Non importa! (It doesn't matter!)

SESSION TWELVE
More Adjectives

12A   Adjectives and Comparatives

There are 80 adjectives in the word list. There is no need to remember them all here, but some indefinite adjectives are in common use and you should try to remember these:

all (**tutto**)
each (**ogni**)
less (**meno**)
many/much (**molto**)
more (**più**)
next (**prossimo**)
other (**altro**)
some (**del**)
too much (**troppo**)

'**Molto**' (much), '**meno**' (less), '**più**' (more) and '**troppo**' (too much) can also be used as adverbs.

Italian

Normally all adjectives have to agree with the noun, but a few such as **'ogni'** (each), **'meno'** (less) and **'più'** (more) do not have a feminine and a plural form.

As we saw in Section 6A (p. 154), all other adjectives ending in -o change to -a in the feminine, those ending in -e do not change at all. All adjectives take an -i ending in the plural except for the feminine plural of the -o adjectives which change to -e.

Remember that all except the very short or very common adjectives follow the noun in word order. Common exceptions are:

good (**buono**)
great/big (**grande**)
long (**lungo**)
old (**vecchio**)
short (**breve**)
small (**piccolo**)
young (**giovane**)

Note that **'buono'** drops the -o and **'grande'** the -de when placed before a masculine noun (**un buon ragazzo**, **un gran generale**), except when the noun starts with s- or z- (**un buono studente**). **'Grande'** drops the -e and takes an apostrophe before any noun starting with a vowel (**una grand' armata** – a great army) whilst **'buono'** only does this before feminine nouns (**una buon' attrice** – a good actress). Also, note that **'grande'** means 'great' when placed before a noun, 'big' when placed after.

The adjective **'bello'** (fine, beautiful or handsome), which crops up quite a lot in Italian, is completely irregular but the endings are the same as for the definite article. The main forms **'bel'** and **'bella'** (m and f sing.) and **'bei'**, **'belle'** (m and f pl) are easy enough to remember. For the other endings, think of the definite article or turn to p. 184, where the same endings for **'quello'** (that) are set out in full.

Comparatives

The Italians use **'più'** (more) or **'meno'** (less) with another adjective to indicate comparison. Where we say 'whiter' they say **'più bianco'** (more white) but **'meno bianco'** (less white) is expressed in the same way in both languages.

If you want to compare one with another, you would use the Italian words **'così . . . come'** or **'tanto . . . quanto'** for 'as . . . as', e.g.

Così bianco come la neve (As white as snow)
(Lui) è tanto ricco quanto Croesus! (He is as rich as Croesus!)

However, note that **'così'** or **'tanto'** are often left out when the meaning is obvious.

So much for ordinary comparatives, how do we show the superlative whit*est*, or *least* white? Just by inserting the definite article (which has to agree) before **'più'** or **'meno'**:

La più bianca neve (The whitest snow)
Il meno rosso (Least red)

Alternative Comparatives

There are a few adjectives and adverbs which have an alternative comparative form. These do not take **'più'** and **'meno'** in front of them, but do add the definite article in the normal way to form the superlative form. Those with an alternative form are shown below.

adj/adv	*comparative*
bad (**cattivo**)	worse (**peggiore**)
badly (**male**)	worse (**peggio**)
big (**grande**)	bigger (**maggiore**)
good (**buono**)	better (**migliore**)
high (**alto**)	higher (**superiore**)
little (**poco**)	less (**meno**)
low (**basso**)	lower (**inferiore**)
much (**molto**)	more (**più**)
small (**piccolo**)	smaller (**minore**)
well (**bene**)	better (**meglio**)

For example:

Questo studente è migliore *di* me (This student is better than me)

Note the use of **'di'** for 'than' in front of the pronoun **'me'**. **'Di'** is used in front of pronouns, nouns and numerals. Otherwise **'che'** is used for 'than'.

Questo studente è migliore *che* (lui) pare (This student is better than he seems)

Superlative Absolute

Finally, the Italians have another form for adjectives and adverbs, called the 'superlative absolute', which they are very fond of using, e.g. **'bellissimo'** (very beautiful). In using the word 'very' you can use the adverb **'molto'**, plus an adjective or adverb, but if you want to emphasize it, use this superlative form. Just drop the final vowel from the adjective and add -**issimo**, remembering that the ending has to agree with the noun or pronoun.

I signori ricc*h*issimi (The very rich gentlemen)

Note that words like **'ricco'** ending in -co or -go have to insert an h, in order to keep the c hard before the i in -issimo.

The same endings apply to adverbs, except where they already end in -mente, in which case the superlative -issimo comes first. For example, **'rapidissimamente'** (very rapidly), but this is such a tongue-twister that it may prudently be avoided by the use of **'molto'**, i.e. **'molto rapidamente'**.

The irregular comparatives shown above also have their own alternative form of the absolute superlative, e.g. **'ottimo'** (the very best), but **'buonissimo'** is perfectly acceptable.

12B Possessive Adjectives and Pronouns

Possessive adjectives and pronouns are the same in Italian. **'Mio'** (m) or **'mia'** (f) can refer to an object, such as 'my hat' or 'my house', or to the statement – 'it's mine'. Whether used as an adjective or a pronoun, it has to agree with the object to which it refers. In most cases it needs to be accompanied by the definite article. A table of Italian possessives is shown below.

	Singular *+ def. article*	*Plural* *+ def. article*
my, mine	**mio/a**	**miei/mie**
his, her/s, its, your/s (sing)	**suo/a**	**suoi/sue**
our/s	**nostro/a**	**nostri/e**
your/s (bus.)	**vostro/a**	**vostri/e**
their/s, your/s (pl)	**loro**	**loro**

All except **'loro'** have masculine and feminine, singular and plural forms, for example:

Il mio amico (My friend)
Le me belle figlie (My beautiful daughters)
La Sua casa (Your house)

Now look at two examples in which the article has been omitted:

Mio fratello (My brother)
Sono vostri (They are yours)

This usually occurs when a pronoun stands on its own, or an adjective refers directly to a single member of one's immediate family. However, if the family is shown in the plural, as in **'le mie belle figlie'**, the definite article still has to be used.

Some confusion may arise over the use of **'suo'** or **'loro'** which has more than one meaning. In writing, you can see when it means 'yours' as **'Suo'** or **'Loro'** are shown with a capital letter. In speaking, you can clarify the meaning by changing the phrase slightly. For example, from **'sua casa'** (his house) to **'la casa di lui'** (literally, the house of him).

SESSION THIRTEEN
Adverbs, Prepositions and Conjunctions

13A   Common Adverbs

To form an adverb in Italian you can add -mente to the feminine singular of the adjective, thus:

felice (happy) becomes **felicemente** (happily)
rapido (quick) becomes **rapidamente** (quickly)

Note that the final vowel is dropped from any adjective ending in -le or -re before adding -mente.

facile (easy)   **facilmente** (easily)

If the adverb gets too long with -mente added, you will find the Italians using the shorter adjective instead – as is sometimes done in English.

Some adverbs, and these are the most common, do not however take -mente endings, such as:

buono (good) becomes **bene** (well)
cattivo (bad) becomes **male** (badly)

There are many other adverbs in our word list, all in common use, which do not have -mente endings and these are shown below.

after, afterwards (**dopo**)
again (**di nuovo**)
ago (**fa**)
almost (**quasi**)

Italian

alone, only (**solo**)
already (**già**)
also/too (**anche**)
always (**sempre**)
before (**prima**)
enough (**abbastanza**)
far (**lontano**)
here (**qui**)
immediately (**subito**)
inside (**dentro**)
late (**tarde**)
near (**vicino**)
never (**mai**)
no (**no**)

now (**ora**)
often (**spesso**)
once (**una volta**)
perhaps (**forse**)
sometimes (**qualche volta**)
soon (**presto**)
then (**allora**)
there (**là**)
therefore (**perciò**)
today (**oggi**)
too much (**troppo**)
unfortunately (**purtroppo**)
very (**molto**)
yes (**sí**)

13B Prepositions and Conjunctions

The classification of English words into adjectives and adverbs, prepositions and conjunctions can become very confusing. Many English words have two or three different uses, like the word 'after', which can be an adverb, a preposition or a conjunction. The simplest advice, to forget about their uses and just remember the Italian, is unfortunately not the best, as the Italians often employ different words for each use.

What we have tried to show is the most common use of the word in English, and then the Italian translation. Where two or three uses are common they are indicated in the text.

Conjunctions

These are words used to link up other words, phrases or sentences. There are only a handful in our word list.

after (**dopo che**)
and (**e**)
as (**come**)
because (**perchè**)
before (**prima che**)
but (**ma**)

if (**se**)
or (**o**)
since (**dacchè**)
so (**perciò**)
when (**quando**)
while (**mentre**)

'Dopo' (after) and 'prima' (before) are also adverbs, but without the 'che'.

Prepositions

These are words indicating position or some other relationship and there are a surprising number in our vocabulary, some of them in constant use.

according to (**secondo**)	in (**in**)
after (**dopo**)	inside (**dentro**)
against (**contro**)	near (**vicino a**)
at, to (**a**)	of (**di**)
before [time] (**prima di**)	on (**su**)
behind (**dietro a**)	opposite (**di fronte a**)
between (**tra**)	over (**sopra**)
during (**durante**)	under (**sotto**)
for, by, through, in order to (**per**)	with (**con**)
from (**da**)	without (**senza**)

'**Prima**' (before), '**dopo**' (after), '**dietro**' (behind), '**vicino**' (near), '**sotto**' (underneath) and '**dentro**' (inside) are also adverbs, dropping the '**di**' or '**a**' of the preposition.

The word 'to' is not usually translated when it is part of the infinitive of a verb,

Vengo vederLa (I am coming to see you)

but there are a number of verbs shown in Section 14B (p. 186) which always take '**a**' after them.

Note that you use an infinitive in place of the present participle after a preposition, e.g.

Sono venuto senza mangi*are*! (I have come without eat*ing*!)

SESSION FOURTEEN
Prepositions and Link Words

14A   This and That

'**Questo**' (this) and '**quello**' (that) can either be used as adjectives or as pronouns (this one, that one or those). In either case they have to agree with the nouns they refer to. Both have different endings for each class of noun, almost copying the endings of the definite article.

Italian

		questo this	*quello* that	*Definite* *article* (for reference only)
Singular	masc	**questo**	quel	il
	fem	**questa**	quella	la
	before vowel	**quest'**	quell'	l'
	before s- or z- masc noun, also emphatic use	–	quello	lo
Plural	masc	**questi**	quei	i
	fem	**queste**	quelle	le
	(masc only) before vowel or s- or z- noun	–	quegli	gli
	(masc only) before i- noun	–	quegl'	gl'

For example,

> **Preferisco questo cappello a quello** (I prefer this hat to that one)
> **Quest' anno prenderò quegli studenti** (This year I shall take those students)
> **Questa è la mia valigia** (This is my suitcase)

Note that **'questi'** and **'quegli'** can have another meaning: **'questi'** means 'this man' and **'quegli'** 'that man'.

The phrase 'this morning' or 'this evening' does *not*, however, use **'questo'**. Here you would say **'stamattina'** or **'stasera'**.

There is also a shortened pronoun **'ciò'** which can be used for 'this' or 'that', providing it refers to things, not people. This has the merit of being invariable – that is to say, there are no other endings!

14B   Use and Form of Common Prepositions

Contractions

A few of the common prepositions which we saw in Section 13B (p. 183), when followed by the definite article, are rolled together and change their spelling. This is done to improve the flow of the Italian language, e.g. **'de'** + **'la'** = **'della'** and **'da'** + **'il'** = **'del'**. The full list is shown in the table opposite. It isn't as complicated as it looks, as all the endings are the same as the definite article. In most cases only one vowel or a consonant is changed.

Definite article ('the')	+ these prepositions				
	to, at	from, by	of	in	on
	a	**da**	**di**	**in**	**su**
il	al	dal	del	nel	sul
la	alla	dalla	della	nella	sulla
l'	all'	dall'	dell'	nell'	sull'
lo	allo	dallo	dello	nello	sullo
i	ai	dai	dei	nei	sui
le	alle	dalle	delle	nelle	sulle
gli	agli	dagli	degli	negli	sugli
gl'	agl'	dagl'	degl'	negl'	sugl'

'**Con**' (with) can also be contracted with '**il**' to make '**col**'.

'Da' and 'In'

Rather more tiresome for the beginner are the different meanings which are given to prepositions in idiomatic use. The most variable of all prepositions is '**da**' which normally means 'by' or 'from' but can also mean 'of', 'with', 'for', 'since', 'to' or 'at' in different contexts. Examples are shown below, together with the rule which applies in each case.

Rule	*Example*
In describing features	**Una ragazza *dai* capelli rossi** (A girl *with* red hair)
In measuring time	***Da* una settimana** (*For* a week)
In measuring time elapsed	***Da* ieri** (*Since* yesterday)
When indicating familiar direction	**Vado *da* lui** (I'm going *to* his place)
When indicating familiar location	**Resto *da* lui** (I'm staying *at* his place)

The preposition '**in**' can also mean 'to' or 'by' when travelling, e.g.

    Vado a Roma *in* treno (I am going to Rome *by* train)

It would be inadvisable to try to learn the idioms, but just be aware of the changes and pick them up as you go along.

    Meanwhile, don't be afraid of getting them wrong!

Italian

'A' and the infinitive

'A' normally means 'to', 'at', or sometimes 'in', thus:

Andiamo al teatro a Roma (Let's go to the theatre in Rome)

but the English word 'to' is usually not translated if it is part of the infinitive of a verb, as we saw in the earlier example:

Vengo vederLa (I am coming to see you)

However, there are some verbs, such as

to begin (**cominciare**), to continue (**continuare**), to invite (**invitare**), to learn (**imparare**), to succeed (**riuscire**), to teach (**insegnare**) which take '**a**' before an infinitive, e.g.

Devo imparare *a* giocare (I must learn to play)

Remember the use of the infinitive in place of the present participle after a preposition:

Non posso parlare italiano senza *apprender*lo prima! (I am not able to speak Italian without learning it first!)

'Di' (of)

You will need to use '**di**' (of) more often in Italian than in English as the Italians do not use the English genitive 's, and so you cannot say 'the girl's father'. You have to say

il padre *della* ragazza (the father *of* the girl)

Some verbs, such as

to believe (**credere**), to finish (**finire**), to hope (**sperare**), to permit (**permettere**), to promise (**promettere**), to say (**dire**) also take '**di**' before an infinitive, e.g.

Spero di finire presto (I hope to finish soon)

One or two prepositions, such as '**prima**' (before), require '**di**' after them, e.g.

Prima *di* arrivare a Roma (Before arriving in Rome)

(Here, note the use of the infinitive '**arrivare**' instead of '**arrivando**', the present participle.)

'**Di**' is *not* used, however, when you translate the phrase 'of them'. Here you use the pronoun '**ne**' before the verb (just like **'en'** in French), and this should not be omitted as it often is in English.

Ne comprerò dieci (I will buy ten *of them*)

Some and None

'Di' plus the definite article is also used in Italian to mean 'some' or 'any'. Literally it just means 'of the'.

Avete del vino? (Have you any wine?)
Comprerò delle arancie (I will buy some oranges)

but if the word 'some' or 'any' is obvious it can be left out:

Non ho denaro (I don't have any money)

You may see **'alcuno'** used for 'some' or 'any' and **'nessuno'** for 'no', 'none' or 'no one', each needing to agree with the noun.

Vedo alcuni soldati (I see some soldiers)
Non vedo nessuna ragazza (I see no girls; literally, I do *not* see *no* girl)

Don't worry about the double negative, this is good Italian!

'Nessuno' behaves like **'uno'**, dropping the final -o before a masculine noun, e.g. **'nessun soldato'** (no soldier).

SESSION FIFTEEN
Numbers and Time

15A   Numbers and Measures

Cardinal Numbers

0	**zero**	10	**dieci**
1	**un/uno/una**	11	**undici**
2	**due**	12	**dodici**
3	**tre**	13	**tredici**
4	**quattro**	14	**quattordici**
5	**cinque**	15	**quindici**
6	**sei**	16	**sedici**
7	**sette**	17	**diciasette**
8	**otto**	18	**diciotto**
9	**nove**	19	**diciannove**

Italian

20	**venti**	100	**cento**
21	**ventuno**	101	**cento uno**
22	**ventidue**	157	**cento cinquantasette**
23	**ventitré**	200	**duecento**
28	**ventotto**	300	**trecento**
29	**ventinove**	400	**quattrocento**
30	**trenta**	500	**cinquecento**
31	**trentuno**	600	**seicento**
32	**trentadue**	700	**settecento**
40	**quaranta**	800	**ottocento**
50	**cinquanta**	900	**novecento**
60	**sessanta**	1,000	**mille**
70	**settanta**	10,000	**dieci mila**
80	**ottanta**	100,000	**cento mila**
90	**novanta**		

157,643 – **cento cinquantasette mila, seicento quarantatré**
1,000,000 – **un milione**
2,000,000 – **due milioni**
1,576,438 – **un milione, cinquecento settantasei mila, quattrocento trentotto**
1,000,000,000 – **un miliardo**

You can see that '**venti**' (20) drops the final -i before 'uno' and 'otto', and the same occurs in every decade up to 100.

One hundred (**cento**) needs no article beforehand and has no plural (**duecent***o*).

Compound numbers over 100 do not need the word '**e**' (and) in the middle.

One thousand (**mille**) also needs no article beforehand but has an irregular plural, '**mila**'.

One million (**un milione**) requires 'of' (**di**) before another noun, but 'one thousand' does not, thus:

due milioni di soldati (two million soldiers)
due mila soldati (two thousand soldiers)

All the other cardinal numbers are invariable, that is to say they have no feminine or plural form.

Numbers showing order are as follows:

first	**primo**
second	**secondo**
third	**terzo**
fourth	**quarto**
fifth	**quinto**
sixth	**sesto**
seventh	**settimo**

eighth	**ottavo**
ninth	**nono**
tenth	**decimo**
thirteenth	**tredicesimo**
twentieth	**ventesimo**

As adjectives, they agree with and precede the noun. For numbers over 10, take the final vowel off the cardinal number (except **'trè'** when stressed) and add -esimo, e.g. cinquantottesimo (58th).

The only fractions you are likely to need at this stage are:

one quarter	**un quarto**
one third	**un terzo**
one half	**una metà** (adjective: **mezzo**)
two thirds	**due terzi**
three quarters	**tre quarti**
one	**un/uno/una**

There is no equivalent to the English words 'once', 'twice', 'thrice'. The Italians say **'una volta'** (one time), **'due volte'** (two times), **'tre volte'** (three times), and so on.

Weights are in chili (kilos) of 1000 grammi (grammes)

un chilo = 35 ounces or just under 2¼ lb
un mezzo chilo = just over 1 lb

If you purchase cheese from a delicatessen, for example, you would ask for 350 grammi, *not* 'un terzo chilo' (one third of a kilo).

Liquid measures are in litri (litres).

un litro (one litre) = cento (100) centilitri (centilitres)
= 35 fluid ounces = 1¾ pints
one pint = approximately 0.6 litro or 60 centilitri

Distances are in chilometri (1000 metres)

un chilometro = 0.6 of one mile
one mile = 1.6 chilometri, ten miles = 16 chilometri

15B   Dates and Time

Un anno (a year) is split into **le quattro stagioni** (seasons):

spring	**la primavera** (f)
summer	**l'estate** (f)
autumn	**l'autunno** (m)
winter	**l'inverno** (m)

Italian

I mesi (the months) are mostly recognizable from the English.

January	**gennaio**	July	**luglio**
February	**febbraio**	August	**agosto**
March	**marzo**	September	**settembre**
April	**aprile**	October	**ottobre**
May	**maggio**	November	**novembre**
June	**giugno**	December	**dicembre**

Ogni mese (each month) **ha quattro settimane** (four weeks) **e ogni giorno** (each day) **si chiama** (calls itself):

Monday	**lunedì**	Friday	**venerdì**
Tuesday	**martedì**	Saturday	**sabato**
Wednesday	**mercoledì**	Sunday	**domenica**
Thursday	**giovedì**		

The Italians do not translate the words 'on' or 'of', thus:

> **Arriverò martedì, l' otto marzo** (I will arrive *on* Tuesday, 8th *of* March)

Ogni giorno è composto (is comprised) **della mattina** (of the morning), **del pomeriggio** (afternoon), **della sera** (evening) **e della notte** (night) **e ci sono** (there are) **ventiquattro ore** (24 hours) **quotidiane** (every day).

> **Ogni ora ha sessanta minuti** (minutes)
> **Ogni minuto ha sessanta secondi** (seconds)
> **Qual' è la data?** (What is the date?)
> **Oggi, è lunedì il diciotto maggio** (Today it is Monday 18th May)

Note that cardinal numbers are used to show dates, except for **'primo'** (the first).

> **Domattina** (tomorrow morning) **sarà martedì** (will be Tuesday)
> **Il giorno prossimo sarà mercoledì** (The next day will be Wednesday)
> **Che ora è?** (What hour [time] is it?)
> **Sono le cinque e mezza** (It is the five and a half i.e. half past five)

The word **'ora'** (hour) is omitted, as in English, but the definite article is always used and has to agree with **'ora'**, or **'ore'** (plural). From two o'clock onwards, 'it is' has to go into the plural: **'sono'** (they are).

'A quarter to six' is translated as:

le sei meno un quarto (*the* six less a quarter)

For minutes past the hour, say

le cinque e ventisette (*the* five *and* twenty-seven)

and for minutes before the hour, just use the word **'meno'** (less)

le sei meno ventisette (*the* six *less* twenty-seven)

Don't bother to say 'minutes' so long as this is understood. Up to 12 noon, say

le sei *di* **mattina** (six in the morning) using **'di'** but no definite article before morning

After **'mezzogiorno'** (midday) and up to **'mezzanotte'** (midnight) say **'le cinque di pomeriggio'** (five in the afternoon) or **'le dieci di notte'** (ten at night)

but remember that published times on the Continent work to a 24-hour clock.

Finally, the weather.

Che tempo fa? (What is the weather like?)
Fa caldo (It is hot; literally, it makes hot)
Fa freddo (It is cold)
but, *Ha* **freddo** (He is cold; literally, he *has* cold)
Piove (It is raining)
Nevica (It is snowing)

Note that **'tempo'** also means length of time.

Non c'è molto tempo! (There is not much time!)
Molto tempo fa (A long time ago)

APPENDIX I

Subjunctives

The subjunctive tenses have been left out of the main text as they can be confusing to those learning Italian. They are little used, even less recognized in English, but they are used much more frequently in Italian. They usually occur in subordinate clauses after the conjunctives **'che'** or **'se'** or the relative pronoun **'chi'**, following verbs of ordering, wanting, expressing fear, doubt or emotion, or after an impersonal verb.

The subjunctive is also used in a conditional sentence starting with **'se'** (if) where the answer is likely to be negative.

The subjunctive is *not* used however when the subject (noun or pronoun) in both the main sentence *and* the subordinate sentence are the same, as in the sentence 'I fear that *I* must leave'.

Typical examples of the subjunctive are as follows:

> **Dubito che Lei abbia del denaro** (I doubt that you have any money)
> **Se fossi ricco, glielo darei** (It I were rich, I would give it to him)

The present and imperfect subjunctive tense endings are set out below for the regular verbs and also for **'avere'** and **'essere'**. The perfect subjunctive can be built up by using the auxiliary verbs, plus the past participle.

As a general rule, the imperfect or perfect subjunctive is used whenever the verb in the main sentence is in the past tense.

Present Tense

	Regular Verbs			*avere*	*essere*
	-are verb endings	*-ere verb endings*	*-ire verb endings*		
1st sing	**-i**	**-a**	**-isca**	**abbia**	**sia**
3rd sing	**-i**	**-a**	**-isca**	**abbia**	**sia**
1st pl	**-iamo**	**-iamo**	**-iamo**	**abbiamo**	**siamo**
2nd pl	**-iate**	**-iate**	**-iate**	**abbiate**	**siate**
3rd pl	**-ino**	**-ano**	**-iscano**	**abbiano**	**siano**

Imperfect Tense

	-are verb endings	-ere verb endings	-ire verb endings	*avere*	*essere*
1st sing	**-assi**	**-essi**	**-issi**	**avessi**	**fossi**
3rd sing	**-asse**	**-esse**	**-isse**	**avesse**	**fosse**
1st pl	**-assimo**	**-essimo**	**-issimo**	**avessimo**	**fossimo**
2nd pl	**-aste**	**-este**	**-iste**	**aveste**	**foste**
3rd pl	**-assero**	**-essero**	**-issero**	**avessero**	**fossero**

Nearly all *irregular* verbs use the -ere verb endings in the present subjunctive, although their stems may change. The imperfect subjunctive endings are the same as the regular verbs, although there too, the stems sometimes change.

When speaking Italian, it is suggested that you start by keeping the sentences fairly simple and avoid too many subordinate clauses, which require the use of the subjunctive.

APPENDIX II

The Use of 'Tu'

In Section 7A we referred to the increasing use of **'tu'**, the 2nd person singular, in everyday language. It is no longer used just for family and close friends. Below we show the different forms of the personal pronoun, the possessive adjective and the appropriate verb endings.

Pronouns

Subject		**tu**	(you)
	direct	**ti**	(you)
Object	indirect	**ti**	(to you)
	stressed after preposition	**te**	(you)
Reflexive		**ti**	(yourself)
Possessive (like **'mio'**, Section 12B, p. 180)		**tuo**	(yours)

Adjective

Possessive (like **'il mio'**, Section 12B, p. 180)	**il tuo** your	

Italian

Verbs

		-are (parlare)	-ere (vendere)	-ire (servire)	-ire (finire)
Present:	**tu**	parli	vendi	servi	finisci
Imperfect:	**tu**	parlavi	vendevi	servivi	finivi
Future:	**tu**	parlerai	venderai	servirai	finirai
Present subj.:	**tu**	parli	venda	serva	finisca
Imperfect subj.:	**tu**	parlassi	vendessi	servissi	finissi
Imperative:		parla	vendi	servi	finisci

		avere	essere
Present:	**tu**	**hai**	**sei**
Imperfect:	**tu**	**avevi**	**eri**
Future:	**tu**	**avrai**	**sarai**
Present subj.:	**tu**	**abbia**	**sia**
Imperfect subj.:	**tu**	**avessi**	**fossi**
Imperative:		**abbi**	**sii**

Irregular verb endings are fairly straightforward, once you are sure of the stem.

		ending
Present:	**tu**	**-i**
Imperfect:	**tu**	**-i**
Future:	**tu**	**-ai**
Present subj.:	**tu**	**-a**
Imperfect subj:	**tu**	**-si**
Imperative:	{ -are verbs	**-a**
	{ others	**-i**

GERMAN

CONTENTS

SESSION ONE
Your Word List

1A 500 Word Vocabulary

a/an **ein/eine** (f)
able, to be **können**
accept, to **akzeptieren**
accident **Unfall -"e** (m)
according to **laut**
account (bill) **Rechnung -en** (f)
address **Adresse -n** (f)
advise, to **raten** (I)
aeroplane **Flugzeug -e** (n)
after **nachdem**
afternoon **Nachmittag** (m)
again **wieder**
against **gegen**
age **Alter** (n)
ago **vor**
agree with, to **über-einstimmen**
air **Luft -"e** (f)
airmail **Luftpost** (f)
airport **Flughafen -"** (m)
all **alle** (pl)
allow (let), to **erlauben**
almost **fast**
alone **allein**
already **schon**
also (too) **auch**
always **immer**
amuse, to **amüsieren (sich)**
animal **Tier -e** (n)
and **und**

angry **zornig**
another **ein anderer** (m)
answer, to **antworten** (I)
anyone **jemand**
arrive, to **an-kommen *S**
art **Kunst -"e** (f)
as . . . as **so . . . wie**
ask, to (question) **fragen**
at **auf, bei, in, zu**
attention **Achtung** (f)
avenue **Allee -n** (f)

bad **schlecht**
bag **Beutel** (m)
baggage (luggage) **Gepäck** (n)
bank **Bank -en** (f)
bath **Bad -"er** (n)
be, to **sein *S**
beach **Strand -"e** (m)
beautiful **schön**
because **weil**
become, to **werden *S**
bed **Bett -en** (n)
before **bevor**
begin, to (start/commence) **beginnen**
behind **hinter**
believe, to **glauben** (I)
between **zwischen**
bicycle **Fahrrad -"er** (n)
big **groß**

Notes: 1 *(I) indicates verbs which take the indirect case: see p. 229.*
2 **S indicates verbs which use 'sein': see p. 230.*
3 *Noun does not change in plural if no ending is shown.*
4 *Where an umlaut is needed on the vowel in the plural, this is shown at the end, thus: -".*
5 *Separable verbs are shown with a hyphen.*
6 *Brackets round the first syllable of a word indicates alternative spelling.*
7 *(a.o.c.) means 'all other cases'.*

German

bill (account)
  Rechnung -en (f)
black **schwarz**
blue **blau**
boat **Boot -e** (n)
book **Buch -¨er** (n)
born, to be **geboren sein**
bottle **Flasche -n** (f)
box **Schachtel -n** (f)
boy **Junge -n** (a.o.c.) (m)
break, to **brechen**
bridge **Brücke -n** (f)
bring, to **bringen**
brother **Bruder -¨** (m)
brown **braun**
building **Gebäude** (n)
bus **Autobus -se** (m)
business **Geschäft -e** (n)
but **aber**
buy, to **kaufen**

cafe/bar **Café -s** (n)
camera
  Fotoapparat -e (m)
can (verb: be able)
  können
car **Auto -s** (n)
car park
  Parkplatz -¨e (m)
caravan **Wohnwagen** (m)
carry, to **tragen**
careful, be! **Vorsicht!**
castle **Schloß** (n)
cat **Katze -n** (f)
certain **sicher**
chair **Stuhl -¨e** (m)
change, to (alter) **ändern**
cheap **billig**
cheque **Scheck -s** (m)
chemist's (pharmacy)
  Apotheke -n (f)
child **Kind -er** (n)
choose, to **wählen**
church **Kirche -n** (f)
cigarette **Zigarette -n** (f)
class **Klasse -n** (f)
clean, to **reinigen**

clear **klar**
clock **Uhr -en** (f)
close, to **schließen**
clothes **Kleider** (n. pl)
coat **Mantel -¨** (m)
cold **kalt**
colour **Farbe -n** (f)
come, to **kommen** *S
comfortable **bequem**
complete **vollständig**
concert **Konzert -e** (n)
continue, to **fort-setzen**
conversation
  Unterhaltung -en (f)
cook, to **kochen**
corner **Ecke -n** (f)
correct **richtig**
cost, to **kosten**
cotton **Baumwolle** (f)
count, to **zählen**
country **Land -¨er** (n)
cover, to **bedecken**
cry, to **weinen**
customs (border)
  Zoll -¨e (m)
cut, to **schneiden**

damage **Schaden -¨** (m)
dance, to **tanzen**
dangerous **gefährlich**
dark **dunkel**
date **Datum,** (pl)
  Daten (n)
daughter **Tochter -¨** (f)
day **Tag -e** (m)
dear (expensive) **teuer**
decide, to **entscheiden**
defend, to **verteidigen**
dentist **Zahnarzt -¨e** (m)
depart, to (leave)
  ab-fahren *S
descend, to (go down)
  herunter-gehen
desire, to (want) **wollen**
die, to **sterben** *S
different **verschieden**
difficult **schwer**

direction (way)
 Richtung -en (f)
dirty **schmutzig**
distance **Ferne -n** (f)
do, to **tun**
doctor (medical)
 Arzt -¨e (m)
dog **Hund -e** (m)
door **Tür -en** (f)
dress **Kleid -er** (n)
drink, to **trinken**
drive, to (a car) **fahren** *S
dry **trocken**
during **während**
duty (customs)
 Zoll -¨e (m)
duty (obligation)
 Pflicht -en (f)

each (every) **jeder** (m)
early **früh**
eat, to **essen**
empty **leer**
end **Ende -n** (n)
engine **Maschine -n** (f)
English **englisch**
enough **genug**
enter, to **ein-treten**
equal **gleich**
evening **Abend -e** (m)
every **jeder** (m)
everything **alles**
excellent **ausgezeichnet**
exchange, to (money)
 wechseln
excuse, to **entschuldigen**
 (sich) (I)
exit **Ausgang -¨e** (m)
expensive (dear) **teuer**
eye **Auge -n** (n)

face **Gesicht -er** (n)
fall, to **fallen** *S
family **Familie -n** (f)
far **fern**
fast (quick) **schnell**
fat **dick**

father **Vater -¨** (m)
feel, to **fühlen**
field **Feld -er** (n)
film **Film -e** (m)
fight, to **kämpfen**
fill, to **füllen**
find, to **finden**
finish, to **auf-hören**
fire **Feuer** (n)
fix, to **befestigen**
floor **Boden -¨** (m)
flight (by air)
 Flug -¨e (m)
fly, to **fliegen** *S
follow, to **folgen** (I)
food **Essen** (n)
foot **Fuß -¨e** (m)
football (game)
 Fußballspiel -e (m)
for **für**
forget, to **vergessen**
free **frei**
French **französisch**
friend **Freund -e** (m)
from **von**
fruit **Obst** (n)
full **voll**

garage **Garage -n** (f)
garden **Garten -¨** (m)
German **deutsch**
gift **Geschenk -e** (n)
girl **Mädchen** (n)
give, to **geben**
glasses **Brille** (f)
glove **Handschuh -e** (m)
go, to **gehen** *S
go down, to
 hinunter-gehen *S
go out, to
 (hin)aus-gehen *S
go up/climb, to
 (hin)auf-gehen *S
god **Gott -¨er** (m)
gold **Gold** (n)
good **gut**
great **groß**

German

ground **Boden -**¨ (m)

hairdresser **Friseur -e** (m)
hand **Hand -**¨**e** (f)
handbag
  Handtasche -n (f)
handkerchief
  Taschentuch -¨**er** (n)
happen, to **geschehen** *S
happy **glücklich**
hard **hart**
hat **Hut -**¨**e** (m)
have (possession of),
  to **haben**
have, to (auxiliary) **haben**
hear, to **hören**
heavy **schwer**
healthy **gesund**
help, to **helfen** (I)
here **hier**
high **hoch**
hill **Berg -e** (m)
hold, to **halten**
holiday (vacation)
  Urlaub -e (m)
hope, to **hoffen**
hospital
  Krankenhaus -¨**er** (n)
hot **heiß**
hotel **Hotel -s** (n)
hour **Stunde -n** (f)
house **Haus -**¨**er** (n)
how **wie**
how much/how many?
  wieviel?
husband
  (Ehe)mann -¨**er** (m)

ice **Eis** (n)
if **wenn**
ill **krank**
immediately **sofort**
important **wichtig**
in **in, auf, an**
include **einschließen**
industry **Industrie -n** (f)

information
  Auskunft -¨**e** (f)
inside **in/innen**
intelligent **intelligent**
interesting **interessant**
is (verb: to be) **ist**
Italian **italienisch**

join, to (be part of)
  beitreten (I)
journey **Reise -n** (f)

keep, to **halten**
key **Schlüssel** (m)
kind **freundlich**
king **König -e** (m)
kiss, to **küssen**
know, to (something)
  wissen
know, to (somebody)
  kennen

lady **Dame -n** (f)
language **Sprache -n** (f)
last **letzt**
late **spät**
lawyer
  Rechtsanwalt -¨**e** (m)
learn, to **lernen**
leave, to (depart)
  ab-fahren *S
leave, to (go out)
  (hin)aus-gehen *S
left **links**
lend, to **leihen**
less **weniger**
let, to (permit)
  (zu)-lassen
letter **Brief -e** (m)
lift **Aufzug -**¨**e** (m)
light (noun) **Licht -er** (n)
like, to **mögen**
liquid **Flüssigkeit -en** (f)
list **Liste -n** (f)
little (small) **klein**
little (a) **ein wenig**
live, to **leben**

live in, to **wohnen**
long **lang**
look at, to **an-blicken**
lorry **Lastkraftwagen** (m)
 (LKW)
lose, to **verlieren**
loud **laut**
love, to **lieben**
luggage (baggage)
 Gepäck (n)

mad **wahnsinnig**
make, to **machen**
man **Mann -¨er** (m)
manner **Art -en** (f)
many **viele** (pl)
map **Landkarte -n** (f)
market **Markt -¨e** (m)
match (light)
 Streichholz -¨er (n)
medicine **Arzneimittel** (n)
meet, to **treffen**
meeting **Treffen** (n)
middle, the **Mitte** (f)
million **Million -en** (f)
minute **Minute -n** (f)
mirror **Spiegel** (m)
mistake **Fehler** (m)
money **Geld -er** (n)
month **Monat -e** (m)
more **mehr**
morning **Morgen** (m)
motorway
 Autobahn -en (f)
mother **Mutter -¨** (f)
mountain **Berg -e** (m)
mouth **Mund -¨er** (m)
move, to **bewegen**
much **viel**
museum
 Museum -seen (n)
music **Musik** (f)
must (verb: to be obliged)
 müssen

name **Name** (m),
 -ns (poss), **-n** (a.o.c.)

near **nahe**
necessary **nötig**
need, to **bedürfen**
never **nie**
new **neu**
newspaper
 Zeitung -en (f)
next **nächst**
night **Nacht -¨e** (f)
no **nein**
noise **Lärm** (m)
nothing **nichts**
now **jetzt**
number (figure)
 Nummer -n (f)

obtain, to **erhalten**
of **von**
offer, to **an-bieten**
office **Büro -s** (n)
often **oft**
oil **Öl -e** (n)
old **alt**
on **an, auf**
once **einmal**
only **nur**
open, to **auf-machen**
opposite **gegenüber**
or **oder**
ordinary **gewöhnlich**
other **anderer** (m)
over **über**
owe, to (be obliged)
 sollen

package **Paket -e** (n)
pain **Schmerz -en** (m)
paper **Papier -e** (n)
park **Park -s** (m)
part **Teil -e** (m)
pass, to (hand to)
 über-reichen
passenger
 Fahrgast -¨e (m)
passport
 Reisepaß -ässe (m)
path **Weg -e** (m)

German

pay, to **(be)zahlen**
pen (ballpoint) **Kuli** (m)
pencil **Bleistift -e** (m)
perhaps **vielleicht**
permit (let) **erlauben**
person/people
  Person -en (f)
persuade, to **über-reden**
petrol **Benzin -e** (n)
pharmacy
  Apotheke -n (f)
photograph **Foto -s** (n)
piece **Stück -e** (n)
place **Ort -e** (m)
play, to **spielen**
please **bitte**
police **Polizei** (f)
point out, to **hinweisen**
poor **arm**
port (harbour)
  Hafen -¨ (m)
porter **Gepäckträger** (m)
possible **möglich**
postcard **Postkarte -n** (f)
post office **Post -en** (f)
prefer, to **vor-ziehen**
prepare, to **(vor)-bereiten**
price **Preis -e** (m)
private (not public)
  privat
probable **wahrscheinlich**
profession **Beruf -e** (m)
programme
  Programm -e (n)
promise, to **versprechen**
put, to (place) **stellen**

quality **Qualität -en** (f)
quantity **Quantität -en** (f)
question **Frage -n** (f)
quick (fast) **schnell**
quiet **ruhig**

rain, to **regnen**
read, to **lesen**
ready **bereit**
receive, to **empfangen**

reception (hotel)
  Empfang -¨e (m)
red **rot**
regret, to (be sorry)
  bedauern
remember, to **sich
  erinnern an**
repeat, to **wiederholen**
reply, to **antworten**
report, to **berichten**
responsible
  verantwortlich
restaurant
  Restaurant -s (n)
return, to
  zurück-kommen
rich **reich**
right (direction) **rechts**
right, to be **recht haben**
river **Fluß -üsse** (m)
road **Straße -n** (f)
room **Zimmer** (n)
run, to **rennen *S**

sad **traurig**
same **derselbe** (m)
save, to **retten**
say, to **sagen**
school **Schule -n** (f)
sea **See -n** (f)
see, to **sehen**
seem, to **scheinen**
sell, to **verkaufen**
send, to **schicken**
serve, to **bedienen** (I)
service **Bedienung -en** (f)
shoe **Schuh -e** (m)
shop **Laden -¨** (m)
short **kurz**
show, to **zeigen**
shower **Dusche -n** (f)
shut, to **schließen**
sign **Zeichen** (n)
silver (adj) **silbern**
since **seit**
sing, to **singen**
sister **Schwester -n** (f)

sit down, to **sich (hin) setzen**
skiing (noun) **Skifahren** (n)
sky **Himmel** (m)
sleep, to **schlafen**
slowly **langsam**
small **klein**
snow **Schnee** (m)
so, thus **also**
soap **Seife -n** (f)
soft **weich**
some **einige** (pl)
someone **jemand**
sometimes **manchmal**
son **Sohn -¨e** (m)
soon **bald**
speak, to **sprechen**
square (town) **Platz -¨e** (m)
stairs **Treppe -n** (f)
stamp **Briefmarke -n** (f)
start, to (begin) **beginnen**
station (railway) **Bahnhof -¨e** (m)
stay, remain, to **bleiben** *S
step (pace) **Schritt -e** (m)
stop, to **auf-hören**
street **Straße -n** (f)
strong **stark**
student **Student -en** (a.o.c.) (m) **-in/innen** (f)
study, to **studieren**
suddenly **plötzlich**
suitcase **(Hand)koffer** (m)
summer **Sommer** (m)
sun **Sonne -n** (f)
suntan **Sonnenbräune** (f)
sweet **süß**
swim, to **schwimmen**
swimming pool **Schwimmbad -¨er** (n)

table **Tisch -e** (m)
take, to **nehmen**
taste, to **schmecken** (I)

taxi **Taxi -s** (n)
tea **Tee -s** (m)
teach, to **lehren**
teacher **Lehrer** (m) **in/innen** (f)
telegram **Telegramm -e** (n)
telephone, to **an-rufen**
television **Fernsehen** (n)
tell, to **sagen**
tennis **Tennis** (n)
thank you! (very much) **danke! (schön)**
theatre **Theater** (n)
then **dann**
there **dort**
there is/are **es ist/sind**
therefore **also, deswegen**
thing **Ding -e** (n)
think, to **denken**
this/that **dieser/der** (m)
through **durch**
ticket **Fahrkarte -n** (f)
time (what time is it?) **Zeit -en** (f) **wieviel Uhr ist es?**
time (one or more) **-mal (ein-, zwei- etc)**
tip **Trinkgeld -er** (n)
tired **müde**
to (direction) **nach**
to (in order to) **um . . . zu**
too (also) **auch**
too much/many **zuviel**
today **heute**
toilet **Toilette -n** (f)
tomorrow **morgen**
tourist **Tourist -en** (m) **-in/innen** (f)
towards **auf . . . zu**
towel **Handtuch -¨er** (n)
town **Stadt -¨e** (f)
traffic **Verkehr** (m)
train (express) **Zug -¨e** (m)
translate, to **übersetzen**
travel, to **reisen** *S

travel agent
  Reisebüro -s (n)
tree **Baum -¨e** (m)
true **wahr**
try, to **versuchen**
typical **typisch**
tyres **Reifen** (m. pl)

umbrella
  Regenschirm -e (m)
under **unter**
underground (rail)
  Untergrundbahn (f)
understand, to **verstehen**
unfortunately **leider**
university
  Universität -en (f)
use, to **benutzen**
useful **nützlich**

vacation (holiday)
  Urlaub -e (m)
very **sehr**
village **Dorf -¨er** (n)
visit, to **besuchen**
voice **Stimme -n** (f)

wait for, to **warten auf**
waiter **Kellner** (m)
walk, to **laufen**
wall **Wand -¨e** (f)
want/wish for, to **wollen**
wash (oneself), to **sich waschen**
watch **an-sehen**
water **Wasser** (n)

way (direction)
  Weg -e (m)
wedding **Hochzeit -en** (f)
week **Woche -n** (f)
weekend
  Wochenende -n (n)
well **gut**
what! **was!**
when? **wann?**
where? **wo?**
which? **welcher?** (m)
which **der** (m)
white **weiß**
who **wer**
why? **warum?**
wide **breit**
wife **Frau -en** (f)
wind **Wind -e** (m)
window **Fenster** (n)
wine **Wein -e** (m)
winter **Winter** (m)
wish/want, to **wollen**
with **mit**
without **ohne**
wood **Wald -¨er** (m)
word **Wort -¨er** (n)
work, to **arbeiten**
world **Welt -en** (f)
write, to **schreiben**

year **Jahr -e** (n)
yellow **gelb**
yes **ja**
yesterday **gestern**
young **jung**

1B 100 Words for Buying Food and Eating Out

Shops

bakery **Bäckerei** (f)
butcher's **Metzgerei** (f)
delicatessen
  Delikatessengeschäft -e (n)
fishmonger's
  Fischladen (m)
grocer's **Lebensmittel-
  geschäft -e** (n)
market **Markt -ˮe** (m)
self service
  Selbstbedienung (f)
shop **Laden -ˮ** (m)
supermarket
  Supermarkt -ˮe (m)
tobacconist's
  Tabakladen (m)

Meals

breakfast **Frühstück -e** (n)
dining room
  Eßzimmer (n)
dinner **Abendessen** (n)
drink **Getränk -e** (n)
food **Essen** (n)
lunch **Mittagessen** (n)
meal **Mahlzeit -en** (f)

Table setting

bottle **Flasche -n** (f)
chair **Stuhl -ˮe** (m)
cup **Tasse -n** (f)
fork **Gabel -n** (f)
glass (table)
  Glas -ˮer (n)
jug **Krug -ˮe** (m)
knife **Messer** (n)
menu **Speisekarte -n** (f)
oil **Öl -e** (n)
pepper **Pfeffer** (m)
plate **Teller** (m)
salt **Salz** (n)

spoon **Löffel** (m)
sugar **Zucker** (m)
table **Tisch -e** (m)
tip **Trinkgeld -er** (n)
vinegar **Essig** (m)
waiter **Kellner** (m)

Drinks

I'm thirsty **ich habe Durst**
beer **Bier -e** (n)
brandy **Kognak** (m)
cider **Apfelwein -e** (m)
coffee **Kaffee** (m)
cream **Sahne** (f)
lemonade
  Limonade -n (f)
milk **Milch** (f)
orange juice
  Orangensaft -ˮe (m)
tea **Tee** (m)
tomato juice
  Tomatensaft -ˮe (m)
water/sparkling water
  Wasser (n)/**Sprudel** (m)
wine **Wein -e** (m)
whisky **Whisky -s** (m)

Food

I'm hungry **ich habe
  Hunger**
apple **Apfel -Ä** (m)
asparagus **Spargel** (m)
aubergine
  Aubergine -n (f)
bacon **Speck** (m)
banana **Banane -n** (f)
bean (French) **grüne
  Bohne -n** (f)
bean (haricot)
  Bohne -n (f)
beef **Rindfleisch** (n)
bread **Brot -e** (n)
broccoli **Brokkoli** (m. pl)

German

butter **Butter** (f)
cabbage **Kohl -e** (m)
cake **Kuchen** (m)
cauliflower
  Blumenkohl -e (m)
celery **Sellerie** (m)
cheese **Käse** (m)
chicken **Hähnchen** (n)
chocolate
  Schokolade -n (f)
cucumber **Gurke -n** (f)
curry **Curry -s** (n)
egg **Ei -er** (n)
fish **Fisch -e** (m)
flour **Mehl -e** (n)
fruit **Frucht -"e** (f)
ham **Schinken** (m)
hors d'oeuvre
  Vorspeise -n (f)
ice cream **Eis** (n)
jam **Marmelade -n** (f)
lemon **Zitrone -n** (f)
meat **Fleisch** (n)
melon **Melone -n** (f)
milk **Milch** (f)
mushroom **Pilz -e** (m)
nectarine **Nektarine -n** (f)
oil **Öl -e** (n)
omelette **Omelett -e** (n)
onion **Zwiebel -n** (f)
orange **Orange -n** (f)
pancake **Pfannkuchen** (m)
pâté **Pastete -n** (f)
peach **Pfirsich -e** (m)
pear **Birne -n** (f)
peas **Erbsen** (f. pl)
pepper **Pfeffer** (m)
pork **Schweinefleisch** (n)
potato **Kartoffel -n** (f)
  chipped potatoes
  Pommes frites (pl)

prawns **Garnele -n** (f)
ravioli **Ravioli**
rice **Reis** (m)
salad **Salat -e** (m)
sauce **Soße -n** (f)
sausage **Wurst -"e** (f)
soup **Suppe -n** (f)
spaghetti **Spaghetti** (pl)
spinach **Spinat** (m)
tart **Torte -n** (f)
toast **Toast -e** (m)
tomato **Tomate -n** (f)
vegetables **Gemüse** (n)
vinegar **Essig** (m)

Cooking

boiled **gekocht**
fresh **frisch**
fried **gebraten**
grilled **gegrillt**
rare **'englisch'**
raw **roh**
sour **sauer**
sweet **süß**
well cooked **durchgekocht**

Containers

bag **Beutel** (m)
bottle **Flasche -n** (f)
bottle opener
  Flaschenöffner (m)
can **Dose -n** (f)
can opener
  Dosenöffner (m)
corkscrew
  Korkenzieher (m)

1C   150 Words for Business Use

interpreter
Dolmetscher (m), **-in** (f)
translate, to **übersetzen**

Organization
Organisation (f)

authority **Autorität** (f)
book-keeper
Buchhalter (m)
chairman **Vorsitzende -n**
(a.o.c.) (m)
company
Gesellschaft -en (f)
company secretary
Vorstandssekretär -e (m)
director **Direktor** (m)
employee **Angestellte -n**
(a.o.c.) (m)
executive
Verwaltungsbeamte -n
(a.o.c.) (m)
management
Geschäftsleitung (f)
manager
Geschäftsleiter (m)
managing director
Geschäftsführer (m)
responsible
verantwortlich
secretary **Sekretär -e** (m)
-in (f)

Office **Büro -s** (m)

agreement
Abkommen (n)
airmail **Luftpost** (f)
authorize, to
genehmigen
bank **Bank -en** (f)
business **Geschäft -e** (n)
computer **Computer** (m)
contract **Vertrag -¨e** (m)

copy **Kopie -n** (f)
data processing
Datenverarbeitung (f)
document
Dokument -e (n)
fax **Telefax -e** (m)
invoice **Rechnung -en** (f)
lease **Mietvertrag -¨e** (m)
legal **gesetzlich**
official **amtlich**
post **Post -en** (f)
private, confidential
privat
receipt (of goods)
Quittung -en (f)
regulations
Regulierung -en (f)
rent **Miete -n** (f)
report **Bericht -e** (m)
requisition
Anforderung -en (f)
shares (in a company)
Aktien (f. pl)
sign, to **unterschreiben**
signatory
Unterzeichner (m)
-in/innen (f)
tariff (customs)
Zolltarif -e (m)

Works/factory
Werk -e (n)/*Fabrik -en* (f)

chemicals
Chemikalien (f. pl)
development
Entwicklung -en (f)
electrician **Elektriker** (m)
electricity **Elektrizität** (f)
engineer **Ingenieur -e** (m)
foreman **Vorarbeiter** (m)
fuel **Brennstoff -e** (m)
gas **Gas -e** (n)
laboratory
Laboratorium -rien (n)

German

machinery
Maschinen (f. pl)
maintenance
Erhaltung (f)
manual worker
Handarbeiter (m)
-in/innen (f)
metal **Metall -e** (n)
oil **Öl -e** (n)
raw materials
Rohstoffe (m. pl)
research
Forschung -en (f)
services (works)
Dienstleistungen (f. pl)
site **Lage -n** (f)
stores (warehouse)
Lager (n)
tool room
Werkzeugslager (n)
warehouse
Lagerhaus -¨er (n)

Production
Produktion (f)

automation
Automatisierung (f)
batch **Schub -¨e** (m)
budget **Budget -s** (n)
construction
Konstruktion -en (f)
consumption
Verbrauch (m)
control, to **verwalten**
effluent **Abwasser** (n)
increase, to **zunehmen**
invest, to **investieren**
job **Arbeit -en** (f)
(new) product **(neues)**
Produkt -e (n)
output **Ertrag -¨e** (m)
performance
Leistung -en (f)
plan **Plan -¨e** (m)
productivity
Arbeitsleistung (f)

quantity **Quantität -en** (f)
reduce, to **vermindern**
schedule **Plan -¨e** (m)
timetable
Stundenplan -¨e (m)
ton **Tonne -n** (f)
utilization
Verwendung -en (f)
volume
Produktionsstärke (f)
waste **Abfall** (m)
works order
Bestellung -en (f)

Marketing *Marketing* (n)

achieve, to **durch-führen**
advertise, to **an-zeigen**
agent (sales) **Agent -en**
(a.o.c.) (m)
agree, accept, to
überein-stimmen
assess, to **schätzen**
brand **Marke -n** (f)
commission (payment)
Provision -en (f)
competition
Wettbewerb -e (m)
customer **Kunde -n**
(a.o.c.) (m)
delivery **Lieferung -en** (f)
demand **Nachfrage** (f)
distribution
Verteilung (f)
economic **ökonomisch**
forecast, to **voraus-sagen**
market objective
Marktziel (n)
market research
Marktforschung (f)
opportunity
Gelegenheit -en (f)
packaging
Verpackung -en (f)
presentation
Präsentation (f)
price **Preis -e** (m)

product test
  Produkttest -e (m)
promote, to **fördern**
quality **Qualität -en** (f)
representative
  Vertreter (m) **-in** (f)
sales **Umsätze** (m. pl)
sales force
  Verkaufspersonal (n)
service (customer)
  Kundendienst -e (m)
share (of market)
  Markanteil -e (m)
target **Ziel -e** (n)

Employment **Arbeit** (f)

assessment
  Bewertung -en (f)
benefit **Nutzen** (m)
bonus **Bonus** (m)
canteen **Kantine -n** (f)
job (for person)
  Stelle -n (f)
pension **Rente -n** (f)
personnel **Personal** (n)
salary **Gehalt -¨er** (n)
skill **Fachkenntis -se** (f)
social security
  Sozialleistung -en (f)
training **Ausbildung** (f)
unemployed **arbeitslos**
vacancy
  offene Stelle -n (f)
wage **Lohn -¨e** (m)

Accounts
  Rechnungen (f. pl)

actual **effectiv**
asset, net **Aktiva** (n. pl)
bad debt **uneinbringlische**
  Forderung -en (f)

balance sheet
  Bilanz -en (f)
borrow, to **sich leihen**
capital **Kapital -ien** (n)
capital expenditure
  Investitions-
  aufwendung (f)
cash **Bargeld** (n)
cash flow **Cash-flow** (m)
cost of sales
  Wareneinsatz -¨e (m)
credit control
  Kreditenkontrolle (f)
creditor **Gläubiger** (m)
debtor **Schuldner** (m)
depreciation
  Abschreibung (f)
dividend **Dividende -n** (f)
expenditure
  Ausgabe -n (f)
grant **Subvention -en** (f)
interest (bank)
  Zinsen (m. pl)
labour cost
  Personalkosten (f. pl)
liability (balance sheet)
  Passiva (n. pl)
liability (damages)
  Haftung (f)
loan **Darlehen** (n)
margin, gross
  Bruttomarge -n (f)
profit, net **Gewinn -e,**
  netto (m)
share capital
  Aktienkapital (n)
stocks, inventories
  Vorrat -¨e (m)
taxation **Steuer -n** (f)
variance **Abweichung** (f)
working capital
  Betriebskapital (n)

German

SESSION TWO
Pronunciation

2A Letters and Sounds

German	Sounds like	Example
a (long)	a in par	Abend
a (short)	a in uncle	Alter
ä (long)	ay in pay	Läden
ä (short)	a in pet	Bäcker
au	ow in now	laut
äu	oi in coin	Käufer
b	b in bar	Farbe
	but p in pat followed by a consonant or at word end	abfahren
c	c in cat	Café
ch	h (exaggerated) as in human	welcher
	but ch in loch after a, au, o and u	auch
	and sh in ship at the beginning of words of French origin	Champagne
	or k in kind at the beginning of words of Greek origin	Chaos
chs	cks in stocks	sechs
d	d in dog	deutsch
	but t in bit at word end or followed by a consonant	und
ee	} ey in fey	See
e (long)		sehen
e (short)	e in fell	wenn
ei	ei in eiderdown	ein
eu	oy in toy	heute
f	f in fast	fern

g	**g** in **g**un	Auge
	but **ck** in ta**ck** at word end or followed by a consonant	genug
h	**h** in **h**at (not pronounced between two vowels, in the middle of a syllable	haben
ie	} **ee** in f**ee**t	wie
i (long)		ihnen
i (short)	**i** in f**i**t	ist
j	**y** in **y**es	jeder
k	**k** in **k**in, must also be pronounced before n	knopf
l	**l** in **l**amp	Land
m	**m** in **m**an	Mädchen
n	**n** in **n**ot	nicht
ng	**ng** in ki**ng**	Angst
oo	} between **oh!** and **or**	Boot
o (long)		rot
o (short)	**o** in n**o**t	Kommen
ö (long)	**ir** in f**ir** with rounded lips	hören
ö (short)	**er** in h**er**	möglich
p	**p** in **p**at	Preis
qu	**kv** (no English equivalent)	Quantität
r	**r** in **r**ight (slightly trilled but almost silent at word end)	Reis
s	**z** in **z**oo before a vowel	sehen
	and **sh** in **sh**ip before p and t	spät
	otherwise **ss** in gla**ss**	Glas
ss or **ß**	**s** in **s**it	schließen
sch	**sh** in **sh**eep	Tisch

German

t	**t** in **t**eeth	**T**axi
u (long)	**oo** in s**oo**n	Br**u**der
u (short)	**ou** in w**ou**ld	L**u**ftpost
ü	**ew** in f**ew**, without the w	f**ü**r
v	**f** in **f**oot	**v**on
w	**v** in **v**an	**W**inter
x	**x** in e**x**it	E**x**amen
y	seldom used	–
z	**ts** in fi**ts**	**z**u

2B Vowels, Accents and Stress

The German language is spoken clearly, sometimes a little harshly to our ears, with each letter given proper diction. It is not slurred, and syllabic sounds are not omitted or rolled over as in English. There are no 'bacon'eggs' in German!

Long and Short Vowels

The simplest way to differentiate between long and short vowels is to remember that vowels are nearly always:

Long when followed by h or a single consonant, or when the vowel is doubled.

There are a few exceptions, in particular where a is used in a prefix or short word like 'am', 'hat', 'man'; or when e is followed by the consonants l, n or r. In those cases the vowel is short.

Umlauts

Umlauts invariably change the sound of the vowels. They may form part of the basic word spelling, or they can be used to indicate the plural of a noun or a change in a verb.

Stress

The German language tends to stress or emphasize the first syllable, or the stem of the verb. Inseparable prefixes like be-, emp-, ent-, er-, ge-, ver- and zer- do *not* take the stress. Imported foreign words tend to keep their own form of stress, whilst very long compound words may need to be stressed in more than one place.

You will soon pick up the rhythm of the language if you listen carefully, and practise speaking it whenever possible.

Punctuation

Commas must be used to separate clauses from each other, as different rules for word order apply to each clause.

Use commas, instead of points, in money and decimals. Do not use commas to split up thousands or millions: just provide spaces, e.g. 3 747 865.

SESSION THREE
Absorbing the Language

This is a practice session, for you to try in your own time.

Go through the main vocabulary in Section 1A and read all the words aloud.

Go through a second time, covering up the English and see how many words you can translate.

Now go through a third time, this time covering up the German and see how many words you can translate from the English. Don't worry if there are only a few. Your vocabulary will develop with regular practice.

SESSION FOUR
Message Builders

4A   Message Builders

The 80 or so *'message builders'* shown below comprise part-phrases, interrogatives or verbs in everyday use, which you can use to build up questions and messages. You can use these *'message builders'* with your own list of key words to find your way round and to give yourself practice in speaking the language. There are no nouns

German

shown in the list below; you get these from your own word list, or the main vocabulary. (Note that nouns and adjectives are shown in the 'subject case' in the vocabulary, and adjectives appear in their masculine form. You will find out in Session Six how to deal with the word endings.)

In Section 4B (p. 216) you will find the commonest forms of address and greetings which will 'top and tail' your messages. Liberal use of 'please' and 'thank you' will add considerably to your communication skills!

English	*German*
Today is.....	**Heute ist** .....
I speak.....	**Ich spreche** .....
Do you speak.....	**Sprechen Sie** .....
Yes.....no	**Ja** ..... **nein**
My name is.....	**Mein Name ist** .....
My number is.....	**Meine Nummer ist** .....
I live in.....	**Ich wohne in** .....
This is my.....	**Das ist mein*** .....
Who is/who are.....	**Wer ist/wer sind** .....
I am/we are.....	**Ich bin/wir sind** .....
Why are we.....	**Warum sind wir** .....
Are you.....	**Sind Sie** .....
Where is/where are.....	**Wo ist/wo sind** .....
a.....	**ein** (m), **eine** (f), **ein** (n)
the.....	**der** (m), **die** (f), **das** (n)
my.....	**mein** (m), **meine** (f), **mein** (n)
Where can I find.....	**Wo finde ich** .....
I have lost.....	**Ich habe** ..... **verloren**
I have broken.....	**Ich habe** ..... **gebrochen**
I have forgotten.....	**Ich habe** ..... **vergessen**
When does.....open	**Wann öffnet** .....
When does.....start	**Wann beginnt** .....
When does.....close	**Wann schließt** .....
Excuse me.....	**Entschuldigen Sie bitte** .....
What is the way to..... (a place)	**Wie komme ich nach** .....
I want to go to.....	**Ich will** ..... **gehen**
Is it far to.....	**Ist es weit bis** .....
Is it.....	**Ist es** .....

* *masculine, subject case*

English	German
It is	**Es ist .....**
It is not	**Es ist nicht .....**
Here is/here are	**Hier ist/hier sind .....**
Is there/are there	**Gibt es .....**
There is/there are	**Es gibt .....**
Is there ..... near here	**Befindet sich hier in der Nähe .....**
Do you have/have you got	**Haben Sie .....**
I have reserved	**Ich habe ..... reserviert**
It's for	**Es ist für .....**
Does it have	**Hat es .....**
I have/we have	**Ich habe/wir haben .....**
Can I have	**Kann ich ..... haben**
Can you	**Können Sie .....**
Would you like	**Möchten Sie .....**
I would like/we would like	**Ich möchte gern/wir möchten gern .....**
Another	**Noch ein* .....**
I am sorry that	**Es tut mir leid .....**
There is no	**Es ist kein* .....**
What ..... do you have	**Welchen* ..... haben Sie**
How many ..... do you have	**Wieviel/e ..... haben Sie**
Anything else?	**Sonst noch etwas?**
I would prefer	**Ich würde ..... vorziehen**
It is too	**Es ist zu .....**
I need/we need	**Ich brauche/wir brauchen .....**
I will take	**Ich nehme .....**
We will take	**Wir nehmen .....**
I like ..... very much	**Ich mag ..... sehr gern**
Give me/give us	**Geben Sie mir/uns .....**
How much is	**Was kostet .....**
More/less	**Mehr/weniger .....**
One/two/three/four/five	**Eins/zwei/drei/vier/fünf**
Ten/twenty/fifty	**Zehn/zwanzig/fünfzig ....**
One hundred/one thousand	**Hundert/tausend .....**
Tell me	**Sagen Sie mir .....**
What time is it?	**Wie spät ist es?**
When does ..... leave	**Wann fährt .....**
When does ..... arrive	**Wann kommt ..... an**
When do we	**Wann (verb) wir .....**

How do we	**Wie (verb) wir .....**
I am going to	**Ich werde ..... (+ infinitive)**
I have just	**Ich bin gerade .....**
Don't go!	**Gehen Sie nicht weg!**
Let's go to ..... (a place)	**Gehen wir nach .....**
Meet me at	**Treffen Sie sich mit mir an .....**
Telephone me at	**Rufen Sie mich um ..... an**
I ought to/we must	**Ich sollte/wir müssen .....**
I can/we can	**Ich kann/wir können .....**
Take care!	**Vorsicht!**
I will come back on	**Ich werde am ..... zurückkommen**
I can't understand	**Ich verstehe nicht**
Speak more slowly	**Sprechen Sir bitte langsamer**
Could you repeat that!	**Könnten Sie das bitter wiederholen!**

4B   Addressing Friends and Strangers

German is a little more formal and polite than English. So:
● It is advisable to remember to shake hands when you meet every day.
● Address adult strangers as **'Herr'** (sir or Mr) or **'Frau'** (Mrs) or **'Gnädige Frau'** (madam; literally, kind or gracious lady) and young girls as **'Fräulein'**, thus:

> **Guten Morgen, Herr Schmidt, können Sie ...?** (Good morning, Mr Smith, can you ... ?)

● **'Bitte'** (please) and **'Danke'** (thank you) or **'Danke schön'** (many thanks) should be used liberally.
● When you meet, or part company, remember the greeting

Good morning	**Guten Morgen**
Good day	**Guten Tag**
Good evening	**Guten Abend**
Good night	**Gute Nacht**
Goodbye! Until we meet again!	**Auf Wiedersehen!**

● Other useful greetings include **'Hallo!'** (Hello!), **'Wie geht's?'** (How are you?). You could reply **'Danke sehr gut!'** (Very well, thank you).

● Other useful expressions which you are likely to need include:

Zum Wohle! (Good health!) or **Prost!** (Cheers!)
Guten Appetit (Enjoy your meal)
Es gefällt mir sehr (I like it very much)

SESSION FIVE
Language Structure

5   Word Order

Word order does differ in certain important respects from English, and you will probably have to refer back several times to this section until the rules for sentence structure become ingrained. There is certainly more flexibility allowed in German in moving words around the sentence to achieve the emphasis you need but one rule remains paramount:

1   **In each main clause, except where shown below, the verb stays in the second position.**

In the simple example **'Frederick liebt Martha'** (Frederick loves Martha) the German and English word order is the same:

Subject – Verb – Object.

But if you start the sentence with an interrogative word, an adverb, a noun or pronoun which is not the subject, an introductory phrase or even a subordinate clause, you have to *reverse* the verb and subject, in order to keep the verb in the second position. Thus:

In Berlin *wohnt* **Frederick** (Frederick lives in Berlin)
Warum *kam* **ich hierher?** (Why did I come here?)
Oft *komme* **ich hierher** (I often come here)
Wenn es Sommer ist, *komme* **ich oft hierher** (When it is summer, I often come here)

However, exclamations, responses like **'ja'** and **'nein'** (yes and no), prepositions and some conjunctions do *not* count as taking the first position. These conjunctions are **'und'** (and), **'aber'** (or), **'sondern'** (but), **'oder'** (or) and **'denn'** (because).

German

2   In the last example shown above two adverbs were used, **'oft'** and **'hierher'**. These adverbs have their own pecking order. Adverbs or adverbial expressions related to 'time' come first, those of 'manner' come second and those of 'place' come third, thus:

Oft fahre ich langsam durch die Stadt (I often drive slowly through the town)

Note that the subject and the verb are not split up, as in English.

3   **In a subordinate clause** (after a relative pronoun or conjunction), the subject usually comes second and the verb goes right to the end of the clause, even after the past participle:

Ich glaube, daß Sie in Berlin wohnen (I understand that you live in Berlin)
Ich höre, daß Sie in Berlin gewohnt haben (I hear that you have lived in Berlin)

4   If you use a compound tense of a verb, the infinitive or past participle goes to the end of the sentence, but the auxiliary verb stays in 2nd position:

Ich habe mein Haus verkauft (I have sold my house)

Where an infinitive and a past participle are both needed, the infinitive goes right to the end. Where there are two infinitives, one will be an auxiliary like **'sein'**, **'haben'** or **'werden'** and that goes right to the end.

5   If you use a separable verb, the prefix goes to the end of the main clause (but not in a subordinate clause) whenever it is separated from the stem (i.e. in the present and past tenses and the imperative).

6   If you ask a question without using an interrogative you just reverse the verb and pronoun as in English, remembering that the words 'do' or 'does' are not translated. In this case the verb can go in first position:

Wohnen Sie in Berlin? (Do you live in Berlin?)

7   If you use a negative, the word **'nicht'** (not) or **'nie'** (never) usually follows the verb, but it can be moved to the beginning or end of the sentence:

Ich wohne nicht in Berlin (I do *not* live in Berlin)

8   If you use a reflexive verb the reflexive pronoun follows the verb:

Ich wasche mich morgens (I wash myself in the morning)

9   The order of precedence for nouns and pronouns is that pronouns come first, as in English:

Ich gab es Frederick (I gave it to Frederick)

10   The order of precedence for nouns themselves is:

Subject – indirect – object, e.g.

Frederick gab Martha das Auto (Frederick gave the car to Martha)

11   The order of precedence for pronouns themselves is:

Subject – object – indirect, e.g.

Ich gab es Ihnen (I gave it to you)

12   Finally, object pronouns usually come before adverbs, as in English:

Ich machte es gut (I made it well)

SESSION SIX
Nouns, Adjectives and The Two Articles

6A   Nouns, Gender and Cases

Nouns may not be the easiest place to start learning German, but as the principles of gender, word endings and cases go right through German grammar, it is best to get them firmly established at the beginning.

Gender

Every noun in German is either masculine (m), feminine (f) or neuter (n), and both the indefinite and definite articles ('a' and 'the') have to agree. For example,

Masculine – **der Mann** (the man)   **ein Mann**
Feminine – **die Frau** (the woman)   **eine Frau**
Neuter   – **das Kind** (the child)   **ein Kind**

Notice that the nouns always start with a capital letter in written German.

There are no easy rules for determining the gender of

German

a noun, so try to learn the gender at the same time as the word itself. However, you may find these guidelines useful:

1   Those people, animals or objects which we clearly identify as masculine or feminine in English are usually the same in German (subject to the other guidelines).

2   Nouns ending in -ig, -ing, -ling, -ich and -lich are masculine, also those ending in -en (except when taken from a verb).

3   Nouns ending in -e, -in, -ung, -heit, -keit, -sion, -tion and -schaft are usually feminine.

4   Nouns which end in -lein, -chen, -tum or start in ge- are usually neuter. So are those words which are lifted from verbs or imported from another language (e.g. **'das Hotel'**).

5   Composite nouns (i.e. two German nouns rolled together) take the gender of the second noun.

6   Nouns which have two meanings (and there are also quite a few in English) are differentiated by having a different gender.

7   Some nouns can be masculine or feminine. The feminine form adds -in to the singular, -innen to the plural.

Run through the word list a few times and both the meaning and the gender of the nouns will start to stick in your mind.

Plurals

The plural endings in German are not quite so simple as in English, although, if you think about it, we too do not always add -s in the plural. For example:

  house – houses,   mouse – mice,   child – children

There are four types (sometimes called declensions) of nouns in German:

(a)   Those which don't change their endings in the plural. Some take an umlaut (¨) over the vowel which changes the sound of the word, such as **'der Vater'** (the father), **'die Väter'** (the fathers).

(b)   Those which add -e in the plural, such as **'der Tag'** (the day), **'die Tage'** (days) and may add an umlaut, such as **'der Zug'** (the train), **'die Züge'** (trains).

(c)   Those which take an umlaut and add -er in the plural, such as **'das Buch'** (the book), **'die Bücher'** (the books).

(d)   Those which add -n or -en in the plural, such as **'die Uhr'** (the clock), **'die Uhren'** (clocks).

These are set out in more detail in Section 6C (p. 223) where we show the rules for plurals *and* case endings.

However, all the plurals are shown in the word list, so look through the list until you become thoroughly familiar with their meaning, gender and plural form.

Cases

Those who have learnt Latin may remember that nouns had 'cases' which meant that their endings changed according to their function in the sentence. This also happens in German. Take for example the simple sentence

He hits *him*

The spelling of the pronoun 'he' changes to 'him' when 'he' becomes the object in the sentence. The same changes occur with the other pronouns, 'I' and 'me', 'she' and 'her', 'we' and 'us', 'they' and 'them'.

In German, the nouns, pronouns, adjectives and the definite or indefinite articles all have endings which show whether they are the subject or the object of the sentence. In Latin and in many grammars they are still referred to as being in the 'nominative' or the 'accusative' case. We shall refer to them simply as the *'subject'* and *'object'* cases.

There are two further cases in German. The *'possessive'*, and the *'indirect'* case (often referred to as the 'genitive' and 'dative' cases).

The *'possessive'* case indicates possession. In English, we add 's to a noun to indicate possession, e.g.

the boy's father

but you can't do that in German. You have to say 'the father of the boy' and the phrase 'of the boy' is in the *possessive case*.

The *'indirect'* case is used where the object is referred to indirectly. In the following example 'car' is the direct object, not 'the house'. 'The house' is the indirect object.

	Parts of speech
The	definite article
father	subject (noun)
of the boy	possessive (noun)

German

	Parts of speech
took	verb
a	indefinite article
new	adjective
car	object (noun)
to the house	indirect object (noun)

The definite article, the noun and the adjective all may change their endings according to whether they are in the *subject*, *object*, *possessive* or *indirect* case.

Some prepositions also determine the case of the nouns which follow them, but we will come to that later in Section 13B (p. 246).

The case endings are set out in the next three sections.

6B   The Two Articles ('A' and 'The')

The definite article 'the' is used in much the same way as in English. The indefinite article 'a' is sometimes omitted if it does not add to the sense, e.g.

Er ist Arzt (He is a doctor)

The definite article is sometimes added to names where we would omit it:

Ich fahre in die Schweiz (I am going to Switzerland)

The definite article and the indefinite article have different endings in German which relate to the gender and the case of the noun to which they refer. These are set out in the table below. (As **'ein'** has no plural, the adjective **'kein'** [no] is shown instead.)

	Singular			Plural
				All genders
	m	*f*	*n*	**(kein)**
a				
Subject	**ein**	**eine**	**ein**	**keine**
Object	**einen**	**eine**	**ein**	**keine**
Possessive (of a)	**eines**	**einer**	**eines**	**keiner**
Indirect (to a)	**einem**	**einer**	**einem**	**keinen**
the				
Subject	**der**	**die**	**das**	**die**
Object	**den**	**die**	**das**	**die**
Possessive (of the)	**des**	**der**	**des**	**der**
Indirect (to the)	**dem**	**der**	**dem**	**den**

The endings can often be a useful guide to the structure of a sentence, particularly in the possessive or indirect case.

As we shall see in the Sections 6D and 12 (pp. 224 and 242), some adjectives and possessives have the same endings as the definite or indefinite articles.

Words which are declined like **'ein'** (a), include **'kein'** (no) and the possessive adjectives **'mein'** (my), **'sein'** (his) etc.

Those which decline like **'der'** (the) include **'dieser'** (this), **'jeder'** (each), **'jener'** (that) and **'mancher'** (many).

6C   Noun Case Endings

The case endings for nouns are not as complicated as they seem, since the changes are fairly universal and generally only affect one or two letters at the end of the word. You will soon get used to the rhythm of the language and find that a noun needs a particular ending to make the sentence flow smoothly. If you make a mistake, don't worry. You are more likely to be understood in German, with an incorrect word ending, than in French for example, where you may get the word exactly right but the pronunciation is incorrect.

There are two main groups of nouns.

1   **Masculine** nouns (except those ending in -e) and **neuter** nouns, generally

– only change endings in the possessive singular, adding -s or -es (as in English), e.g.

$$masc \begin{cases} \textbf{der Vater} \text{ (the father)} \\ \textbf{der Tag} \text{ (the day)} \\ \textbf{der Zug} \text{ (the train)} \end{cases} becomes \begin{cases} \textbf{des Vaters} \\ \textbf{des Tages} \\ \textbf{des Zuges} \\ \textbf{des Buches} \end{cases}$$
$$neut \quad \textbf{das Buch} \text{ (the book)}$$

– add -e or -er in the plural and may take an umlaut over the vowel, e.g.

die Tage, die Züge, die Bücher

But those masculine nouns ending in -el, -en and -er and neuter nouns ending in -chen and -lein do *not* change their ending, although they can take an umlaut in the plural, such as **'die Väter'** which changes the pronunciation of the vowel.

German

– add -n in the indirect plural, e.g.

den Vätern, den Tagen, den Zügen, den Büchern

2 **Feminine** nouns do not change at all in the singular, but mostly add -en in the plural (or just -n if the noun ends in -e, -el or -er). Those ending in -in change to -innen.

die Uhr (the clock)			**die Uhren**
die Katze (the cat)	*becomes*		**die Katzen**
die Frage (the question)			**die Fragen**
die Freundin (the friend [f])			**die Freundinnen**

3 A very few masculine nouns ending in -e, such as **'der Junge'** (the boy) and one or two common words like **'der Herr'** (the gentleman) or **'der Student'**, add -n or -en to *every* case except the subject singular. These are marked a.o.c. (all other cases) in the word list.

To help you imprint these rules into your memory, we have set down all the cases for the examples shown on the previous page and above.

Gender Noun	Masc (father)	Masc (day)	Neuter (book)	Fem (clock)	Masc (boy)
Subject sing	**Vater**	**Tag**	**Buch**	**Uhr**	**Junge**
Object sing	**Vater**	**Tag**	**Buch**	**Uhr**	**Jungen**
Possessive sing	**Vaters**	**Tages**	**Buches**	**Uhr**	**Jungen**
Indirect sing	**Vater**	**Tag**	**Buch**	**Uhr**	**Jungen**
Subject pl	**Väter**	**Tage**	**Bücher**	**Uhren**	**Jungen**
Object pl	**Väter**	**Tage**	**Bücher**	**Uhren**	**Jungen**
Possessive pl	**Väter**	**Tage**	**Bücher**	**Uhren**	**Jungen**
Indirect pl	**Vätern**	**Tagen**	**Büchern**	**Uhren**	**Jungen**

As you can see, the cases are not too difficult to remember, and you can pick up the plurals from the word list. (Note that the plural is *only* shown in the word list where it changes from the singular.)

6D Adjectives

When an adjective is used with the verb **'sein'** (to be) or **'werden'** (to become) the endings do not change, regardless of the case or gender of the noun or pronoun.

Die Frau ist schön (The woman is beautiful)

Here **'schön'** does not take a different ending even though 'the woman' is feminine.

However, when the adjective is preceded by the indefinite or definite articles ('a' or 'the') and certain other adjectives, they *do* have to agree with the gender and case of the noun. The endings are fairly simple and are set out in the table below.

Adjectival endings

Case and gender	After **'ein'** (a) **'kein'** (no) **'mein'** (mine) and all possessive adjectives	After **'der'** (the) **'alle'** (all) **'dieser'** (this) **'jeder'** (each) **'jener'** (that) **'mancher'** (many)
SINGULAR	*Ending*	*Ending*
Subject		
Masculine	-er	-e
Feminine	-e	-e
Neuter	-es	-e
Object		
Masculine	-en	-en
Feminine	-e	-e
Neuter	-es	-e
Possessive { all	-en	-en
Indirect { genders	-en	-en
PLURAL { all genders all cases	-en	-en

If there is *no* definite article used, the adjective takes on both the role and the *endings* of the *definite* article, which you can see in Section 6B (p. 222). The only difference is that the ending -en is preferred to -es in the possessive case, although -es is still grammatically acceptable. For example:

Ein braver Junge (A good boy) subject singular
Jedes kleine Mädchen (Each little girl) object singular
Allen guten Männern (To all good men)
  indirect plural
Roter Rosen (Of red roses) possessive plural –
  no article

Obviously it takes time to get used to the endings of nouns, adjectives and the two articles, as the endings are very often the same for different cases and genders. But don't let it deter you. Keep the sentences short until you become more practised. Start by getting the endings right for 'a' and 'the', then master the subject and object cases. Remember, the stem or main body of the word will nearly always get the message across.

Finally, note that adjectives can be used as nouns, with a capital letter at the beginning and the same endings as for ordinary adjectives.

SESSION SEVEN
Personal Pronouns and Verbs

7A   Subject Pronouns

Before moving on to verbs, we should run through the personal pronouns – I, he, we, you and they – which are the *subject* of the verb. We usually describe the subject pronouns as being in the 1st, 2nd or 3rd person singular, or plural, and modify the verb endings accordingly. The subject pronouns are as follows:

1st person singular	I	**ich**
2nd person singular	you (informal)	**du**
3rd person singular	he/it (m)	**er**
3rd person singular	she/it (f)	**sie**
3rd person singular	it (n)	**es**
3rd person singular	you (formal)	**Sie**
3rd person singular	one	**man**
1st person plural	we	**wir**
2nd person plural	you (informal)	**ihr**
3rd person plural	you (formal)	**Sie**
3rd person plural	they	**sie**

In everyday speech, for 'you' the Germans use the old-fashioned word **'Sie'** (with a capital S), and this requires the use of the 3rd person, *not* the 2nd person singular or plural. The words for 'you' in German, **'du'** (singular) and **'ihr'** (plural) are mainly used amongst family and close friends (or for animals) and can be left out of the main text. However, notes on the use of **'du'** and **'ihr'** can be found in Appendix II (p. 255).

7B Regular Verbs

This section deals with regular German verbs, which are easy to learn. They just use two tenses, present and past, in which the verb endings change according to the subject pronoun used. All the other tenses are made up, just as in English, by adding the verbs **'sein'** (to be), **'haben'** (to have) or **'werden'** (to become) to the infinitive or past participle of the verb used. These are called 'compound' tenses.

In the table below, we set out the tenses of the regular verb **'leben'** which is the infinitive of the German verb 'to live'.

The infinitive always ends in -en, or just -n (after r or l) which is tacked on to the stem of the verb. The past participle of **'leben'** is **'gelebt'** (lived) which adds the prefix ge- and the ending -t.

All the regular verbs are conjugated like **'leben'**, but if the stem ends in -n or -t (or a consonant followed by m or n) and it becomes impossible to pronounce, you need to insert an e before the final -t, thus:

Ich habe vor sieben Jahren dort gelebt (I lived there seven years ago)
Ich habe die Tür geöffnet (I have opened the door)

The other exception is that the ge- prefix is not used in verbs which already have a prefix like be-, ge-, er-, ver-, zer-, emp-, ent-, mis-, or those whose infinitive ends in -ieren, e.g.

verkaufen (to sell)   **verkauft** (sold)
studieren (to study)   **studiert** (studied)

Finally, note that **'Sie'** (you) always takes the *plural* form of the verb, even though 'you' may be either singular or plural.

Present

I	live	ich		lebe
he/she/it	lives	**er/sie/es**		**lebt**
we/you/they	live	**wir/Sie/sie**		**leben**

Past

I/he/she/it	lived	**ich/er/sie/es**		**lebten**
we/you/they	lived	**wir/Sie/sie**		**leben**

Future

I	will/shall live	ich	werde	leben
he/she/it	will/shall live	**er/sie/es**	**wird**	**leben**
we/you/they	will/shall live	**wir/Sie/sie**	**werden**	**leben**

German

Conditional

I/he/she/it	would/should live	**ich/er/sie/es**	**würde**	**leben**
we/you/they	would/should live	**wir/Sie/sie**	**würden**	**leben**

Perfect

I	have lived	**ich**	**habe**	**gelebt**
he/she/it	has lived	**er/sie/es**	**hat**	**gelebt**
we/you/they	have lived	**wir/Sie/sie**	**haben**	**gelebt**

Pluperfect

I/he/she/it	had lived	**ich/er/sie/es**	**hatte**	**gelebt**
we/you/they	had lived	**wir/Sie/sie**	**hatten**	**gelebt**

For the regular verbs, the subjunctive tenses (present and past) are the same (with one exception) as the indicative tenses shown above. Subjunctive tenses are used in a subordinate clause after certain verbs or conjunctions and these are shown in Appendix I, p. 254.

Although **'werden'** is literally translated 'to become' it is commonly used to mean 'will' or 'would'.

You can build up further tenses, like 'shall have' or 'would have', by using the auxiliary verbs **'haben'** and **'werden'**. **'Haben'** is conjugated as follows:

Present

I	have	**ich**	**habe**
he/she/it	has	**er/sie/es**	**hat**
we/you/they	have	**wir/Sie/sie**	**haben**

Past

I/he/she/it	had	**ich/er/sie/es**	**hatte**
we/you/they	had	**wir/Sie/sie**	**hatten**

Future

I	will have	**ich**	**werde haben**
he/she/it	will have	**er/sie/es**	**wird haben**
we/you/they	will have	**er/Sie/sie**	**werden haben**

Conditional

I/he/she/it	would have	**ich/er/sie/es**	**würde haben**
we/you/they	would have	**wir/Sie/sie**	**würden haben**

Note that the future and conditional tenses are split up when the past participle of another verb is used. For example:

Ich *würde* dort gelebt *haben* (I *would have* lived there)

Finally, to form the present participle of an English verb we add -ing to the stem. In German we just add -d to the infinitive, for example, leben**d** (living). You do *not* use this form for 'I am liv*ing*' or 'we are liv*ing*'. As you can see from the table above, this requires the present tense 'I live', 'we live', etc. The present participle is used when the verb is on its own, for example:

In London wohnend (Living in London)

7C Verbs Taking the Indirect Case

Whilst the object of most transitive (active) verbs is usually shown in the object case, some verbs require the *object* to be placed in the indirect case. Thus:

Ich möchte meinen Freunden danken (I wish to thank my friends)

Those verbs which take the indirect case are marked (I) in the word list. They are:

to advise (**raten**)
to answer (**antworten**)
to believe (**glauben**)
to excuse (**verzeihen**)
to follow (**folgen**)
to help (**helfen**)
to serve (**bedienen**)
to taste (**schmecken**)
to thank (**danken**)

The indirect case also needs to be used where there are two objects, one of which is given, shown, passed or sent to the other, thus:

Er gab es mir (He gave it *to me*)

In this case **'es'** is the neuter object and **'mir'** (to me) has to be put into the indirect case.

This is not always apparent where you might say 'Show me it' instead of 'Show it to me'. So remember to use the indirect case where this occurs after verbs such as

to allow (**erlauben**)
to bring (**bringen**)
to give (**geben**)
to lend (**leihen**)
to offer (**bieten**)
to order (**befehlen**)
to pass (**reichen**)
to say (**sagen**)
to send (**schicken**)
to show (**zeigen**)
to write (**schreiben**)

German

SESSION EIGHT
To Be

8   Sein and the Passive Mood

Sein (to be)

'Sein' is in constant use, and needs a separate section which should be memorized. The past participle is 'gewesen' and the tenses are conjugated as follows:

Present

I	am	ich	bin
he/she/it	is	er/sie/es	ist
we/you/they	are	wir/Sie/sie	sind

Past

I/he/she/it	was	ich/er/sie/es	war
we/you/they	were	wir/Sie/sie	waren

Future

I	will/shall be	ich	werde sein
he/she/it	will/shall be	er/sie/es	wird sein
we/you/they	will/shall be	wir/Sie/sie	werden sein

Conditional

I/he/she/it	would be	ich/er/sie/es	würde sein
we/you/they	would be	wir/Sie/sie	würden sein

Perfect

I	have been	ich	bin gewesen
he/she/it	has been	er/sie/es	ist gewesen
we/you/they	have been	wir/Sie/sie	sind gewesen

Pluperfect

I/he/she/it	had been	ich/er/sie/es	war gewesen
we/you/they	had been	wir/Sie/sie	waren gewesen

Note that the perfect and pluperfect tenses of 'sein' also use 'sein' not 'haben' (to have) as an auxiliary verb. This is true of a number of German verbs, just as we use 'être' for the perfect tense in French, and these are shown below. They include most of the verbs describing motion, as well as a few others, all of which are marked *S in the word list.

to arrive (**ankommen**)	to die (**sterben**)
to be (**sein**)	to fall (**fallen**)
to come (**kommen**)	to fly (**fliegen**)
to depart (**abfahren**)	to go (**gehen**)

to go, travel (**fahren**)   to stay (**bleiben**)
to run (**laufen**)   to travel (**reisen**)

Passive Mood

When the subject of the sentence is impersonal or the action is happening to the subject, we use the passive mood, thus:

Ich habe gebeten (I have requested) is active
Ich werde gebeten (I am requested) is passive
Das Glas wurde gebrochen (The glass was broken) is impersonal and passive

In the passive mood, we nearly always use '**werden**' in place of '**sein**' although '**sein**' can be used when the action is complete or a verb is used adjectivally to describe a subject. It is therefore much safer to use '**werden**'!
The passive tenses of '**werden**' can be summarized as follows:

am being	...ed	**werde**	
was	...ed	**wurde**	plus past
have been	...ed	**bin worden**	participle
will/shall be	...ed	**werde werden**	
would/could be	...ed	**würde werden**	

As you can see the double use of '**werden**', once for the passive mood and once for the future or conditional tense, sounds rather strange, so you might be well advised to avoid these last tenses until you have the confidence to use them.

SESSION NINE
Object Pronouns

9   Object Pronouns

We have already seen how nouns, adjectives and the two articles change their form, according to their position in the sentence, and the same happens to pronouns.
In English, pronouns also change when they become the object of a sentence. To take a simple case:

He hits *him* is translated **Er schlägt ihn**

German

He changes to *him* in English, *er* changes to *ihn* in German.

Where in English we would say 'to him' (or 'to' any other pronoun) the Germans put the pronoun into the indirect case, thus:

Er gab es *mir* (He gave it to me)

Where two pronouns are used, as above, the pronoun in the indirect case takes second place.

A table of personal pronouns is set out below:

	Subject	*Object*	*Indirect Case*
I	**ich**	**mich**	**mir**
he/it (m)	**er**	**ihn**	**ihm**
she/it (f)	**sie**	**sie**	**ihr**
it (n)	**es**	**es·**	**ihm**
one	**man**	**(einen)***	**(einem)***
we	**wir**	**uns**	**uns**
you	**Sie**	**Sie**	**Ihnen**
they	**sie**	**sie**	**ihnen**

* Rarely used

Note that the German form of 'it' depends on the gender of the noun, m, f, or n.

After certain prepositions such as 'out of' (**aus**), 'with' (**mit**), and 'to' or 'after' (**nach**), the pronoun always goes into the indirect case even though it is the object of the sentence. More details are given in Section 13B on prepositions (p. 245).

SESSION TEN
Imperatives, Reflexives and Irregular Verbs

10A   The Imperative and Reflexive Verbs

If you instruct someone to do something, you use the imperative. There are only two forms which you need:

You must (do something)
Let us (do something)

In the first case, just follow the infinitive by **'Sie'**, whether singular or plural. In the second, use **'wir'**, thus:

Sprechen Sie! (Speak! – 'you' is understood in English)
Gehen wir! (Let's go!; or, let *us* go!)

Only one verb has an irregular imperative and that is
'sein' (to be). In this case the imperative is **'seien'**, e.g.

Seien Sie still! – Be quiet!

However, the imperative should be used with discretion.
It is more polite to say **'Sollen wir'** (Shall we) or **'Wollen
sie . . . bitte'** (Would you like to . . . please)

Reflexive Verbs

Some verbs can be changed to 'reflexive' by changing the
pronouns, thus:

Ich ziehe Frederick an (I dress Frederick)
Frederick zieht sich an (Frederick dresses himself) is
reflexive

The verb needs to be followed, just as in English, by
'myself', 'himself', 'yourself' etc. Some verbs such as
'wash' or 'get dressed' are nearly always used in the
reflexive form and these are preceded by **'sich'** in the
word list. The present tense of 'to get dressed' is as follows:

ich ziehe mich an (I dress myself)
er/sie/es zieht sich an (he/she/it dresses him/her/
itself)
wir ziehen uns an (we dress ourselves)
Sie/sie ziehen sich an (you/they dress yourself/selves/
themselves)

or sometimes

Ziehen Sie sich an! (Get dressed!)

As you will see in the section on irregular verbs (below), a
few require the object to be placed in the 'indirect' case. In
that case, all you need to do is to change **'mich'** (myself)
to **'mir'** (to myself). All the other reflexive pronouns stay
just the same.

10B Irregular Verbs

There are 54 irregular verbs (sometimes called 'strong' or
'old' verbs) in our word list and these include some of the
most commonly used words. For an English student they

should not be too difficult to remember, although it would be unwise to try to learn them all at once.

The difference between regular and irregular verbs can be quickly spotted by looking down the list set out on pp. 235–7. They mainly comprise vowel changes in the present tense (3rd person singular), the past tense and the past participle. The past tense, for example, rarely uses the endings -te or -ten which are used in regular verbs but changes the stem vowel instead. This is also what we do in English, e.g.

English – I beg**in**   I beg**an**   I have beg**un**
German – ich begi**nn**e ich beg**ann** ich habe beg**o**nnen

Some of the verbs do change more than the vowel itself, but so they do in English, e.g.

I bring (**ich bringe**)   I brought (**ich brachte**)

Notice that some of the past participles do not start with the prefix **ge-**. Those which take the auxiliary verb **'sein'** rather than **'haben'** in the perfect tense are marked *S against the past participle.

Any compound verb such as **'ausgehen'** (to go out), **'hinuntergehen'** (to go down) or **'hinaufgehen'** (to go up) is conjugated like the verb it is based on. But see Section 10C (p. 239) for the treatment of separable verbs in which the preposition (or adverb) is split up from the main stem and transferred to the end of the sentence.

See the list of irregular verbs on pages 235, 236 and 237.

10C   Modal and Separable Verbs

'Modal' Verbs

We now come on to what are called 'modal' verbs (verbs of mood) which express one's ability, willingness, licence or obligation to do or acquire something. There are six modal verbs, one or two of which are fairly similar in meaning, and so they need careful use. They are:

dürfen (may, am allowed to)
können (can, am able to)
mögen (like, like to)
müssen (must, ought to)
sollen (should, am supposed to)
wollen (want to, am willing to)

They all behave as auxiliary verbs which need to be

(Continued on p. 238)

Infinitive		Present tense 1st sing	3rd sing	plural	Past tense sing	plural	Past Participle
beginnen	*begin*	beginne	beginnt	beginnen	begann	begannen	begonnen
bitten	*ask for*	bitte	bittet	bitten	bat	baten	gebeten
bleiben	*remain*	bleibe	bleibt	bleiben	blieb	blieben	*S geblieben
brechen	*break*	breche	bricht	brechen	brach	brachen	gebrochen
bringen	*bring*	bringe	bringt	bringen	**brachte**	**brachten**	**gebracht**
denken	*think*	denke	denkt	denken	**dachte**	**dachten**	**gedacht**
dürfen	*be allowed to*	darf	darf	dürfen	durfte	durften	gedurft
empfangen	*receive*	empfange	empfängt	empfangen	empfing	empfingen	**empfangen**
essen	*eat*	esse	ißt	essen	aß	aßen	gegessen
fahren	*drive (vehicle)*	fahre	fährt	fahren	fuhr	fuhren	*S gefahren
fallen	*fall*	falle	fällt	fallen	fiel	fielen	*S gefallen
finden	*find*	finde	findet	finden	fand	fanden	gefunden
fliegen	*fly*	fliege	fliegt	fliegen	flog	flogen	*S geflogen
geben	*give*	gebe	gibt	geben	gab	gaben	gegeben
gehen	*go*	gehe	geht	gehen	**ging**	**gingen**	*S **gegangen**
geschehen	*happen*	–	geschieht	geschehen	geschah	geschahen	*S geschehen
haben	*have*	habe	hat	haben	hatte	hatten	gehabt
halten	*hold*	halte	hält	halten	hielt	hielten	gehalten

235

German

Infinitive		Present tense 1st sing	3rd sing	plural	Past tense sing	plural	Past Participle
heißen	to be called	heiße	heißt	heißen	hieß	hießen	geheissen
helfen	help	helfe	hilft	helfen	half	halfen	geholfen
kennen	know (someone)	kenne	kennt	kennen	kannte	kannten	gekannt
kommen	come	komme	kommt	kommen	kam	kamen	*S gekommen
können	be able to	kann	kann	können	konnte	konnten	gekonnt
lassen	let, allow	lasse	läßt	lassen	ließ	ließen	gelassen
leihen	lend	leihe	leiht	leihen	lieh	liehen	geliehen
lesen	read	lese	liest	lesen	las	lasen	gelesen
mögen	like to	mag	mag	mögen	mochte	mochten	gemocht
müssen	owe, have to	muß	muß	müssen	mußte	mußten	gemußt
nehmen	take	nehme	nimmt	nehmen	nahm	nahmen	genommen
rennen	run	renne	rennt	rennen	rannte	rannten	*S gerannt
schlafen	sleep	schlafe	schläft	schlafen	schlief	schliefen	geschlafen
schließen	shut	schließe	schließt	schließen	schloß	schloßen	geschlossen
schneiden	cut	schneide	schneidet	schneiden	schnitt	schnitten	geschnitten
schreiben	write	schreibe	schreibt	schreiben	schrieb	schrieben	geschrieben
schwimmen	swim	schwimme	schwimmt	schwimmen	schwamm	schwammen	geschwommen
sehen	see	sehe	sieht	sehen	sah	sahen	gesehen

Infinitive		Present tense 1st sing	3rd sing	plural	Past tense sing	plural	Past Participle
sein	*be*	**bin**	**ist**	**sind**	**war**	**waren**	*S gewesen
senden	*send*	sende	sendet	senden	sandte	sandten	gesandt
singen	*sing*	singe	singt	singen	sang	sangen	gesungen
sitzen	*sit*	sitze	sitzt	sitzen	saß	saßen	gesessen
sollen	*be supposed to*	soll	soll	sollen	sollte	sollten	gesollt
sprechen	*speak*	spreche	spricht	sprechen	sprach	sprachen	gesprochen
stehen	*stand*	stehe	steht	stehen	**stand**	standen	gestanden
sterben	*die*	sterbe	**stirbt**	sterben	starb	starben	*S gestorben
tragen	*carry*	trage	trägt	tragen	trug	trugen	getragen
treffen	*meet*	treffe	trifft	treffen	traf	trafen	getroffen
trinken	*drink*	trinke	trinkt	trinken	trank	tranken	getrunken
tun	*do*	tue	tut	tun	tat	taten	getan
vergessen	*forget*	vergesse	vergißt	vergeßen	vergaß	vergaßen	**vergessen**
verlieren	*lose*	verliere	verliert	verlieren	verlor	verloren	**verloren**
waschen	*wash*	wasche	wäscht	waschen	wusch	wuschen	gewaschen
werden	*become*	werde	**wird**	werden	wurde	wurden	*S geworden
wissen	*know (something)*	weiß	weiß	wissen	wußte	wußten	gewußt
wollen	*want to*	will	will	wollen	wollte	wollten	gewollt

237

German

followed by the infinitive of the verb they serve, the latter usually placed at the end of the sentence, thus:

Ich soll nach Berlin gehen (I am supposed to go to Berlin)
Ich muß jetzt gehen (I must go now)
Ich kann mit Ihnen kommen (I can come with you)

Modal verbs in English such as 'may', 'might', 'will', 'could', 'should', 'ought to' and a few others, are probably more difficult for foreigners, as many of our words have double meanings. The Germans are rather more precise in their use, and there is no doubt that the modal verbs help to soften the language and make the expression of one's wishes or requests more polite. Note that one very common use of **'mögen'** (to like) is taken from its past subjunctive, e.g.

ich möchte (I would like)
wir möchten (we would like)

How much better to say:

Ich möchte ein Bier bitte (I *would like* a beer please)

rather than,

Ich will Bier (I want some beer)

(Note that 'some' is omitted in German, where quantity is indicated.)

Apart from the use of the subjunctive of **'mögen'**, the tenses which you are most likely to need are set out below.

Present Tense	*Singular*	*Plural*
can/am able to	**kann**	**können**
like/like to	**mag**	**mögen**
may/am allowed to	**darf**	**dürfen**
must/ought to	**muß**	**müßen**
am supposed to	**soll**	**sollen**
want to/am willing to	**will**	**wollen**

Past Tense		
could/was able to	**konnte**	**konnten**
liked to	**mochte**	**mochten**
could/was allowed to	**durfte**	**durften**
had to/ought to have	**mußte**	**mußten**
should have/was supposed to	**sollte**	**sollten**
wanted to/was willing to	**wollte**	**wollten**

The other tenses are built up using **'werde/werden'** for

'will/shall', **'würde/würden'** for 'could/should', **'habe/ hat/haben'** for 'have', and **'hatte/hatten'** for 'had'. Whichever you use has to be followed by the infinitive (not the past participle) of the modal verb, and the infinitive of the active verb, thus:

Ich werde kommen können (I will be able to come)

The use of the double infinitive is not uncommon in German, but if its use makes you feel uncomfortable, stick to the present and past tenses.

Separable Verbs

Both the German and English languages attach prepositions (or adverbs) to verbs to establish a different meaning, e.g.

to go (**gehen**)
to go *out* (*aus*gehen)

but the German language tends to incorporate them into the verb, in the form of a prefix. In some cases the verb and the prefix are split up, with the prefix sent to the end of the sentence, e.g.

Heute *gehe* ich mit meinen Freunden *aus* (Today I am going *out* with my friends)

Putting the preposition at the end of the sentence is not as odd as it looks. We do it in English, e.g.

He *knocked* his opponent *out*

The verbs which are split up in this way are called separable verbs. They are shown in the word list with a hyphen, but this should *not* appear in writing. They include verbs starting with

ab-, an-, auf-, aus-, ein-, fern-, mit-, nach-, vor-, weg-, zu-, zurück-, and **zusammen**

However verbs starting with **be-, emp-, ent-, ge-, er-, ver-, zer-,** and **miß-** prefixes are *in*separable. A few starting with **um-, durch-, über-** and **wieder-** and other common prepositions can be separable or inseparable. If in doubt look them up in the word list or a dictionary.

The rules for using a separable verb are fairly straightforward.

1   The prefix is split up *only* in the main clause, not in subordinate clauses. In the following case the verb 'to go

out' is in a subordinate clause. The prefixes are in italic type in each case.

> When I go out, come back quickly! (**Wenn ich** *aus***gehe, kommen Sie schnell** *zurück***!**)

2　The prefix is split up only in the present and past tenses, and the imperative.

3　The letters **-ge-** are interposed between the prefix and the verb in the perfect and pluperfect tenses, but the word order is not changed.

4　The letters **-zu-** (to) are interposed between the prefix and the verb, when the English word 'to' would normally be used before the infinitive (*to* do something). Where the infinitive forms part of a compound tense, it does not include '**zu**', e.g.

Verb	*ausgehen*	*to go out*
Present	**ich gehe . . . aus**	I go out
Past	**ich ging . . . aus**	I went out
Future	**ich werde ausgehen**	I will go out
Conditional	**ich würde ausgehen**	I would go out
Perfect	**ich bin* aus**ge**gangen**	I have gone out
Pluperfect	**ich war* aus**ge**gangen**	I had gone out
Imperative	**gehen Sie aus!**	go out!
Infinitive	**ich will ausgehen**	I wish to go out

* Note the use of 'sein' (not 'haben') with 'gehen' and its compound verbs in the perfect and pluperfect tenses.

SESSION ELEVEN
Questions and Negatives

11　Questions and Negatives

German and English are fairly similar in the way in which they deal with questions and negatives.

Questions

Just reverse the verb and the noun (or pronoun), with or without an interrogative at the beginning. The past participle or the infinitive go to the end of the sentence. For example,

Haben Sie es gesehen? (Have you seen it?)
Wo sind Sie gewesen? (Where have you been?)

Remember that the English words 'do', 'does', 'did', 'will' and 'would' are incorporated in the verb itself.

Kam er heute zurück? (Did he come back today?)

(Remember also that **'zurückkommen'** is a 'separable' verb and the prefix goes to the end of the sentence.)

The most common interrogative words which you will need are shown in the word list. These are

wer?	– who
wann?	– when
wo?	– where, **'wohin'** (where to), **'woher'** (where from)
warum?	– why
wie?	– how, **'wieviel'** (how much, how many)
was?	– what, **'was für'** (what kind of)
welch?	– which

Another way of asking a question is to make a statement, and then say, 'isn't it?'. In German this is translated 'nicht wahr?'

Heute ist Montag, nicht wahr? (Today is Monday, isn't it?)

Negatives

Use **'nicht'** after the verb, for example:

Haben Sie nicht es gesehen? (Have you not seen it?)
Nein, ich habe nicht es gesehen (No, I have not seen it)
Ist der Student nicht zurückgekommen? (Has the student not returned?)
Kam das Fräulein nicht? (Did the girl not come?; literally, 'Came the girl not?')

As in English, there is quite a vocabulary of negatives:

nein (no)
nicht (not)
nichts (nothing)
nie *or* **niemals** (never)
niemand? (no one)
weder . . . noch (neither . . . nor)

German

For example,

> **Ich habe ihn nie geliebt** (I have never loved him)
> **Ich liebe weder dieses Mädchen noch jenes** (I neither love this girl nor that one)

'Kein' is the German for 'not any'. It is classed as an adjective whose case endings match those of the indefinite article ('ein'), as shown on p. 222.

To contradict a negative with an affirmative, do not use the German 'ja' for yes, but use 'doch' instead, e.g.

> **Verstehen Sie nicht? Doch!** (Don't you understand? Yes I do!)

Finally:

> **Es macht nichts!** (It doesn't matter!)

SESSION TWELVE
More Adjectives

12 Adjectives, Comparatives and Possessives

There are 80 adjectives in the word list. There is no need to remember them all here, but some are indefinite adjectives which are in common use and you should try to remember these:

all (**alle**)
each (**jeder**)
enough (**genug**)
little (**wenig**)
many/much (**viel**)
more (**mehr**)
other/another (**ander**)
some (**manche**)

'Genug' (enough), 'viel' (much), 'mehr' (more) and 'wenig' (not much) can also be used as adverbs.

As we saw in Section 6D (p. 224) adjective endings vary according to the article or other adjective which precedes it, and whether the verbs 'sein' or 'werden' are used.

Comparatives

The Germans seldom use the word **'mehr'** (more) in making a comparison. Instead they use the other English method, adding -er or -ste (+ the definite article) to the adjective, thus:

kalt (cold)   **kälter** (colder)   **der kälteste** (coldest)

Note that the vowel in **'kalt'** takes an umlaut in the comparative, as do most adjectives, and that **'kälteste'** inserts an e- before -ste in its superlative form in order to make the word easier to pronounce. The e is usually needed in adjectives ending -d, -t, -s, -ß and -z.

Adjectives ending in -el, -en, and -er usually drop the first e in the comparative forms to make the word easier to pronounce, e.g.

dunkel (dark)   **dunkler** (darker)
der dunkelste (darkest)

If a superlative stands on its own, i.e. without a noun, the word **'am'** is inserted at the beginning, and the letter n is tacked on to the end, e.g.

Er rennt am besten! (He runs best!)

When comparatives come before the noun, they have to agree like any other adjective, e.g.

Mein älterer Bruder (My elder brother)
Meine ältere Schwester (My elder sister)
Meine ältesten Freundinnen (My oldest girlfriends)

A few comparatives are thoroughly irregular as in English:

gut (good)   **besser** (better)   **der beste** (best)
hoch (high)   **höher** (higher)   **der höchste** (highest)
viel (much)   **mehr** (more)   **der meiste** (most)

If you have to compare one object with another, either use **'so . . . wie'** (as . . . as), or **'als'** (than), thus:

Ihr Wagen ist nicht so gut wie meiner (Your car is not as good as mine)
Mein Wagen ist besser als Ihrer (My car is better than yours)

Possessives

The last two examples bring us on to possessive adjectives and pronouns, as follows:

German

Adjectives		*Pronouns*	
my	**mein**	mine	**meiner**
his/its	**sein**	his/its	**seiner**
her/its	**ihr**	hers/its	**ihrer**
our	**unser**	ours	**unserer**
your	**Ihr**	yours	**Ihrer**
their	**ihr**	theirs	**ihrer**

The possessive adjective has to agree with the noun and is declined first just like **'ein'** on p. 222, e.g.

Mein Wagen (My car)

The possessive pronoun still has to agree with the noun (not the person) to whom it refers, even though it stands on its own, and it is declined like **'der'** on p. 222, e.g.

Der Wagen ist meiner (The car is mine)

There is another form of the possessive pronoun which you will hear used quite often. This uses the same stem, **'mein'**, **'sein'**, etc, but ends in -ige or -igen and needs the definite article. You don't have to use it, only to recognize it. For example,

Dieser Wagen ist der meinige (This car is mine)

SESSION THIRTEEN
Adverbs, Prepositions and Conjunctions

13A   Common Adverbs

Whereas English adjectives usually add -ly when they change to adverbs, German adjectives and adverbs are usually the same. A few adjectives can be shown with a -weise ending (or -*er*weise or -*s*weise) like **'unglücklicherweise'** (unfortunately) to turn them into adverbs, but it is best to avoid this form.

The comparative form for an adverb is the same as for an adjective (as shown in Section 12, p. 243), with one or two irregularities. But all adverbs use the 'am . . .-sten' endings in their superlative.

A list of 38 other adverbs (or adjectives) which appear in our word list is shown below. Remember, also, the rule on positioning of adverbs which we dealt with in Section 5, p. 217. If there is more than one adverb in the sentence, those of 'time' come first, those of 'manner' second, and those of 'place', last.

again (**noch einmal**)	no (**nein**)
ago (**vor**)	now (**jetzt**)
almost (**fast**)	often (**oft**)
already (**schon**)	once (**einmal**)
also/too (**auch**)	only (**nur**)
always (**immer**)	perhaps (**vielleicht**)
bad (**schlecht**)	quickly (**schnell**)
before (**zuvor**)	slowly (**langsam**)
enough (**genug**)	so, thus (**so**)
far (**fern**)	sometimes (**manchmal**)
happy (**glücklich**)	soon (**bald**)
here (**hier**)	suddenly (**plötzlich**)
immediately (**sofort**)	then (**damals**)
inside (**drinnen**)	there (**dort**)
late (**spät**)	therefore (**also**)
later (**später**)	today (**heute**)
much (**viel**)	too much (**zuviel**)
near (**nahe**)	very (**sehr**)
never (**nie**)	yes (**ja**)

13B Prepositions and Conjunctions

The classification of English words into adjectives and adverbs, prepositions and conjunctions can become very confusing. Many English words have two or three different uses, like the word 'after', which can be an adverb, a preposition or a conjunction. The simplest advice, to forget about their uses and just remember the German, is unfortunately not the best, as the Germans often employ different words for each use.

What we have tried to show is the most common use of the word in English, and then the German translation. Where two or three uses are common they will both be shown, either in the text or in the vocabulary.

Conjunctions

These are words used to link up other words, phrases or sentences. There are only a handful in our word list.

after (**nachdem**)	but (**aber**)
and (**und**)	if (**wenn**)
as/when (**als**)	or (**oder**)
because (**weil**)	since (**seit**)
before (**bevor**)	so (**also**)

German

'Nachdem' is also an adverb, **'seit'** an adverb and a preposition.

Prepositions

These are words indicating position or other relationship and there are a surprising number in our vocabulary, some of them in constant use. (For the code in brackets, see below.)

according to **laut** (p)
against **gegen** (o)
at, near, by **bei** (i)
at, on **auf** (oi)
at, towards **an** (oi)
behind **hinter** (oi)
between **zwischen** (oi)
during **während**
for **für** (o)
from, out of **aus** (i)
in, into **in** (oi)
in front of (oi) before (i) **vor**
in order to **um . . . zu**

inside **innerhalb** (p)
near **in der Nähe von** (i)
of, from **von** (i)
opposite **gegenüber** (i)
over **über** (oi)
since **seit** (i)
through **durch** (o)
to **zu** (i)
to, towards, after **nach** (i)
under **unter** (oi)
until **bis** (o)
with **mit** (i)
without **ohne** (o)

Prepositions govern the case of the noun, adjective or article which follows. Some have to be followed by the 'object' case, some by the 'possessive' case and some by the 'indirect' case. These are marked above by o (object), p (possessive) and i (indirect).

Those marked (oi) can take either case according to the verb used. If the verb indicates motion the object case is required. If the verb does not indicate motion, use the indirect case, thus:

Ich gehe in (I go into) – use the object case
Ich wohne in (I live in) – use indirect case

Some of the shorter prepositions, when they are placed next to the definite article, join up and get contracted in the process. The most common contractions are between

an + dem = am
in + dem = im
bei + dem = beim
von + dem = vom
zu + dem = zum

an + das = ans
in + das = ins
auf + das = aufs

zu + der = zur

Other contractions using **'durch'**, **'über'** and **'unter'** are also used in German speech, but not in writing.

A familiar problem arises in German, as in other

languages, in translating the simple little words 'at', 'to' or 'in'. You have to be careful which preposition to use, and which case must follow. The table below should be sufficient to guide the beginner:

English	Meaning	German	Case needed
in	inside	**in**	indirect
in	into	**in**	object
to	towards a town/s or country	**nach**	indirect
to	towards (other)	**zu**	indirect
at	the premises of	**bei**	indirect
at	home	**zu Hause**	
at	an address	–	(no preposition used)
at	inside	**in**	indirect

SESSION FOURTEEN
Link Words

14A   Relative Pronouns

The relative pronoun 'who', 'which' or 'that', used to join clauses together, is translated by one word **'der/die/das'** which is similar to the definite article but differs in the possessive and indirect cases, as shown below.

		Singular		Plural
	m	*f*	*n*	*all*
Subject	**der**	**die**	**das**	**die**
Object	**den**	**die**	**das**	**die**
Possessive	**dessen**	**deren**	**dessen**	**deren**
Indirect	**dem**	**der**	**dem**	**denen**

The relative pronoun has to agree with the noun or pronoun used earlier in the sentence, to which it refers, and *not* the noun which follows. For example,

Hier ist das Kind, das ich verlor (Here is the child whom I lost)

In this case **'das Kind'** is the neuter object, and the relative pronoun must agree.

The possessive case is used to translate the English 'whose', e.g.

Das Kind, dessen Vater hier ist (The child whose father is here)

German

Remember that clauses are always marked off by commas, and the verb in subordinate clauses has to go to the end of the sentence. The relative pronoun must not be omitted, as it can be in English, e.g.

Das Haus, *das* ich kaufte (The house I bought)

Notice how '**das**' is used twice with two different meanings. You will sometimes hear '**welcher**' (which) used to avoid this repetition, but its use is restricted, and it is both easier and more correct to say '**das**'.

The relative pronoun is often used together with a preposition such as '**bei**' (at, near, by), '**an**' (at, to), '**mit**' (with), '**in**' (in) or '**auf**' (at, on), in which case the relative pronoun must take the case governed by the preposition.

Das Kind, mit dem ich lebe (The child with whom I live)

14B   It and Some

It and Impersonal Verbs

Impersonal verbs, without an object, are used just as much in German as in English, e.g.

Es regnet (It is raining)   **Es ist schade** (It's a pity)
Es schneit (It is snowing)   **Es ist nötig** (It is necessary)
Es macht nichts (It doesn't matter)   **Es ist wichtig** (It is important)

There is also an impersonal and polite way of saying 'I like':

es gefällt mir (literally, it pleases me)

'**Es ist**' can either mean 'it is' or 'there is':

es ist (it is, there is)   **es war** (there was)
es sind (there are)   **es waren** (there were)

You will also hear '**es gibt**' or '**es gab**' used for 'there is/are', or 'there was/were'. Be careful, however, not to use '**es ist**' plus the present participle of another verb. Where we might say 'there *is* a dog *playing* in the road', the Germans would only use the one verb, 'to play':

Da spielt *der* Hund . . . (there plays the dog . . .)

Some

There are a number of different words for 'some' or 'any'

in different contexts – **'einige'**, **'etwas'**, **'manche'** and **'welche'**. For the beginner, the easiest way to deal with it is to avoid its use altogether, which is permissible in expressions of quantity, e.g.

Haben Sie Geld? (Do you have any money?)

Otherwise, use **'etwas'** for 'something', **'manchmal'** for 'sometimes' and **'jemand'** for 'someone'.

SESSION FIFTEEN
Numbers and Time

15A   Numbers and Measures

Cardinal Numbers

0	null	30	dreißig
1	eins	31	einunddreißig
2	zwei	32	zweiunddreißig
3	drei	40	vierzig
4	vier	50	fünfzig
5	fünf	60	sechzig
6	sechs	70	siebzig
7	sieben	80	achtzig
8	acht	90	neunzig
9	neun	100	hundert
10	zehn	101	hunderteins
11	elf	157	hundertsiebenundfünfzig
12	zwölf	200	zweihundert
13	dreizehn	300	dreihundert
14	vierzehn	400	vierhundert
15	fünfzehn	500	fünfhundert
16	sechzehn	600	sechshundert
17	siebzehn	700	siebenhundert
18	achtzehn	800	achthundert
19	neunzehn	900	neunhundert
20	zwanzig	1,000	tausend
21	einundzwanzig	10,000	zehntausend
22	zweiundzwanzig	100,000	einhunderttausend

157 643 – **hundertsiebenundfünfzigtausend-sechshundertdreiundvierzig**
1 000 000 – **eine Million**
2 000 000 – **zwei Millionen**

German

1 576 432 – **eine Million fünfhundertsechsundsiebzig-
tausendvierhundertzweiunddreißig**
1 000 000 000 – **eine Billion**

1   From 20 to 99 the smaller numbers precede the larger,
e.g.

zweiundzwanzig (two and twenty)

2   Compound numbers are joined together although
you can take a break after millions!

3   'Ein' is generally omitted before **'hundert'** (hundred)
and **'tausend'** (thousand).

4   'Eine Million' and 'eine Billion' are nouns adding -en
in the plural. 'Hundert' and 'tausend' are nouns only
when they stand on their own, and they take an -e in the
plural.

5   Add **'mal'** to the cardinal number to indicate 'times'.
e.g.

einmal (once), **zweimal** (twice), **zehnmal** (ten times),
hundertmal (hundred times)

Ordinal Numbers

Ordinal numbers up to 20 add -te as we add -th,
e.g. **'zehnte'** (tenth) but **'erste'** (first), **'dritte'** (third)
and **'siebte'** (seventh) are irregular. Numbers over 20 add
-ste, thus:

einundvierzigste (forty-first)
hundertzwanzigste (one hundred and twentieth)

As ordinal numbers are adjectives they have normal endings, as set out in Section 6D (p. 224).
    Add -ns to the ordinal numbers to create an adverb, e.g.

erstens (firstly)   **zweitens** (secondly), and so on.

Fractions

The only fractions you are likely to need at this stage are:

one quarter	**ein Viertel** (n)	
one third	**ein Drittel** (n)	
one half	**halb** (adjective)	**die Hälfte** (noun)
two thirds	**zwei Drittel**	
three quarters	**dreiviertel**	
one	**ein/s**	
one and a half	**eineinhalb**	

Weights and Measures

Weights are in Kilo (literally 1000 Gramm [grammes])

ein Kilo = 35 ounces or just under 2¼ lb
ein halbes Kilo = just over 1 lb

If you purchase cheese from a delicatessen, for example, you would ask for '350 Gramm', *not* 'ein drittel Kilo' (one third of a kilo).

Liquid measures are in Liter (litres).

ein Liter (one litre) = hundert (100) Zentiliter = 35 fluid ounces = 1¾ pints
one pint = approximately 0.6 Liter or 60 Zentiliter

Distances are in Kilometres (1000 metres).

ein Kilometer or Km = 0.62 of one mile
one mile = 1.6 Kilometer, ten miles = 16 Km

15B Dates and Time

Ein Jahr (a year) is split into four seasons:

spring	**der Frühling**
summer	**der Sommer**
autumn	**der Herbst**
winter	**der Winter**

Die Monate (the months) are almost the same as in English.

January	**Januar**	July	**Juli**
February	**Februar**	August	**August**
March	**März**	September	**September**
April	**April**	October	**Oktober**
May	**Mai**	November	**November**
June	**Juni**	December	**Dezember**

Jeder Monat (each month) **hat vier Wochen** (four weeks) **und jeder Tag** (each day) **heißt** (is called):

Monday	**Montag**	Friday	**Freitag**
Tuesday	**Dienstag**	Saturday	**Samstag**
Wednesday	**Mittwoch**	Sunday	**Sonntag**
Thursday	**Donnerstag**		

If you want to say 'on' a day of the week, use **'am'**, but if something always happens on, say, Tuesdays, add -s to the day of the week, thus:

German

Ich werde am Dienstag ankommen (I will arrive on Tuesday)

Ich werde Dienstags kommen (I will come on Tuesdays)

Jeder Tag (each day) **hat vierundzwanzig Stunden** (hours)

Jede Stunde (each hour) **hat sechzig Minuten** (minutes)

Jede Minute (each minute) **hat sechzig Sekunden** (seconds)

Den wievielten haben wir heute? (What date do we have today?)

Heute ist Montag der achtzehnte Mai neunzehnhundertachtundachtzig (Today it is Monday 18th May 1988)

Morgen früh (tomorrow morning) **ist Dienstag** (will be Tuesday)

Der nächste Tag ist Mittwoch (The next day will be Wednesday)

Am Mittwoch (on Wednesday) **sind wir im Monat Mai** (we will be in the month of May)

Wieviel Uhr ist es? (What time is it?)

Es ist Viertel *vor/nach* **fünf** (It is a quarter *to/past* five)

For minutes past or before the hour, again use **'vor'** or **'nach'**, e.g.

es ist siebenundzwanzig Minuten *nach* **fünf** (twenty-seven minutes past five)

siebenundzwanzig Minuten *vor* **sechs** (twenty-seven minutes to six)

If you want to meet at six o'clock, say **'***um* **sechs Uhr'** (at six o'clock – note **'Uhr'** stays in the singular).

Don't get confused by **'halb sechs'**. This is *not* half past six, as in English, but half *before* six, therefore only half past five.

Remember that published times on the Continent work to a 24-hour clock. **'Sechs Uhr abends'** (six o'clock in the evening) is achtzehnhundert (1800) on the timetable.

Times of the day are **'der Morgen'** (morning) up to **'der Mittag'** (midday), then **'der Nachmittag'** (afternoon), **'der Abend'** (the evening) and lastly **'die Nacht'**.

Note the prepositions used for the times of day:

um **sechs Uhr** (at six o'clock) **nachmittags** (in the afternoon)

Finally, the weather.

> **Was ist der Wetterbericht?** (What is the weather forecast?)
> **Es ist warm** (warm) **trocken** (dry) **sonnig** (sunny) **heiss** (hot) **oder wolkig** (or cloudy)
> **Im Winter regnet es oft!** (In winter it often rains!)

German

APPENDIX I

Subjunctives

The subjunctive tenses have been left out of the main text as they can be confusing to those learning German. Subjunctives are little used, even less recognized in English, but they are used more frequently in German. The subjunctive is used principally in reported speech, in conditional sentences starting with **'wenn'** (if), after verbs expressing wishing or doubt, or when you make a polite request, for example:

1	**Ich glaube nicht daß er reich sei**	I do not believe (that) he is rich
2	**Wenn ich reich wäre**	If I were rich
3	**Er sagte er sei reich**	He said he was rich
4	**Könnten Sie mir bitte . . . Leihen**	Could you please lend me . . .

The first example uses the verb **'glauben'** (to believe) in the negative, expressing doubt.

In the second example, 'If I were rich', it is assumed that 'I' am not. This is sometimes called the conditional negative, and the past subjunctive is generally required.

In the third example of reported speech, 'He said he *was* rich', we have used the present, not the past tense of **'sein'**. This is because the speaker himself used the present tense when he said, 'I *am* rich'. So the present subjunctive is also used in reported speech.

The past subjunctive is also used for polite requests, as in the last example. This form is most commonly used with the two auxiliary verbs **'haben'** and **'sein'**, and also the modal verbs (p. 234).

For most purposes the present and past subjective will be sufficient and the verb endings are simple to learn:

Present Tense

	Regular verb ending	Irregular verb ending	sein
singular	**-e**	**-e**	**sei**
plural	**-en**	**-en**	**seien**

Past Tense

singular	**-te**	**¨-e**	**wäre**
plural	**-ten**	**¨-en**	**wären**

254

You can see that the present subjunctive is the same as the present indicative, except for the 3rd person singular where no -t ending is required.

The past subjunctive is the same as the past indicative for regular verbs. Irregular verbs just add -e or -en to the past indicative, but the a, o and u vowels in the stem take an umlaut. Those ending in -e already only add the umlaut.

	Indicative	*Subjunctive*
I thought	**ich dachte**	**ich dächte**
you thought	**Sie dachten**	**Sie dächten**

APPENDIX II

The Use of 'Du' and 'Ihr'

In section 7A (p. 226), we referred to the use of **'du'** and **'ihr'**, the second person singular and plural, which are mainly used in a family context, or for close friends. Be very careful with its use, which should not change once a 'du' relationship has been established. Below, we show the different forms of the personal pronouns, the possessive adjective and the appropriate verb endings.

Pronouns

	Case	*Singular*	*Plural*	
Personal	subject	**du**	**ihr**	thou/you
	object	**dich**	**euch**	
	indirect	**dir**	**euch**	
Reflexive	object	**dich**	**euch**	yourself/selves
	indirect	**dir**	**euch**	
Possessive	(as **'der'**)	**deiner**	**eurer**	yours
(alternative)	(as **'der'**)	**deinige**	**eurige**	

Adjective

Possessive	(as **'ein'**)	**dein**	**euer**	your

Regular Verbs

e.g. **'leben'** (to live)

German

Tense		Singular	Plural
Present	you live	**du lebst**	**ihr lebt**
Past	you lived	**du lebtest**	**ihr lebtet**
Future	you will live	**du wirst leben**	**ihr werdet leben**
Conditional	you would live	**du würdest leben**	**ihr würdet leben**
Perfect	you have lived	**du hast gelebt**	**ihr habt gelebt**
Pluperfect	you had lived	**du hattest gelebt**	**ihr hattet gelebt**
Imperative	live!	**leb(e) (du)!**	**lebt (ihr)!**

In the imperative, the use of the personal pronoun gives extra emphasis. In speaking the -e in **'leb(e)'** is usually dropped after most verb stem endings. In writing, don't forget the exclamation mark!

Irregular Verbs

Irregular verbs also need an -st ending in the singular and -t in the plural. But watch out for the stem changes, e.g.

> **ich gebe, du gibst, ihr gebt** (present)
> **ich gab, du gabst, ihr gabt** (past)

The most important irregular verbs which you need to remember are **'haben'**, **'sein'** and **'werden'**.

Present	**du hast**	**du bist**	**du wirst**
	ihr habt	**ihr seid**	**ihr werdet**
Past	**du hattest**	**du warst**	**du wurdest**
	ihr hattet	**ihr waret**	**ihr wurdet**